Behold the Man

Behold the Man

Jesus and Greco-Roman Masculinity

COLLEEN M. CONWAY

OXFORD
UNIVERSITY PRESS

2008

OXFORD

UNIVERSITY PRESS

Oxford University Press, Inc., publishes works that further
Oxford University's objective of excellence
in research, scholarship, and education.

Oxford New York
Auckland   Cape Town   Dar es Salaam   Hong Kong   Karachi
Kuala Lumpur   Madrid   Melbourne   Mexico City   Nairobi
New Delhi   Shanghai   Taipei   Toronto

With offices in
Argentina   Austria   Brazil   Chile   Czech Republic   France   Greece
Guatemala   Hungary   Italy   Japan   Poland   Portugal   Singapore
South Korea   Switzerland   Thailand   Turkey   Ukraine   Vietnam

Copyright © 2008 by Oxford University Press, Inc.

Published by Oxford University Press, Inc.
198 Madison Avenue, New York, New York 10016

www.oup.com

Oxford is a registered trademark of Oxford University Press

Library of Congress Cataloging-in-Publication Data
Conway, Colleen M.
Behold the man : Jesus and Greco-Roman masculinity / Colleen M. Conway.
    p. cm.
Includes bibliographical references and index.
ISBN: 978-0-19-532532-4
1. Men in the Bible.   2. Bible. N.T. Gospels—Criticism, interpretation, etc.
3. Masculinity—Religious aspects—Christianity—History of doctrines—Early church,
ca. 30–600.   4. Men (Christian theology)   5. Jesus Christ—Person and offices.   I. Title.
BS2545.M39C66 2008
225.8'30531—dc22   2007035820

9 8 7 6 5 4 3 2 1
Printed in the United States of America
on acid-free paper

To David,
vir bonus

Preface

When I wrote my dissertation on the male and female characters in
the Gospel of John, I had originally planned to include a chapter on
Jesus. Instead, my first teaching position and the birth of my two
children took the place of that chapter, which in any case had seemed
a daunting task. Still, I was never quite satisfied with omitting consideration of Jesus as a gendered character in the Gospel of John, and
I suppose it was inevitable that I would return to the topic. When I
did, my interests took me beyond John to consideration of the gendered aspect of Jesus across the New Testament. Soon, I found myself
involved in what, once again, seemed a very daunting task. And
once again, I found myself having to limit the scope of the work so that
it might actually be published before my children had children of
their own. For this reason, I have had to restrict my focus to the
presentations of Jesus in the Gospels, the Pauline literature, and the
Book of Revelation. I have also had to limit my research on the
enormous amount of literature devoted to New Testament Christology. Instead of reviewing this scholarship in every chapter, I have
focused on illustrating what a gender-critical approach helps us learn
about the presentations of Jesus in the New Testament. That is to say,
the chapters devoted to the New Testament material are intended
primarily as gender-critical analyses of the figure of Jesus, rather than
comprehensive treatments of the Christology of each writing. Even
in the case of gender analysis, there is certainly more to learn than
what I offer here. It is my hope that this initial sustained reading of

ancient gender ideology and New Testament depictions of Jesus will stimulate more work and further conversation on these topics.

For style and references I have followed the *SBL Handbook of Style: For Ancient Near Eastern, Biblical, and Early Christian Studies* (Patrick Alexander et al., eds., 1999). Translations of primary classical sources are from Loeb Classical Library volumes unless otherwise noted. Translations of biblical material are from the NRSV unless otherwise noted.

Many people have assisted in this project over the past six years. I shared early versions of chapters with the Gender and Theory group that met in our apartment for two years. I benefited greatly from my conversations with Dale Martin, Diana Swancutt, Virginia Burrus, Stephen Moore, and David Carr. I am also grateful for the many opportunities I have had to present the research that led to the completion of this book. Before the book was fully conceived, the Philo of Alexandria Group at the American Academy of Religion (AAR) and Society of Biblical Literature (SBL) annual meeting in Denver in 2001 gave me the chance to venture outside my research on John and explore gender issues in relation to Philo's depiction of Moses. Early versions of my work on Paul were presented at the annual meeting of the Catholic Biblical Association in 2002. Martti Nissenen and Risto Uro generously invited me in 2003 to give a lecture at the University of Helsinki on my work on John and masculinity. Initial work on the Gospels was presented as a research report at the annual meeting of the Catholic Biblical Association in 2004. Later that year I presented a revised version of this work for the Jesus Traditions, Gospels and Negotiating the Roman Imperial World Consultation at the annual meeting of the AAR/SBL in San Antonio. The seeds of the chapter on Luke were sown for a presentation to the Synoptic Gospel Section at the 2005 AAR/SBL annual meeting in Philadelphia. As my work on Paul developed, I had another opportunity to present it to the Pauline Epistles Section at the 2006 AAR/SBL meeting in Washington, DC. Initial work on the Book of Revelation was presented at the 2007 Mid-Atlantic Regional AAR/SBL meeting. Finally, Deirdre Good and Stephen Moore both graciously invited me to discuss my work with their students at General Theological Seminary and Drew University, respectively. Seton Hall University granted me a yearlong sabbatical without which I could not have completed this book.

My thanks also to the Society of Biblical Literature and Brill for granting me permission to include revised versions of two previously published articles. Portions of chapter 3 were first published as "Philo of Alexandria and Divine Relativity," *Journal for the Study of Judaism* 34 (2003): 471–91. Chapter 8 appeared in an earlier version as " 'Behold the Man!' Masculine Christology in the

Fourth Gospel," in *New Testament Masculinities,* ed. Stephen D. Moore and Janice Capel Anderson (2003), 163–89.

I am also extremely grateful to several individuals who read portions of the manuscript along the way. Jennifer Glancy, Todd Penner, Dale Martin, and Janice Capel Andersen all read several chapters and provided highly useful feedback and encouragement. Stephen Moore was also very supportive, reading the entire manuscript in a short period of time. He not only pushed me to work harder in places; he also saved me from some embarrassing oversights. If I'd had more time and energy to follow through on all his suggestions, no doubt the book would be the better for it. Many thanks also to Cynthia Read, Meechal Hoffman, Christi Stanforth, Liz Smith, and others at Oxford University Press with their expert help on the editing and production of my manuscript. Most of all thanks to my husband, David Carr, who cheerfully and promptly read every chapter (sometimes more than once) and always gave me more to think about. Meanwhile, he regularly volunteered to perform unsavory household tasks because I was "working on my book." This book is far better than it might have been without his continual love and support.

Contents

Behold the Man

I

Introduction

Jesus and Gender

Christ stands for the highest type of a strong, virile man, and
there was nothing effeminate about him.
— R. Warren Conant, *The Virility of Christ*

In 1915, Dr. R. Warren Conant wrote a book titled "The Virility of
Christ: A New View," with an additional note printed in bold capitals:
"A BOOK FOR MEN." The book addressed the problem of the absence
of men in the church. Dr. Conant's thesis was that men were not
populating the pews because of the "feminizing of Christianity."
"Consider," he says, "the conventional Christ as presented by Christian art and Christian preaching":

> From lovely illuminated church windows and from Sunday-
> school banners he looks down upon us, "meek and lowly,"
> with an expression of sweetness and resignation, eyes of-
> ten down-cast, soft hands gently folded, long curling hair
> brushed smoothly from a central parting—all feminine,
> passive, negative. Although he lived in a country where the
> sun's heat during a large part of the year made some cov-
> ering for the head necessary, art requires that Christ should
> always go bareheaded; probably in order to give full effect to
> his womanish hair and appearance.
>   Then for fear that they might not give him sufficient
> appearance of sanctity and purity Christ must present to us

a languid pose and smooth line-less features, destitution of expression save a pensive melancholy, no character, no virility.[1]

As an antidote, Conant contends that "Christian art and Christian preaching need a strong tonic of Virility. . . . Why not hold up to the world a portrait drawn to the life of the Manly Christ in place of the womanish? Why have we no Christ of the Denunciation, towering majestic, tense with righteous wrath; the eye flashing, the arm stretched forth in judgement—the impersonation of masterful virility! Are the painters and preachers afraid of it?"[2]

Conant was not the only author calling for a "muscular Christianity" during this period. Bruce Barton begins his book *The Man Nobody Knows* with a story of his boyhood struggle to love the Jesus pictured on his Sunday-school wall. "It showed a pale young man with flabby fore-arms and a sad expression. The young man had red whiskers." He knew Jesus was the Lamb of God, but that sounded like "something for girls—sissified."[3] Similarly, Warner Sallman, painter of the ubiquitous *Head of Christ*, was reportedly influenced by the following conversation with E. O. Sellers, faculty member of Chicago's Moody Bible Institute:

> "I understand you're an artist, Sallman, and I'm interested in knowing why you're attending the institute."
>
> "Well, I'm here because I wanted to increase my knowledge of the Scriptures. I want to be an illustrator of biblical subjects."
>
> "Fine! There is a great need for Christian artists. Sometime I hope you give us your conception of Christ. And I hope it's a manly one. Most of our pictures today are too effeminate."
>
> "You mean to say you think Jesus was a more rugged type? More of a man's man?"
>
> "Yes, according to the way I read my Bible. We know he walked great distances and slept out under the stars; he was rugged and strong. He preached in the desert, so he must have been tanned. More than that, the Word says he set his face 'like a flint' to go down to Jerusalem, so he wasn't soft or flabby. We need a picture of that kind of Christ, Sallman, and I hope you will do it some day."[4]

Such accounts reveal many things about the gender ideology of early twentieth-century America. One could note the equation of a particular type of physical appearance with ideal masculinity, the notion of "character" as synonymous with virility, and the anxiety about the church going "soft." Indeed, this last point—the threat of ecclesial impotence—is what drives the quest for a manly Jesus in this period. Thus, Conant and Barton repeatedly attest to the masculinity of Christ by pointing to qualities such as courage, nerve, force (physical, mental, and moral), sound judgment, persistence, endurance, and so on.

Fast-forward to the mid- to late twentieth century and the emergence of a different combination of gender ideology and Christology. As women began to find their voices in the public sphere and feminist theologies began to claim authority for women in the church, new questions about the gender of Jesus emerged. In this context, women wrestled with the question of the maleness of Jesus, with feminist theologian Rosemary Radford Ruether asking directly, "Can a male savior save women?"[5] With such a question in mind, scholars sought the "feminine side" of Jesus and focused on the presence of women in the Gospel traditions.[6] At the same time, the image of Jesus as liberator of the oppressed (including women) was emphasized. Not surprisingly, Ruether's conclusions regarding the gender of Jesus were different from those reached by Conant and Barton some sixty years earlier. Whereas Conant and Barton see the virility of Jesus as essential to the life of the church, Ruether saw it as ultimately insignificant. She argued:

> Theologically speaking, then, we might say that the maleness of Jesus has no ultimate significance. It has social symbolic significance in the framework of societies of patriarchal privilege. In this sense, Jesus as the Christ, the representative of liberated humanity and the liberating Word of God, manifests the kenosis [emptying] of patriarchy.[7]

Since the initial wave of feminist challenges to biblical patriarchy, there have been numerous attempts to construct a feminist Christology.[8] Several of these attempts have drawn on New Testament associations of Jesus with the Wisdom traditions of the Hebrew scriptures.[9] For example, Elizabeth Johnson interprets the story of Jesus as that of Wisdom's child, Sophia Incarnate.[10] Such an interpretation, she suggests,

> leads to the realization that as Sophia incarnate Jesus, even in his human maleness, can be thought to be revelatory of the graciousness of God imaged as female. . . . Not incidentally, the typical stereotypes of masculine and feminine are subverted as female Sophia represents creative transcendence, primordial passion for justice and knowledge of the truth while Jesus incarnates these divine characteristics in an immanent way relative to bodiliness and the earth.[11]

Such arguments, coupled with the earlier concerns about "muscular Christianity," should make clear that the way one interprets and portrays the gender identity of Jesus makes a difference. They also demonstrate that for at least the past one hundred years, gender and Christology have been viewed as closely related categories. Indeed, from certain perspectives in this history, it seemed that the very future of the church depended on how one viewed the gender of Jesus. The saving power of the Christ was either inextricably linked to his gendered identity, his "manliness," or totally distinct from it.

But the interest in gender and Christology is not limited to the past century. Caroline Walker Bynum has explored the attention given to the gendered nature of Christ in the medieval period, especially the literary and visual expressions of Jesus as a mother.[12] Such images conveyed the nurturing aspects of Christ to the believer, especially to the Cistercian monks of the twelfth century. Moving back earlier still in the history of the church, one finds an explicit interest in the role of gender in Gnostic accounts of creation and the saving power of Christ.[13]

The subject of this book is the intersection of gender ideologies and representations of Christ at a still earlier stage of Christological reflection. It explores the relationship between gender ideologies of the first-century Roman imperial world and conceptions of Jesus as the Christ in the New Testament. In particular, the book examines how cultural ideas of masculinity informed the various representations of Jesus in the writings of the New Testament.

I should make clear at the outset that my goal is not to establish the influence of patriarchy on New Testament Christology. At this point in the history of biblical scholarship, that hardly needs doing. Indeed, the accumulated work of feminist biblical scholars during the past several decades has made the patriarchal nature of the biblical text abundantly clear.[14] By studying the intersection of masculinity and New Testament Christology, my aim is to provide an additional resource for evaluating the role of gender in the Christian church as it relates to the broader culture. Cultural ideologies often function below the radar of those who are affected by them. This is true whether one unconsciously embraces this ideology or feels the strain of its imposition. By examining the influence of ancient gender ideologies in the Greco-Roman period, we might become ever more conscious of the multiple ways contemporary gender ideologies function in our own lives. Moreover, an examination of the construction of masculinity in relation to New Testament Christology allows new perspectives on the familiar question of the relationship between Christ and culture. By examining the complex relationship between ancient masculine ideology and New Testament images of Jesus, I hope to provide an additional resource for further feminist Christological reflection and construction.

Thus, I propose an analysis of the various ways the New Testament authors related to the ideology of masculinity that was dominant during this particular historical period. As chapter 2 will make clear, depictions of Jesus or understandings of the Christ would have to relate in some way to the cultural demands of ideal masculinity in order to have any credibility in the broader culture. Moreover, what one might identify as the "fact" of biological sex— Jesus was a man and not a woman—would not be proof enough to satisfy these demands. Instead, one would need to establish the ways in which Jesus Christ fulfills, redefines, rejects, or does something else entirely to Greco-Roman cultural ideals of masculinity.

In fact, there were many types of cultural interactions available to the early Christians who wrote about Jesus. On this point, the work of Greg Woolf is informative. Speaking on the complicated relationship between Rome and Greece, he states, "Roman responses to Hellenism consisted of a complex and partly incoherent mixture of adoption, adaptation, imitation, rejection, and pro-hibition, while the rhetorical poses repeatedly struck include assertions of admiration, of condemnation and of reconciliation."[15] I suggest that the New Testament contains a range of similarly complex responses to the ideology of masculinity. At times, one finds what seems like a clear rejection of the notions of power and strength that were so closely linked to definitions of manliness. At other times, these very concepts are used to construct a picture of Jesus that is a challenge to imperial power. Still other times, the lines between masculine and feminine constructs are blurred, for instance when Jesus is portrayed as a powerful, authoritative male figure speaking in the language of Wisdom, a concept that was traditionally personified as female. In every case, however, one can discern ways in which the New Testament authors both engaged in and contributed to the ideal of masculinity that coursed through the veins of the Roman Empire.

This leads to two hermeneutical points that are important for the approach taken here. First, a fundamental premise of my approach concerns the com-plex reciprocal relationship between text and context. Rather than assuming that literary texts reflect historical reality, I follow literary critics in considering how texts take part in the construction of reality, both in the past and in the present. Texts help to shape the context of which they are a part. This means that the New Testament writings are both shaped by and helped shape cultural expressions of masculinity, divinity, power, and authority.[16] Although this work will not extend much beyond the New Testament period in terms of textual focus, it will point to ways in which early Christian engagement with dominant gender ideologies has had an ongoing influence on contemporary understandings of Christology, gender, and sexuality.

The second point concerns the context in which the New Testament engagement with dominant gender ideologies takes place. Because I am interested in Greco-Roman articulations of masculinity, much of this study will concern the imperial context of the New Testament writings. In considering the ways that early Christian writers produced their images of Jesus in this context, I have learned from the work of postcolonial theorists. These theorists have analyzed the effects of colonizing power on indigenous peoples at multiple levels, such as the portrayal of the "native" in colonial texts and the influence of colonization as reflected in indigenous literature.[17] Biblical scholars who engage postcolonial theory often analyze how the Bible was deployed in the service of European expansion and colonization.[18] Here I am interested in how the Roman imperial context (particularly its ideology of imperial masculinity) affected the presentations of Jesus. Of special interest will be the concept of "mimicry," in which the indigenous subject reproduces rhetoric and ideologies of the dominant power.[19] So, while I would not call my overall approach "postcolonial" and I do not engage postcolonial theory in any extended way, its hermeneutical influence will nevertheless be clear at various points of the analysis.

Jesus and Greco-Roman Masculinity

The subtitle of this book points to the two matrices that give shape to this study. The first is the presentation of Jesus in the New Testament, or New Testament Christology. The second is the cultural construction of masculinity in the Greco-Roman period. Chapter 2 will detail what is meant here by "Greco-Roman" masculinity. First, however, it is necessary to clarify what is meant by the term "masculinity" and how this category will be used in an analysis of the New Testament presentation of Jesus. Clearly, any use of gender as a category of Christological analysis will move beyond traditional approaches to the topic. Nevertheless, situating this study in the context of earlier studies of New Testament Christology will demonstrate how gender analysis might also inform long-standing scholarly debates.

Theorizing Masculinity

The study of masculinity entered biblical studies through several different paths, including feminist analysis and the mythopoetic men's movement of the early nineties.[20] But by far the most influential work on study of masculinity in the New Testament has come from studies of masculinity in the classical world.[21] In large part, these studies grew out of the work of Michel Foucault, whose three-volume *History of Sexuality* includes an analysis of sexuality in the ancient Greek and Roman imperial world. While Foucault and those influenced by his work have been thoroughly critiqued by some feminist scholars, his work remains foundational for contemporary studies of gender and sexuality.[22]

For instance, Judith Butler's groundbreaking *Gender Trouble* draws on Foucault to argue for a performative theory of gender.[23] From this perspective, gender is something one *does* rather than something one *is*. In Butler's now oft-quoted words, "Gender ought not to be construed as a stable identity or locus of agency from which various acts follow; rather, gender is an identity tenuously constituted in time, instituted in an exterior space through a stylized repetition of acts."[24] This insight has proved enormously helpful in considering the ways that gender is performed in various times and places, including the Roman imperial period, in which the New Testament was written. Moreover, such an approach has made possible an awareness of how "normative" gender identities function in a given culture vis-à-vis other marginalized articulations of gender.

Although some feminist scholars have been suspicious of a move that seemingly puts men at the center once more, the absence of an analysis of masculinity as a constructed category reinforces the notion that masculinity is a natural, normative, or essential mode of being—a category immune to deconstruction. This study is founded on the conviction that gender categories are deeply embedded and entangled in the symbolic systems of any culture. It also assumes that such symbolic systems are open to analysis, critique, and deconstruction.

As with feminist studies, current publications with an interest in masculinity studies reach across multiple disciplines in the humanities and social sciences.[25] Two key ideas that have emerged in such studies will be operative throughout this investigation. First, I draw on the notion of a "hegemonic masculinity." As far as I can tell, the term was first used in a sociological study by Carrigan, Connell, and Lee that described the relationship between versions of masculinity and power. According to the authors of this study, hegemonic masculinity refers to a "particular variety of masculinity to which others ... are subordinated."[26] Thus, to understand how hegemonic masculinity functions is to explore "how particular groups of men inhabit positions of power and wealth and how they legitimate and reproduce the social relationships that generate their dominance." They go on to argue:

> An immediate consequence of this is that the culturally exalted form
> of masculinity, the hegemonic model, so to speak, may only corre-
> spond to the actual characters of a small number of men. ... Yet very

large numbers of men are complicit in sustaining the hegemonic model.[27]

This conception of hegemonic masculinity will prove especially useful for study of the Greco-Roman world. One of the frequent critiques made of studies of the ancient world is that the data are skewed in the direction of the elite culture, because such studies draw primarily on textual traditions to reconstruct the social world. In other words, whatever concept of masculinity one finds in such texts would not necessarily apply to the lower classes.[28] But the notion of hegemony suggests that, while the dominant ideology may be fully realized only in a small group of people, it is nevertheless supported in multiple ways by other, much larger groups. A similar point is made by Sally Robinson, as she reflects on her experience of teaching masculinity studies:

> Studying masculinity means studying the rewards men reap for reproducing the dominant fictions and the punishments they suffer for violating them. While it is certainly the case that a large number of men—maybe even most—feel that they suffer such punishments, it is also the case that the survival of a dominant fiction of masculinity means that some people are reproducing, acting out, performing it. Although individual men never easily measure up to an impossible standard of pure masculinity, dominant masculinity nevertheless keeps reproducing itself.[29]

Robinson observes an important aspect of the way hegemonic masculinity functions. In both historical and theoretical studies of masculinity, one finds a repeated emphasis on a threatened or unstable masculinity, or a "masculinity in crisis." Bryce Traister has traced this crisis theory of masculinity as it comes to expression in multiple studies on masculinity in American history. In the post-Revolutionary period, the antebellum period, the Civil War, after the Civil War, the early twentieth century, the Depression, the two World Wars, and so on—at seemingly every stage of American history—studies find that men faced a "crisis of masculinity." This crisis left them adrift in a sea of gender confusion.[30] Notably, this same focus on crisis extends to studies in the ancient world as well. Foucault identified a "crisis of subjectivity" brought on by a change in marriage practices and political structures in the imperial period.[31] Others, too, have suggested that in the emerging Roman Empire, the loss of autonomy under the Principate initiated a crisis for elite Roman men.[32]

There are many ways to interpret such a continuous historical account of gender crisis. One could see it as a phenomenon of contemporary theories of masculinity that predispose the historian to find evidence of gender crises in his or her sources.[33] Or, perhaps less cynically, one could understand the account to reflect the lived experience of males across the centuries. A third possibility is to see the evidence for a crisis in masculinity in historical sources as the result of rhetorical constructions necessary for the maintenance of hegemonic masculinity.[34] And, of course, these possibilities are not mutually exclusive. It may well be a combination of each of the above factors that have produced such consistent accounts of masculinity in crisis.

Nevertheless, whether in spite of or because of the focus on crisis, hegemonic masculinity has remained a powerful cultural force in the Western tradition for thousands of years. Indeed, as Traister has argued, accounts of failed or deconstructed masculinity fail to take adequate account of the historical masculinity that has and continues to dominate the culture. Focusing in particular on American masculinity studies as influenced by Butler's performative gender theory, he notes that the demystification of "all things powerful, stabile, and erect . . . cannot change the fact that American enterprise was driven by the very men whose masculinity now appears a masquerade."[35]

In short, the study of masculinity has produced a paradox: the rhetoric of instable and threatened masculinity juxtaposed with the reality of stable and continuous masculine power. As indicated above, one way to make sense of this paradox is to see "threat" and "failure" as an inherent part of the symbolic world of hegemonic masculinity. In other words, the threat of a failed masculinity and (perhaps) the lived experience of an inferior manliness is one of the ideological tools necessary for the maintenance of hegemonic masculinity. This idea will be explored in more depth with respect to the rhetoric of masculinity that pervades the literature of the Roman Empire. While notions of inferior masculinity and worries about feminization pervade the literature, they are all situated in the context of a highly successful imperial masculine rule.

The same can be said about alternative or competing expressions of masculinity or about contradictions that exist in the dominant discourse of ideal masculinity. It is not that such alternatives or fractures in the ideology do not exist. The next chapter will make clear that those qualities that counted for "manliness" were sometimes contradictory and sometimes contested. Alongside a dominant discourse of masculinity, there were often alternative discourses in play. But the existence of alternative masculinities does not mean that hegemonic masculinity was any less of an ideological force in the ancient world. Instead, such alternatives could function to clarify and further strengthen the dominant masculine posture. Likewise, internal contradictions may do little more than relieve the stress of the dominant ideological structure and keep it standing, "stabile and erect." In this way, contradictions need not indicate weaknesses in a system, but instead may contribute to its strength. As Dale Martin puts it, "Just as earthquake-resistant buildings must contain within themselves a certain amount of flexibility, a 'give and take,' so ideologies must be malleable and flexible."[36]

Finally, what is particularly fascinating about the study of Christology from a gender-critical perspective is that at its root the Christian myth is not only a story of a fallen and redeemed "mankind"; it is also a story of failed and redeemed masculinity. Coming out of this ancient context, the story of a tortured and crucified man is the story of his emasculation. As Stephen Moore aptly puts it, "Jesus' passivity, his submissiveness, his stripping and whipping, his role as plaything in the rough hands of the soldiers, his ... penetration and abject helplessness on the cross would all have conspired, in complicity with the hegemonic gender codes, to throw his masculinity into sharp relief—precisely as a problem."[37]

As the examination of texts from Paul and the Gospel narratives will show, each of these texts contends with the problem of an emasculated Jesus, and each tells the story of a revirilized Christ. The texts do so in different ways, as their authors draw from and contribute to a range of cultural discourse at their disposal. Overall, however, a common concern to restore the masculine honor of Jesus Christ resulted in a tradition that could appeal to a wide range of potential adherents. A further result was the emergence of a religious tradition that could more easily wend its way from the margins to the very center of the empire.

New Testament Christology

Finally, a word about how this study relates to other studies of New Testament Christology. Traditionally and broadly defined, New Testament Christology has involved the study of the person and work of Christ as understood by the New Testament writers and their early Christian communities. As would be expected, there are a variety of methods that have been used for such a study, and vast amounts of literature devoted to the task. Here I provide only the briefest of reviews in order to situate my own approach in light of major scholarly trends.

One major trend in the study of Christology in the twentieth century involved a focus on titles used for Jesus in the New Testament. Oscar Cullman's work is the classic example of this approach, but many others have engaged in a similar project.[38] Although one still commonly finds discussions of titles such as "Son of Man" or "Son of God" in commentaries, generally the titles approach has been left behind. One problem with a focus on titles concerns the malleability of language across time and space—the meaning of a particular title changes depending on the context. "Son of Man" means one thing in 1 Enoch and something else in Ezekiel, for example. Another problem with the approach is discerning what constitutes a "title." For example, in the Gospel of Mark, Jesus is often described as one having authority, although this is not a title per se. Similarly, in the Gospel of John, Jesus is one who "comes from above"—again not a formal title or recognizable office, but highly significant to the Christology of the Gospel. Finally, the major objection to the study of Christological titles in the New Testament is that the approach ignores the narrative context in which the titles are situated. As many have noted, it is the immediate literary context that reveals the author's understanding of the title as applied to Jesus, more than a definition abstracted from other sources.

For this reason, the most recent trend in studies of New Testament Christology has been a more contextual or literary approach to the problem. Marinus de Jonge's work represents an early stage of this turn, as he examines the earliest responses to Jesus through a form-critical analysis of the text.[39] He looks to early layers of tradition to understand how communities first responded to and defined the meaning of Christ with respect to their own lives. Taking a more literary approach, Frank Matera has concentrated on the idea of narrative as the vehicle through which New Testament Christology finds expression. From his perspective, "we can learn how the writings of the New Testament understand the person and work of Jesus Christ by paying attention to the explicit and implicit stories of Christ in the New Testament."[40] A number of recent studies of New Testament Christology reflect a similar interest in what has been termed "narrative christology."[41]

This particular study of the gendered presentations of the person and work of Jesus in the New Testament will draw on the insights from all of the approaches listed above. The analyses that follow will at times explore particular titles applied to Christ, at times consider early Christian responses to the death of Christ, and at times analyze the unfolding of the story of Jesus in a particular text. Holding this eclectic approach together is an interest in gender. I examine the presentations of Jesus in these early Christian writings with a particular interest in how these early Christologies interact with ancient ideologies of masculinity.

Thus, there is no attempt to offer a comprehensive discussion of the Christology of any particular writing, much less of the entire New Testament. When it is relevant, more detailed attention will be given to scholarship on issues of Christology pertaining to particular New Testament writings. Moreover, for the most part, the analysis is not a theological one, insofar as I am not exploring the implications of gender and Christology in the New Testament with respect to a transcendent reality. There are others who are better equipped than I for such a task. Instead, the aim here is a historical and cultural focus: situating presentations of Jesus and God in their broader sociocultural setting with respect to gender ideologies. This also means that, in general, my interest lies more in the potential reception of the writings, rather than their conception.[42] While I do not ignore questions of origin for particular ideas found in the New Testament, I focus more on how the language and imagery of the text might have been perceived by the ancient Greco-Roman audience.

In the next chapter, the study begins with an overview of Greco-Roman masculinity. This is followed by a series of "case studies" of ideal divine men in antiquity. With this preparation, the focus turns to New Testament writings, in particular Paul, the Gospels, and the Book of Revelation. By examining the presentation of Jesus in light of Greco-Roman masculine ideology, these chapters are in one sense additional "case studies," although focused on a common figure, Jesus. Together, the chapters illustrate the multiple ways that New Testament authors engaged various rhetorics of ancient masculinity in their presentations of Jesus. In this way, they also contribute to the overall picture of Greco-Roman masculinity in its diverse articulations.

2

How to Be a Man in the Greco-Roman World

Thales . . . used to say there were three blessings for which he was grateful to Fortune: "First, that I was born a human being and not one of the brutes; next, that I was born a man and not a woman; thirdly, a Greek and not a barbarian."

—Diogenes, *Thales*, 1.33

This expression of gratitude reported by Diogenes of the pre-Socratic philosopher, Thales, provides an apt gateway into the hierarchal world that we are about to enter. A person ranks higher than an animal, a man higher than a woman, and a Greek higher than a non-Greek; and, by the time of the Principate, a Roman higher than a non-Roman.[1] To these oppositions we could also add that of free versus slave—slaves, too, were like animals, women, and foreigners insofar as they lived lives of submission. In short, understanding what it meant to be a man in the Greco-Roman world meant understanding one's place in a rationally ordered cosmos in which free men were placed at the top and what fell beneath could all be classified as "unmen."[2]

 The purpose of this chapter is to make evident the ideology of masculinity that contributed to the construction of this order. It highlights the image of the ideal man that runs across a full range of Greek and Latin texts throughout the Greco-Roman period.[3] While places of difference and resistance to this ideology exist, as well as certain internal contradictions, I am primarily interested in showing the consistent and pervasive nature of the ideology that any such deviations were up against. The image of ideal masculinity presented in this chapter is gleaned from philosophical, anatomical, and physiognomic treatises, moral discourses, legal codes, and biblical commentary, as well as material evidence from ancient coins, altars, statues and inscriptions. I draw on texts that span several centuries ranging from the first century B.C.E. (and sometimes earlier) to texts from the fourth century C.E. This breadth is intentional, as it demonstrates the persistence and endurance of this version of masculinity. The aim is a thick and detailed description of what it meant to be masculine in this hyper-masculine culture. Together, the textual and material evidence testifies to the values and ideals of the ruling class, values which, as I argued in the introduction, undoubtedly played a role in the broader culture. Even if this picture of manliness did not represent the lived reality of most men in the empire, it had an effect on them. No matter where one lived in the empire, one would not have to look hard to find an image of masculinity that was intended to evoke admiration and honor, and to which one was supposed to aspire. When the New Testament writers worked out their Christological formulations, they did so alongside this dominant ideology of masculinity.

The Paradoxical Body

The body is perhaps the most obvious entrée into issues of sexuality and gender, because for most people, the relationship between sexual anatomy and gendered identity seems clear-cut. Male bodies equal men and masculinity; female bodies equal women and femininity. However, just as many now recognize the complexity of the relationship between physical anatomy and gendered identity in our contemporary society, so scholars are uncovering a similar complexity in the ancient world. What has become increasingly clear is that ancient masculinity was constituted more by the shape of one's life than by the shape of one's body. In fact, as we will eventually show, it is actually *incorporeity* that was viewed as the ultimate in masculine achievement.

To be sure, the body was foundational in the Greco-Roman construction of gender, insofar as Roman law required an infant's classification at birth as male or female. As one would expect, such classification was done by visual observation of the external appearance of the genitalia.[4] Thus, initially the body did determine whether one was male or female. Still, once this classification was made, there was no guarantee that a given boy would grow to become a man. The problem was not just one of infant mortality, but whether the boy would live up to the requirements of masculinity. As Carlin A. Barton puts it, "one was ontologically a male but existentially a man. Born a male (*mas*) or a human (*homo*), one made oneself a man (*vir*). A *vir* was not a natural being."[5]

In this sense, the body was ultimately not of primary importance in the achievement of ideal masculinity. While the male body launched one on the way toward this goal, it provided no guarantee of success. Indeed, from the ancient perspective, the body lacked stability; there was no certainty that a masculinity earned was a masculinity saved. The specter of lost manliness, of a slide into effeminacy, was frequently raised before the eyes of the literate male audience.

Perhaps one reason this fear was evoked so regularly was that from an Aristotelian perspective, the male body did not provide assurance of being completely different in kind from the female body. Instead, the male body was viewed as the perfected, more complete body when compared to the female. As Aristotle explains:

> In human beings the male is much hotter in its nature than the female. . . . It is due to this . . . that the perfecting of the female embryos is inferior to that of male ones (since their uterus is inferior in condition). (*Gen. an.* 775a)

So, too, writing in the second century c.e., the physician Galen comments:

> Now just as mankind is the most perfect of all animals, so within mankind the man is more perfect than the woman, and the reason for his perfection is his excess of heat, for heat is Nature's primary instrument. (*On the Usefulness of the Parts*, 2.630)

In other words, from the perspective of these influential authors, there was actually only one set of reproductive organs, "one sex," as Laqueur argues.[6] Biologically, in this view, the difference between male and female anatomy amounted to the presence of adequate heat. Indeed, pointing to the essential sameness of male and female reproductive organs, Galen encourages his reader to imagine the male genitalia turned outside in and the woman's reproductive organs inside out. The biological implication of this thought experiment is that "instead of being divided by their reproductive anatomies, the sexes are linked by a common one."[7]

The pervasiveness of this perspective can be seen in the way a Hellenistic Jewish writer like Philo readily assimilates this view in the context of his biblical commentary. Explaining the sex-specific requirement for the Passover lamb, Philo remarks, "Male . . . because male is more perfect than female. . . . [I]t is said by the naturalists that the female is nothing else than an imperfect male"

(*QE* 1.7; cf. also *Spec. Laws* 1.200–201). One could hardly find a more concise statement of the Greco-Roman understanding of sex/gender categories. Maleness is associated with completion and perfection. "Female" is a non-category apart from its definition as imperfect male.[8]

For the ancient authors, the disturbing implication of this "one-sex model" of humanity, to borrow Laqueur's term, is the possibility of gender slippage, particularly from male to female. If women were not different in kind, but simply a lesser, incomplete version of men, what was there to keep men from sliding down the axis into the female realm? As John Winkler has pointed out, the fear behind this question created an ethos in which the cultural polarity between the genders was made internal to one gender, the male.[9] It was not enough to be clear that one was a man rather than a woman. One also needed to ensure that one was a manly man rather than a womanly man. As Maud Gleason argues, one's masculine status had to be constantly maintained and proven through a demonstration of manly deportment. In her words, "Manhood was not a state to be definitely achieved but something always under construction and constantly open to scrutiny."[10]

And here is the paradox. Although the presence of male reproductive organs could not prove one's manliness, there were other aspects about the body that could betray it. Particular bodily traits were open to scrutiny, and the "science" of physiognomy was devoted to their analysis. Physiognomy was the discipline of discerning a person's character, disposition, or destiny through the study of external appearances. Highlighting this link between body and character (or "soul"), the earliest treatise on physiognomy posits, "For no animal has ever existed such that it has the form of one animal and disposition of another, but the body and soul of the same creature are always such that a given disposition must necessarily follow a given form."[11] Both the instability of the body and the danger of gender slippage can also be seen in this text, as the author notes, "It seems to me that the soul and body react on each other; when the character of the soul changes, it also changes the form of the body, and conversely, when the form of the body changes, it changes the character of the soul."[12] In other words, if one behaved badly, demonstrating weakness of character, the body would react in turn: it would become more womanly.

In spite of this clear link between body and disposition, the extent to which gender was nevertheless distinct from male and female anatomy is apparent in the way this same text designates certain animals as male and female types, without correspondence to the male and female of the species. For example, the lion exhibits the most perfect male type, with its well-proportioned features (mouth, nose, eyes, forehead, neck mane, etc.), slow majestic walk, gentility and affection coupled with love of victory. The panther, on the other hand, with its ill-articulated and ill-proportioned body (long, thin neck, narrow chest, thick and fleshy loins and hips) and its correspondingly small, furtive, tricky soul, is the most feminine of animals.[13] All of this translates to the study of human physiognomy as well. Working up the human body, the same text treats the appearance of feet, ankles, lower legs, knees, thighs, buttocks, waist, and so on, up to the head with all its features. Also discussed are gestures, mobility of eyes, quality of voice, and stature. Being well proportioned is most critical, indicating an upright and brave man. Thus, the premise of this text, and of the entire physiognomic corpus, circles back to the paradox with which we began. While sexual anatomy does not necessarily make the man, certain physical characteristics reveal him.

In this sense, the ancient physiognomist understood that when it came to basic anatomy and gender identification, the body could be deceptive. But, if one knew how to read certain corporeal clues, one could unmask a person's real gender identity. Along this line, the work of both Maud Gleason and Tamsyn Barton explores how ancient physiognomy actually functioned in determining gender identity.[14] The discussion of corporeal clues to gender identity most often takes the form of detailed analysis of gender deviance. To this end, Barton notes that "For easy reference all the treatises from Peripatetic Physignomonica onwards offer Κιναίδου /Ανδρογύνον σημεῖα (signs of the *kinaidos* or androgyne)."[15] Gleason summarizes Polemo's signs of the effeminate androgyne as follows:

> You may recognize him by his provocatively melting glance and by the rapid movement of his intensely staring eyes. His brow is furrowed while his eyebrows and cheeks are in constant motion. His head is tilted to the side, his loins do not hold still, and his slack limbs never stay in one position. He minces along with little jumping steps; his knees knock together. He carries his hands with palms turned upward. He has a shifting gaze, and his voice is thin, weepy, shrill, and drawling.[16]

Eyelids, eyebrows, gaits, limbs, voices—such are the reliable bodily characteristics that determine gender if one knows how to read them. The task was not always easy, however, even for the experts. Consider the story told by Dio Chrysostom of an unnamed expert in physiognomy who is nearly baffled by a particular case. Attempting to stump him, the people bring to the physiognomist a person whom Dio Chrysostom describes as follows:

> a person of rugged frame and knitted brows, squalid and in a sorry state and with callouses on his hands, wrapped in a sort of coarse

gray mantle, his body shaggy as far as the ankles and his locks
wretchedly shingled ... (Dio Chrysostom, 1 Tars. [Or. 33] 54)

The expert studies the man closely for a long time, but is unable to solve the
case and sends him away. As the man goes, however, he sneezes. At this, the
game is up, and the physiognomist immediately cries out that he is a *kinaidos*.[17] The moral of the story, according to Dio, is that one "must not
think ... that movements and actions do not vary according to sex and afford
no clue to it." For Dio, these movements and actions include "voice, glance,
posture ... style of haircut, model of walking, elevation of the eye, inclination of
the neck, the trick of conversing with upturned palms" (1 Tars. [Or. 33] 52).
These are the indicators of gender identity rather than physical anatomy or
even basic physical appearance.

Similar ideas are found in Philo, when he connects such physical characteristics with a degenerate soul. He argues:

> Just as bodily properties are seen in mirrors, so those of the soul (are
> seen) in the face and countenance. But a shameless look and an
> elevated neck and a continuous movement of the eyebrows and a
> womanish walk and not blushing at, or being ashamed of, any evil at
> all is the sign of a lewd soul, which clearly pictures and describes the
> forms of its invisible disgraces on its visible body. (QG 4.99)

Like the ancient physiognomist, Philo links certain physical traits with masculinity (or the lack of it) and the state of one's soul. In this case, the already-
degenerate soul is reflected in an effeminate body, but the concept can be
expressed in reverse as well. Philo worries about the effects of effeminate
behavior, or the "female disease," on both body and soul, a point that will be
explored further in the next chapter.

The Body and the Law

Some elements of the Roman legal code confirm the relative unimportance of
the body for determining masculine status and the absolute importance of
social—and, in many cases, sexual—conduct. Jane Gardner's work on Roman
law is especially informative in this respect. As mentioned earlier, at birth, a
child's male genitalia are the deciding factor in granting male legal privilege.
Yet, Gardner's work suggests that once the boy becomes an adult, the presence
or absence of male reproductive organs is not what endangers that privilege.
Instead, it is *acting* like a woman. That is to say, in analyzing the legal problems
that resulted from physiological deficiency in persons legally classified as male,

Gardner finds that such deficiency would warrant no change in legal status. Indeed, her findings suggest that at least in principle, as long as one has (or had at one time) the theoretical possibility of generative capacity, an important aspect of male identity, one's legal privileges as a man could be maintained.[18] Even in the case of *castrati*, Gardner argues, their condition was not grounds for curtailment of their legal rights as male citizens. While the literature suggests that there was social disdain for their emasculated condition, the legal code focused on shameful behavior (*infamia*) rather than anatomical state. As Gardner puts it, "Castrati were not, simply as castrati, *infames*, though they might be for other reasons."[19]

But here is the main point: an adult male, castrated or not, who played the part of a "passive" female *did* risk losing the rights and privileges that accompanied proper masculinity. For example, catamites (that is, "*qui corpore suo muliebria passus est*," or "someone who has been physically treated like a woman") were banned, like women, from representing others in court (*Dig.* 3.1.1.6).[20] Moreover, Gardner notes, "In later Roman law, a man who voluntarily submitted to a homosexual act lost half his property and the capacity to make a will (Paulus, Sent 2.26.13 = Col. 5.2.2)."[21] The importance of active versus passive behavior for the construction of masculinity will be discussed more fully in the next section, including ways in which these categories tend toward oversimplification. Still, what such laws indicate is that the core of masculine identity resided not in the body per se but rather in what one did with, and allowed to be done to, one's body.

Considering the legal code from another angle, Walters argues that the active/passive opposition meant not only that free men were defined as the active members of society, but also that they enjoyed legal protection from being acted upon. Bodily violations such as beatings and sexual penetration of free men were forbidden. In this way, true men were essentially "impenetrable penetrators" in a context that characterized "those of high social status as being able to defend the boundaries of the body from invasive assaults of all kinds."[22] In contrast, "unmen," to recall Walters's term, were those who were subject to, or who subjected themselves to, bodily penetration. In other words, a penetrated body signaled the loss or absence of true manliness.[23]

Acting Like a Man: Masculinity, Sexuality, and the Virtues

As discussed in the opening chapter, Michel Foucault and Judith Butler argue in different ways that gender is always a performance, always an already-scripted role that one plays. As we have seen, in the ancient Roman world it was not enough to be born a male, even a free Roman male citizen. One also had to *act* the part of the man. Yet, if the body was paradoxical in the way it did and did not reveal gender identity, so also the role that men were asked to play contained certain contradictions. On the one hand, acting like a man required one to assume the active role in private sexual practice as well as one's public life. At the same time, such a role also required the careful display of control and restraint, both with respect to one's passions—sexual and otherwise—and in terms of treatment of the other.[24] Both aspects of this manly role will be explored below.

With respect to sexual practice, the first demand meant quite literally that one must be the actor, rather than one acted upon. This was because from the philosophical sphere to the social, masculinity was understood to be the active, rational, generative principle of the cosmos. Thus, Aristotle can speak of males as more divine or "godlike" (θειότερον) due to their active role in creation (*Gen. an.* 732a9). Similarly, Philo explains that "the female gender is maternal, passive, corporeal and sense-perceptible while the male is active, rational, incorporeal and more akin to mind and thought" (*QE* 1.8). Thus, the activity of men was linked to the creative activity of the gods.

Second, and related to the first point, to be active often involved expressing one's dominion over another. To be passive meant to submit to this domination. In the Roman setting, the popularity of the god Priapus illustrates the importance of this aspect of masculinity. Priapus was an extraordinarily well-endowed fertility god, frequently depicted in paintings and statues with his oversized member ready to defend the garden or household against intruders through penetration of the enemy.[25] Aside from depictions of Priapus, phallic images were found throughout the empire on a wide variety of objects, such as jewelry, pottery, masonry, and street-corner plaques. As a sign of fertility and strength, the phallus was venerated, and the symbol was used as an apotropaic charm. Phallic wind chimes and front-door plaques graced the home, so that the phallic image was ever present in one's comings and goings in the Roman world. Its ubiquity reminded those who would be men that generation and domination through penetration was an essential part of the act.[26]

Yet, in spite of this pervasive presence of the phallus, there were other acts, besides or instead of sexual ones, that defined masculinity. Sexual penetration was not the only way for members of the Greco-Roman elite to demonstrate manliness; nor was it even the preferable way. Instead, to become a *vir* in the Greco-Roman world, one was required to demonstrate manliness through the practice of particular virtues. Indeed, as Williams and others have pointed out, *virtus*, often translated as "virtue," is etymologically equivalent to "manliness."[27] As one popular (if incorrect) etymology ran:

So the male was named man [*vir*], because strength in him is greater than in woman. Hence, too, courage (or valor) [*virtus*] has received its name. Likewise, woman . . . is from the word for softness, one letter changed and one taken away, as though (it should have been) *mollier* [softness], rather than *mulier* [woman]. (Lactantius, *Opif.* 12.16–17)

Such an etymological claim makes explicit the perceived relationship between true man and virtue. In Kuefler's words, "Virtue was so intimately linked to maleness in the Roman universe that it is impossible to separate Roman definitions of masculinity from more general notions of ideal human behavior."[28]

Moreover, the link between masculinity and virtue, especially the virtues of leading elite men, had a long history before its use in Roman imperial ideology. As J. R. Fears illustrates, Xenophon's *Cyropaedia*, written in the fourth century B.C.E., uses the life story of Cyrus as a cipher for defining the ideal Hellenistic king. As Fears summarizes:

The good king must be a model to his subjects; by his virtues he ensures the continued well-being of the commonwealth. Hence, through his actions he shows himself possessed of the noblest virtues: piety towards gods and men, wisdom, courage and prowess in battle, temperance, generosity, faithfulness, and love of truth.[29]

This ideological heritage, Fears goes on to argue, enters the Roman Republic and builds to a crescendo in the Principate of the late first and early second centuries, especially through the cult of Virtues propagated by the successive emperors.[30] The next chapter will examine the degree to which Caesar Augustus was a key figure in construing the emperor as a model of all the best of Roman masculinity. For now, the accolade given the Roman Emperor Julian by the fourth-century historian Ammianus Marcellinus is enough to demonstrate Fears's point:

Julian must be reckoned a man [*vir*] of heroic stature, conspicuous for his glorious deeds and his innate majesty. Philosophers tell us that there are four cardinal virtues [*virtutes*]: self-control, wisdom, justice, and courage; and in addition to these certain practical gifts: military skill, dignity, prosperity, and generosity. All these Julian cultivated both singly and as a whole with utmost care. (*Amm. Marc.* 25.4.1)[31]

Among the virtues listed by Ammianus, it is no coincidence that self-control is listed first. Cicero had already described *ordo et moderatio* as that which "dreads rashness; it shrinks from injuring anyone by wanton word or deed; and it fears to do or say anything that may appear unmanly [*parum virile*]" (*Fin.* 2.47). By the first century, largely under the influence of Stoic teaching, self-control emerges among the most important keys to ideal masculinity. The notion finds its way into multiple cultural discourses—not only the teachings of the moral philosophers, but also the evaluations of historians, the romance novels from this period, and the literature of the Jewish and Christian communities.[32] Moderation, or self-mastery, was frequently discussed in terms of mastery of the passions, especially lust and anger, but also self-restraint in eating, drinking, and luxury in general.

If Julian serves as a positive example of the connection between virtue and masculinity, Nero provides a negative one with respect to self-control. Suetonius goes on at length about Nero's "acts of wantonness, lust, extravagance, avarice and cruelty" (*Nero* 26.1). It is just these vices that call into question one's masculinity and suggest a "softness" in character.[33] To these vices are added complaints of Nero's sexual improprieties with freeborn boys and married women (*Nero* 28.1), precisely the two categories there were off limits to the sexual exploits of Roman men. Dio Cassius's account of rebellion against Nero also includes a challenge to Nero's manliness. In his *Roman History*, Dio describes Nero's opponent, Gaius Julius Vindex, as one "powerful in body, shrewd intelligence, skilled in warfare," as Gaius rallies his followers and challenges the virility of Nero:

> Believe me, I have seen that man (if man he is who has married Sporus and been given in marriage to Pythagoras) in the circle of the theatre, that is, in the orchestra, sometimes holding the lyre and dressed in loose tunic and buskins, and again wearing high-soled shoes and mask. (*DioCass* 63.4)

Thus is Nero repeatedly charged with lack of self-control in all areas of his life. He represents the opposite of self-restraint, the submission to one's desires and a sliding down the scale from man to unman. Julian, in contrast, exhibits only manly traits, including, as Ammianus includes in his description, his chastity after the death of his wife, his moderation in eating and sleeping, and his frugality of living. Chapter 3 will return to this notion of the emperor being a measure of masculinity for the empire. Indeed, as shown in the examples of Nero in the first century C.E. and Julian in the fourth, following Augustus, the connections between imperial leadership, masculinity, and virtue become commonplaces in Roman historians' descriptions of reputable and disreputable emperors.[34]

As mentioned above, the emphasis on self-control complicates the ideology of masculinity, insofar as it seems to push against the idea of generativity and reproduction. In this sense, Greco-Roman masculinity cannot be reduced strictly to the notion of activity vs. passivity in sexual roles. In fact, by the first century and beyond, self-control appears to trump the active/passive binary when it came to defining ideal masculinity. This is seen, for example in accusations of effeminacy even if one's sexual desires were for one's wife.[35]

Plutarch, for example, reports the public mockery of Pompey, who "weakly succumbed to his passion for this young wife," apparently spending too much time in villas and gardens with her. Pompey's opponent asks, "Who is this autocrat with no self-control?" (αὐτοκράτωρ ἀκόλαστος, my translation). The word choice seems intentionally ironic here, since one who had absolute power over others was expected to have control over himself. Even more telling are the questions that follow: "Who is the man who seeks other men? Who scratches his head with one finger?" (*Pomp.* 48.5–7, my translation). Here Pompey's desire for his wife, certainly active desire, is nevertheless put in the same category as other effeminate behavior.[36] The reference to scratching with one finger was a commonplace in the literature—a gesture associated with unmanliness.[37] Regarding the charge of "seeking after other men," the object of the seeking is less of an issue than the seeking itself, that is, Pompey's general lack of control over his sexual passion.[38]

In fact, charges of effeminacy are frequently accompanied by charges of adultery, because adultery was another case of a lack of restraint. Apparently, Romans did not think twice about the idea of an effeminate man seeking voraciously after women.[39] Richlin points out that this was simply the Roman sexual stereotype: "effeminate men were thought to be more interested in sex of any kind than were more rugged types."[40] Again, this suggests that to think of masculinity merely in terms of active versus passive is an oversimplification. As Edwards puts it, "Accusations of effeminacy . . . need not be seen as essentially concerned with sexual 'passivity.' . . . 'To be male' was a rather more complex business even in specifically sexual contexts."[41]

Moving outside the sexual arena, one finds further critique of excess and lack of self-control pertaining to luxury, greed, and avarice. All were thought to make a man soft. Cicero mocks Verres, who, instead of spending his summer inspecting his province or going to sea like other respectable governors, had daily dinner parties for women. On remarking that only Verres and his young son would accompany the women at the table, Cicero continues, "and as they were the men, I might well have said that no men at all were present" (*Verr.* 2.5.81). Similarly, Pliny complains that Antony outdid the proverbial extravagance of both women and foreigners with his shameful use of a golden toilet (*Nat.* 33.50).

On the topic of avarice, Gellius records an interesting discussion of a passage from Sallust's *Catiline*. The passage in question reads:

> Avarice implies a desire for money, which no wise man covets; steeped as it were with noxious poisons, it renders the most manly body and soul effeminate; it is ever unbounded, nor can either plenty or want make it less.

The puzzled Favorinus asks:

> How does avarice make a man's body effeminate? For I seem to grasp in general the meaning of his statement that it has that effect on a manly soul, but how it also makes his body effeminate I do not yet comprehend.

The conversation continues until a certain learned man weighs in,

> We observe that almost all those whose minds are possessed and corrupted by avarice and who have devoted themselves to the acquisition of money from any and every source, so regulate their lives, that compared with money they neglect manly toil and attention to bodily exercise, as they do everything else. For they are commonly intent upon indoor and sedentary pursuits, in which all their vigour of mind and body is enfeebled and, as Sallust says, "rendered effeminate." (*Noct. att.* 3.1)

As with Philo's discussion of the degenerate soul being reflected in the body, here is an instance of a particular vice resulting in the emasculating of both soul and body.

The gendered implications of anger present another case of cultural contradictions. In what follows, I discuss the gender complexities of anger in some detail because, as we will see, it is a problem on both the human and divine levels. As such, it provides an example of the way masculine ideology did not just involve men but had implications for the gods as well. The basic problem is whether anger should be regarded as a loss of control and therefore effeminizing, or as an active display of one's convictions—a manly act.

For many, it was obvious that true men should not lose their dignity through a violent display of anger against another. Appealing to the physiognomic argument, Plutarch points to how the "countenance, color, gait, and voice" change when someone is angry (*Cohib. ira.* 455f), so that he appears in a state "contrary to nature" (*Cohib. ira.* 456b). The angry man's conduct turns him into an undignified and unmanly figure. Marcus Aurelius reflects the same position in his mediations on anger:

> In moments of anger, let the thought always be present that loss of temper is no sign of manliness, but that there is more virility, as well as more natural humanity, in one who shows himself gentle and peaceable; he it is who gives proof of strength and nerve and manliness, not his angry and discontented fellow. Anger is as much a mark of weakness as is grief; in both of them men receive a wound, and submit to a defeat. (*Meditations* 11.18)[42]

Given this view, it should come as no surprise that anger is associated with women. So Plutarch argues:

> Just as with the body a bruise results from a great blow so with the most delicate souls the inclination to inflict pain produces a greater outburst of anger in proportion to their greater weakness. That is why women are more irascible than men. (*Cohib. ira.* 457a)

Similarly, Seneca evokes a woman/animal comparison when he says, "it is for women to rage in anger, for wild beasts doubtless—and yet not even the noble sort of these—to bite and worry their prostrate victims" (*Clem.* 1.5.5). Or, as he puts it more bluntly, "anger is a most womanish and childish weakness" (*Ira.* 1.20.3).[43]

From this position, the philosophers make the next logical step. If true men should not display their anger, God especially should not be subject to anger.[44] Cicero claims that "it is the commonly accepted view of all philosophers that God is never angry, never hurtful" (*Off.* 3.102). He reflects such views as handed down from Epicurus that God "is exempt form outbursts of anger and partiality, for all such things are weaknesses" (in other words, effeminizing).[45] Clearly, for the Jewish or Christian Greek who knew anything of the biblical portrait of God, this aspect of Greco-Roman masculine ideology presented difficulties.

Philo, for one, understands the dilemma. In his essay *On the Unchangeableness of God*, he denies that God was susceptible to any pathos or passion whatsoever, in spite of Genesis 6:7: "I will blot out man from the face of the earth . . . because I have grown angry that I made them." This means that Philo must explain why the author (Moses) misrepresented God, who has no human weakness. His solution lies in the need for instruction and discipline. Just as an ill-disciplined slave needs a frightening master to train them, so Moses understands that a fool must be admonished through depiction of a threatening and angry god (*Deus* 60–68).[46] In this way, Philo preserves the reputations of

God, Moses, and the scripture. He also solves the problem of an angry, effeminate god.

But there were other, competing claims regarding the relationship between anger and manliness. Even as he refutes the position, Plutarch admits
that some do understand anger as a manly act. Apparently, there are "many" for
whom the drive and ferocity produced by anger indicate "activity," "boldness,"
"force of character," "firmness of resolution," even "hatred of evil" (*Cohib. ira.*
456f). In this view, rather than threatening one's masculinity, anger actually
displayed it. As David Brakke puts it:

> Because anger motivated a man to action in righting wrongs to
> himself and others, because its opposite appeared to be passivity in
> the face of challenges from other males, because—to put it simply—
> it raised the body's temperature, anger appeared to be a characteristic
> of masculinity, a sign that a man was indeed a manly man.[47]

Philo might have drawn on this competing perspective to exonerate the
biblical deity. By the fourth century, the Christian writer Lactantius does just
this. He comments, "I have often noticed... that many people believe that
which even some philosophers have held, namely, that God does not get
angry" (*Ir.* 1.1). Lactantius goes on to dispute both the Epicurean and the Stoic
arguments about God's lack of anger, which points both to the popularity of
this position and to the problem it caused for Christians.[48] The biblical God
clearly became angry on a regular basis throughout the Old and New Testament. Did this impugn God's virtuous character, his masculinity?

Lactantius refutes both the Epicurean notion that the gods have no emotions and the Stoic reasoning that God, as an exemplar of moral virtue, would
never get angry. Instead, he asserts that God's anger is a consequence of his
kindness (*Ir.* 6). One cannot exist without the other. Unlike humans, however,
God has power over his anger, not vice versa. Moreover, God's anger is not
temporal. He has eternal anger at those who continue in sin (*Ir.* 21). The
fourth-century bishop Basil extends this notion to men. While he is opposed to
the unseemly display of anger in most cases, he also suggests the possibility of
a "proper anger," one that is linked to "hatred of sin." Moreover, Basil makes
clear with not-so-subtle imagery that this type of anger actually aids the cause
of masculinity. "If the soul should become enervated from pleasure," he argues, "anger hardens it as with a tincture of iron and restores it from a most
weak and flaccid state to strictness and vigor" (*Against Those Prone to Anger,*
456).[49]

Thus, with the case of anger, as with the tension between generativity and
sexual restraint, one finds another place of contradiction. It is another instance,

as Brakke suggests, in which the Greco-Roman ideology of masculinity is at odds with itself. Also notable is the degree of attention devoted to a cultural perspective that might impugn the gendered identity of Christian men, and even worse, the masculinity of God.

Masculinity, Courage, and Pain

If true men avoided anger, lust, luxury, avarice, and excess of any kind, on the positive side they sought opportunities for manly displays of courage. Whereas the Latin *vir* is a cognate of *virtus*, the Greek *andreia* can be rendered either courage or manliness. They are one and the same. Such displays were often expressed in terms of courage in battle with a formidable opponent. So, for example, Cicero defends the reputation of Murena, disputing Cato's claims that he fought a war "against a lot of women" (the Mithridates). Cicero speaks instead of the "hard fighting" and the officer's unquestionable courage in battle (*Mur.* 31).

Noble acts of suicide were also counted as displays of bravery. There are many such examples to draw on, but one notable example is the suicide of Otho as described by Suetonius. According to Suetonius, the courageous suicide of Otho was enough to overcome the reputation of effeminacy that he had gained during life. Suetonius begins the account of Otho's suicide by opining that "neither Otho's person nor his bearing suggested such great courage." According to Suetonius, Otho was most womanly in personal hygiene—having his body hair plucked, wearing a wig, shaving his face every day. Given this effeminate behavior, Suetonius notes that his manly death that was "so little in harmony with his life excited the greater marvel." He describes the reaction to his death as follows:

> Many of the soldiers who were present kissed his hands and feet as he lay dead, weeping bitterly and calling him the bravest of men and an incomparable emperor, and then at once slew themselves beside his bier. . . . In short, the greater part of those who had hated him most bitterly while he lived lauded him to the skies when he was dead . . . " (*Otho* 12)

Otho's willingness to take his life for the good of others by circumventing more death and civil strife made him a true man.

To have courage, or to be "manly," also meant one should bear pain bravely. A true man should not exhibit tears or distress when in pain. Cicero writes at length on this topic, exhorting Publius Sittus to bear his pain bravely, reminding him that he is a *vir*, even while being a *homo* (*Fam.* 5.17.3).[50] In a similar way, he tells of Gaius Marius, who underwent surgery without constraints for one leg, but opted out of surgery on the other. As Cicero puts it, "Thus being a man [*vir*], he bore pain, being a human [*homo*] he refused to bear greater without actual necessity" (*Tusc.* 2.22.53). Again, pointing to the larger principle at work, Cicero concludes, "The whole point then is to be master of yourself" (*Tusc.* 2.22.53). Drawing on the familiar contrast, Cicero makes clear that to do otherwise would be to act in a "slavelike" or "womanish" way (*Tusc.* 2.22.55).

To summarize the discussion thus far, concepts of masculinity and effeminacy were part of a larger system designed to separate true men from everyone else. In this system, as Williams observes, "the oppositional pair masculine/effeminate can be aligned with various other binarisms such as moderation/excess; hardness/softness; courage/timidity; strength/weakness; activity/passivity; sexual penetration/being sexually penetrated; and encompassing all of these, domination/submission."[51] Indeed, as was clear in the accusation against Pompey, the point of self-mastery was ultimately mastery over others. Dio Chrysostom makes this explicit when he asks, "If a man is not competent to govern a single man, and that too a man who is very close to him, in fact his constant companion, and if, again, he cannot guide a single soul, and that his own, how could he be king?" (*Regn. tyr.* Or. 62.1). Or, in Williams's words, "A man must exercise dominion over his own body and his own desires as well as the bodies and desires of those under his jurisdiction—his wife, children and slaves—just as the Roman citizenry as a whole ideally dominates most of the rest of the world."[52]

Learning to Be a Man

Having detailed the dominant ideology of masculinity that coursed through the veins of the Greco-Roman world, it may be useful to examine the process of transfusion from culture to individual. Apart from whatever enculturation a boy received from his family, the primary place where a young boy would begin to learn how to be a man would be the educational system. As W. Bloomer has aptly put it, "When first the child puts pen to paper, or stylus to wax, he practices a kind of social distinction."[53]

Boys (and some girls) from elite families were schooled at an early age with gnomic school texts. Thus, their training in literacy involved the copying and recopying of literary maxims.[54] Not surprisingly, many of these maxims concern virtue, either general statements such as "Practice virtue" or "Flee blame," or statements regarding particularly virtuous behavior—being truthful, just, and so on.[55] But a large portion of these literary quotes also concern women. Teresa Morgan cites the following: "Touch a woman and open your tomb." "Don't trust a woman with your *bios*." "For an old man to become a lover is the final catastrophe." She goes on to summarize the overall point of these maxims:

> Women are wild, evil, uncontrollable. They should always be silent and are dangerous when they confer; life would be carefree if it were not for the talk of women. They know nothing but what they want, but an educated woman is a dangerous anomaly. Woman is the beginning of *hamartia*. She must be ruled.[56]

Here is a place where one could say much about the misogynistic construction of women. But what do such texts do for the construction of masculine identity? In part, they present young boys with a negative image of women, thereby reinforcing all that is positive about the pursuit of a manly identity. To become a man means becoming the opposite of wild, evil, and uncontrollable. It is to be the ruler rather than the ruled.

In addition to these negative examples, boys were also schooled with stories of men to emulate. The degree to which such stories were repeated is reflected in Seneca's instructions on facing death fearlessly. After illustrating his point through the example of the courageous Mucius, Seneca voices the objections of his interlocutor, Lucilius: "Oh," you say, "those stories have been droned to death in all the schools; pretty soon, when you reach the topic, 'On Despising Death,' you will be telling me about Cato." Seneca goes on to do just that ("And why should I not?" he asks), relating the story of Cato's noble suicide in the face of a life under Caesar's triumvirate (*Ep.* 24.6).

This education through school drills using maxims and models was the first step in constructing men of status and distinction. Indeed, Cicero claims that the two professions that raise men to the highest level of distinction are the successful general and the good orator (*Mur.* 30). According to Quintilian, to become a perfect orator what is most essential is to be a good man (*vir bonus*). "Consequently," he says, "we demand of him not merely the possession of exceptional gifts of speech, but of all the virtues of character as well" (*Inst.* 1.Pr. 9). For this reason, Quintilian explains, he "shall frequently be compelled to speak of such virtues as courage, justice, self-control" (*Inst.* 1.Pr.12). Highlighting the association between rhetoric and true masculinity, Quintilian complains about a declamatory style that has lost its vigor and become "flaccid and nerveless":

> Declaimers are guilty of exactly the same offence as slave-dealers who castrate boys in order to increase the attractions of their beauty. For just as the slave-dealer regards strength and muscle, and above all the

beard and other natural characteristic of manhood as blemishes, and soften down all that would be sturdy if allowed to grow, on the ground that is it harsh and hard, even so we conceal the manly form of eloquence and power of speaking closely and forcibly by giving it a delicate complexion of style and, so long as what we say is smooth and polished, are absolutely indifferent as to whether our words have any power or no. (*Inst.* 5.12.18)

In contrast, Quintilian urges that a young man in training should strive for victory in the schools, equipping himself with weapons and learning "how to strike the vitals of his foe and protect his own" (*Inst.* 5.12.20).

Such training in rhetoric constituted the highest level of education and was reserved for the most elite class. To accentuate the vigor of this training and its ultimate goal, the educational process was often described as a steep road leading to virtue. This link between the arduous educational journey and the attainment of masculinity is obvious in such texts as Lucian's *Rhetorum praeceptor*. In this amusing parody, Lucian's narrator, a teacher of rhetoric, offers two roads to rhetoric: one difficult, one easy. While seemingly skewering both paths, Lucian provides useful insight into the gendered connotation of rhetorical training. His "teacher" urges the student to choose the quick and easy route. But it soon becomes clear that if one avoids long, hard educational training and "takes the road that is easy and downhill" toward the mastery of rhetoric, among the causalities will be one's masculinity. The downhill road can lead only to becoming a ridiculously absurd and womanly imposter of rhetoric.

Such gender implications are clear as the teacher describes the guide for the difficult road as "a vigourous man with hard muscles and a manly stride, who shows heavy tan on his body, and is bold-eyed and alert"(*Rh.Pr* 9). Along with making the student "dig-up long buried speeches as if they were something tremendously helpful," this guide "will say that hard work, scant sleep, abstention from wine, and untidiness are necessary and indispensable; it is impossible, says he, to get over the road without them" (*Rh.Pr* 9–10). But the teacher urges the student to "bid a long good-bye to that hairy, unduly masculine fellow, leaving him to climb up himself, all blown and dripping with sweat and lead up what others he can delude" (*Rh.Pr* 10). Instead, the student should turn to the easy road. On this path, the guide to rhetoric will be "a wholly clever and wholly handsome gentleman with a mincing gait, a thin neck, a languishing eye, and a honeyed voice, who distils perfume, scratches his head with the tip of his finger, and carefully dresses his hair"; in short, a wholly effeminate man (*Rh.Pr* 11). The equipment necessary for the training includes "ignorance; secondly, recklessness, and thereto effrontery and shamelessness. Modesty, respectability, self-restraint and blushes may be left at home, for they are useless and somewhat of a hindrance to the matter in hand." Clothing should either be brightly colored or transparent, and sandals should be the high Attic type that women wear, with many slits (*Rh.Pr* 15). And so Lucian goes on with tongue firmly in cheek, making his point abundantly clear.

In a more serious vein, the elder Seneca also links lack of rhetorical skill with effeminacy. He bemoans the absence of this skill in the youth of the day, blaming their effeminate lifestyle:

> Look at our young men: they are lazy, their intellects asleep; no-one can stay awake to take pains over a single honest pursuit. . . .
> Libidinous delight in song and dance transfixes these effemina-
> tes. Braiding the hair, refining the voice till it is as caressing as a
> woman's competing in bodily softness with women, beautifying
> themselves with filthy fineries—this is the pattern our youths set
> themselves. Which of your contemporaries—quite apart from his
> talent and diligence—is sufficiently a man? Born feeble and spine-
> less, they stay like that throughout their lives: taking others' chastity
> by a storm, careless of their own. (*Controv.* 1, Pr. 8–9)

In keeping with the elder Seneca's perspective, Roman oratory is replete with warnings against an effeminacy that might be detected in phrasing, syntax, or use of rhetorical figures.[57] Often these warnings came by way of reference to woman and slaves. So, for example, Quintilian urges that instructors "should not permit the student's hand to be raised above the level of the eyes or lowered beneath the belly," lest the youth appear to imitate the "lively movements common among maidservants and unmarried women" (*Inst.* 11.3.112). Or, as Joy Connolly puts it, training in rhetoric involved "erasing any traces of fem-inine and servile practice, disciplining [the student's] body to maintain an upright posture, unwavering gaze, restrained gestures, and other signs that enacted his social dominance." Such discipline "was paramount to the project of transforming a youth into a master."[58]

In the early part of a boy's *paideia*, this disciplining of the body involved physical as well as mental discipline. Indeed, there is abundant evidence to suggest that physical beatings were a common part of a young boy's education from classical Greece through the empire. Catherine Atherton points to the categorical overlap between children, animals, and slaves that may have con-tributed to this practice. Plutarch seems to be the exception to typical practice when he advises that children ought to be led by encouragement and reason, rather than by "blows or ill treatment," since the latter are "more fitting for slaves rather than freeborn" (*Lib. ed.* 8.12). As Atherton notes, Plutarch's "anxious protestations against the (over-)use of force suggest the practice of treating children in much the same way as slaves was widespread."[59] The point of such treatment, as Atherton notes, was to further mastery of the skills that would allow young boys to take their place among the adult elite. Moreover, by climbing the "the ladder of eloquence" and moving from boy to man, or from *grammaticus* to *rhetor*, one also rose above the susceptibility to corporeal punishment.[60]

But there seem to be even higher aspirations associated with education. This difficult journey to rhetorical mastery also drew one closer to the gods. As one school poem expressed this idea: "Would that I could complete my general education. I long to rise up in the air and come near Zeus's abode."[61] In contrast, Cribiore notes the implication of a lack of education: "The uneducated man was marked not only by insignificance but also by this inability to rise above and fly 'aloft to the region where the gods dwell' (Plato *Phdr.* 246d)."[62] In this way, education and masculine formation is linked to divinity. And this is not the only way that masculinity and divinity are connected. The next chapter will explore more fully the relationship between masculinity and divinity through examination of three different "ideal men" from the Greco-Roman world.

3

Constructing the Lives
of Divine Men

Divus *Augustus, Philo's Moses,*
and Philostratus's Apollonius

But in truth, except for a widespread fondness for apotheosis of great
men, there is no set type or model of theios aner.
—Howard Clark Kee, *Jesus in History*

This statement by Howard Clark Kee is intended as a critique of the
use of the "divine man" category for understanding New Testament
Christology. For him, the "widespread fondness for apotheosis of
great men" is little more than an aside to his more significant point
regarding the lack of a set type of divine man. Kee's point that there
was "no set type or model" of divine man in the ancient world is
certainly correct. But for this study, his observation of widespread
divinization of whoever was considered a "great man" is more interesting. In fact, both points are what make the examination of divine
men in antiquity a critical part of understanding representations of
Jesus in the New Testament.

First, the lack of a "set type" of divine man hardly renders the
concept useless. The fact that there was more than one type of divine man points instead to the rich array of possibilities that were
available to early Christians as they contemplated and presented their
own divine man—Jesus Christ. Second, the widespread fondness
for divinizing great men points precisely to the importance of understanding what constituted a great man. Past studies of the category
tended to focus on aspects that reflected the divinity of these figures,
especially the miracle traditions. But the common denominator of

these erstwhile divine men may lie more in what rendered them divine in the first place, namely their ideal masculinity. In this sense, when Kee points to the "widespread fondness for apotheosis of great men," he says more than he realizes about the construction of masculinity in the ancient world.

Masculinity, Status and Divinity: The Cosmic Gender Hierarchy

Chapter 2 illustrated how achieving masculinity had less to do with a biologically male body than with personal conduct. Moreover, the training by which one became a man was limited, in large part, to the elite classes of society. At least within the ideology of the elite class, perfect masculinity formed the apex of the social hierarchy, with all other categories defined in relation to it. In this sense, masculinity was fundamentally concerned with status. The higher the social status one achieved, the more masculine one became and vice versa. True men were distinct from and positioned above all others, whether these "others" were slaves, women, boys, foreigners, or men who assumed a passive role in sexual relations.

This social hierarchy was part of the great cosmic hierarchy that extended beyond the realm of animals, slaves, women, and men, to daemons, demigods, and finally to the one most powerful god residing at the top. What also extended into the higher regions of the hierarchy was the equation of masculinity with perfection. As already noted, Aristotle assumes that masculinity is more godlike than femininity. He also suggests that surpassing virtue changes men into gods (ἐξ ἀνθρώπον γίνονται θεοὶ δἰ ἀρετῆς ὑπερβολήν, Eth. nic. 7.1.2). Plato speaks of the nature of god as that which is least liable to be altered by external influences, that is, one who is most courageous/manly (ἀνδρειοτατην), having the wisest type of ψυχή (Rep. 381a). In discussing this passage, Angela Hobbs wonders whether in this case it is accurate to equate courage with manliness. She asks, "In what sense can god be said to be manly? Or is courageous here supposed to transcend gender?"[1] Such questions reflect contemporary ways of connecting masculinity with biology more than ancient concepts of masculinity did. From this perspective, God cannot be a male (person), so God cannot be described as manly. God transcends gender. But if masculinity is equated with perfection, unity, rationality, order, and completeness, as it was in the ancient world, God would *necessarily* be masculine, even while incorporeal and asexual. Rather than transcending gender, God is the perfect example of masculinity.

Another important aspect of this cosmic gender hierarchy is its fluidity.[2] If one could move up and down a gender hierarchy in terms of one's manly status, it stands to reason that this would also pertain to one's godly status. And one hardly needs to make a case for relativity and fluidity in the divine/human hierarchy within Greco-Roman religions. From the hero cult of ancient Greece to the imperial cult of the Romans, the idea of a person becoming a god was a part of the cultural ethos of the ancient Mediterranean world. With respect to Philo's era, the authors of *Religions of Rome* point out, "The boundary between gods and men was never as rigidly defined in Roman paganism as it is supposed to be in modern Judaeo-Christian tradition. . . . There was no sharp polarity, but a spectrum between the human and divine."[3] A good illustration of the fluidity between humanity and divinity during this period is the famous Prima Porta statue, with its simultaneous depiction of the emperor Augustus at different points on the hierarchy ascending from human to hero to god. The statue celebrates Augustus as military conqueror while making clear his divine ancestry. His sandaled feet are not those of a mortal; they recall gods and heroes. The details of his breastplate depict images that turn the historical event of the victory at Parthia into a paradigm of salvation. As Paul Zanker puts it, "the princeps who wears this new image of victory on his breastplate becomes the representative of divine providence and the will of the gods. It is not a question of heroic deeds; through his very existence, the offspring of the gods guarantees the world order."[4] It is images such as this that reveal an ancient cultural worldview that entertained the idea of movement from man to god (and god to man).

Moreover, this fluid continuum was not limited to Roman paganism, but was present within Judaism as well. For example, the notion of intermediary beings that populate the cosmos was common to Jewish literature. Hurtado has grouped such divine agents into three categories: personified divine attributes such as Wisdom or Philo's Logos, exalted patriarchs, and principal angels such as Michael.[5] Apocalyptic literature is filled with divine intermediaries and heavenly ascents that enable the transformation of human beings into angels.[6]

But even a nonapocalyptic writer like Philo can refer to biblical heroes like Abraham and Jacob becoming "equal to the angels" (*Sacr.* 1–10). Isaac proves to be higher than the angels (*Sacr.* 6) and Moses higher still (*Sacr.* 8). Clearly, this Alexandrian Jewish philosopher shares with the rest of the Roman world the idea of a divine continuum. From his perspective, there are beings who are more or less divine, and there are exceptional men who are capable of becoming more divine than they formerly were.

Even more pertinent is the institutional practice of promoting Roman emperors to gods, either at their deaths or sometimes while still living. Past scholarship sometimes downplayed the divinization of the emperor as little more than political propaganda. The imperial cult was often viewed as a transplant from the east that no Roman mind could readily accept, so that any ritual of deification was done with a wink. However, more recent work has analyzed the phenomenon through the lens of the Roman religio-political system, rather than through Judeo-Christian categories. Doing so has made possible new insight into the nature of the imperial cult practice.

For example, Ittai Gradel's work on emperor worship resists a fundamental distinction between religion and politics with respect to the Roman world.[7] He argues that whether the emperor was viewed as god or man when worshipped in divine rites, or whether he was a political or religious figure, would not be relevant questions for the Romans. What mattered in the ancient sociopolitical context, according to Gradel, was one's status vis-à-vis others. The more power one had, the higher the honors bestowed. The point of divine honors, then, was to express "a superhuman status of absolute power, divinity in a relative sense."[8] In this sense, "the man-god divide in a pagan context was a distinction in status between the respective beings, rather than a distinction between their natures or 'species'."[9] Concretely, Gradel points out the case of Augustus. "In terms of the traditional, republican social hierarchy there could be little doubt: Augustus had burst out of the top of the social structure, into the level of the gods; his power was divine, that is, absolute in his sphere of control."[10]

In this chapter, the relationship between masculinity, status, and divinity is explored further through examination of Caesar Augustus and two other "divine men" from antiquity—Philo's Moses, and Philostratus's Apollonius of Tyana. Whereas chapter 2 provided an overview of qualities that identified someone as a true man, this chapter presents three different examples of ideal men—case studies, in a sense—that illustrate these qualities in particular figures. Taken together, the three examples cover much of the empire geographically—Rome proper, Egypt, and the Greek East. Temporally, the figures span the beginning of the empire through the third century c.e. While these men (both authors and their subjects) differ in significant ways, they nevertheless illustrate the overall consistency and pervasiveness of certain aspects of Greco-Roman masculinity and its links to divinity.

Consideration of these diverse and divine men will show that while there is no set model or requirement for achieving godly status, there are certain consistent demonstrations of ideal masculinity in their literary representations. For example, each of these men shows special promise in his childhood. Each shows little, if any, interest in sex. Each is a model of virtue and piety. Each figure engages in critiques of others that involve gender slurs and attacks on their opponents' masculinity. And, of course, each is regarded as divine in some sense. Such similarities should not be surprising. All of the authors who wrote about these figures were members of the elite literate culture. All of them would have received some form of the education discussed in the last chapter. It is no wonder that all three heroic figures—Moses, Augustus, and Apollonius—are presented with many of the traits of ideal masculinity discussed in the previous chapter. These divine men and their "biographers" illustrate the temporal and spatial range of the ideology of Greco-Roman masculinity and the multiple ways that this ideology found literary expression. The divine men discussed here form part of the cultural fabric into which the New Testament writers wove their own presentations of Jesus.

Caesar Augustus: The Model of Masculinity

There is an enormous amount of scholarship devoted to Augustus and the Augustan age.[11] Much of this work has focused on the ways that Augustus shaped and displayed his public image during his thirty-seven-year reign.[12] Many have noted his skill in presenting himself as a conserver of traditional Roman values, even as he shaped and defined the new office of Principate and introduced new legislation to promote his social agenda. With the gender construction of Augustus, one finds a similar mix of tradition and innovation. On the one hand, the public portrayal of Augustus is deeply rooted in the traditions of Greco-Roman masculinity. Both Augustus and his supporters were fully formed by the gender ideology outlined in the preceding chapter. On the other hand, Augustus also brought something new. With the Principate, all the ideals of masculine deportment, and the honor and authority that accompany them, were concentrated in one man. This ideal man was to be a model of Roman masculinity for all other aspiring men.

From Octavian to Augustus, or, In Defense of Manliness

As with all men of the Greco-Roman period, Caesar Augustus, the *princeps*, or "first man" of the empire, was not born but was carefully constructed through education, cultivation, and especially through representation. From the young boy, Octavian, emerged the carefully constructed man who was to be Augustus. Insight into both the boy and the man comes through literary and historical reconstructions of these figures, as well as through the material remains of statues, coins, altar friezes, and inscriptions. In what follows, the line between "history" and "representation" is not carefully drawn, nor could it be. The interest here is on the cultural creation of "Caesar Augustus," itself a mix of historical "fact" and orchestrated fiction.

The earliest glimpses of the man, Augustus, come by way of gendered attacks by Octavian's enemies. Perhaps the most graphic of these attacks are found in inscriptions on a collection of ancient sling bullets uncovered from Octavian's historical siege of Perusia in 41/40 B.C.E.[13] Sling bullets were often cast with messages for the enemy, and much can be said of the gendered nature of this particular war based on the sling bullets that were discovered on site. The war was waged against Fulvia, wife of Mark Antony, and Antony's brother, Lucius Antonius, and the sling bullets contain sexual slander against both sides of the struggle.[14] Of particular interest here, however, are the sling bullets that attack the gender identity of Octavian. The bullets contain crude references to Octavian's submission to anal and oral penetration, referring to him not as "Caesar" or Octavian, but rather using the feminine name, "Octavia."[15]

Further evidence for gendered attacks against Octavian comes from Suetonius's collection of accusations pointing to his sexual deviance (*Aug.* 68).[16] Suetonius begins his account with the claim that "in early youth, he was harassed with charges of various disgraceful acts" (*prima iuventa variorum dedecorum infamian subiit*, my translation). Among these, Suetonius lists Mark Antony's claim that Octavian earned adoption by Julius Caesar through illicit sexual relations with him. The term used to describe these relations is *stupro*, a word that is difficult to translate, but which, as Craig Williams has argued, typically connotes "the violation of the sexual integrity of the freeborn Roman, male or female."[17] Thus, along with casting Octavian as a penetrated man, the term challenges his status as a freeborn male, associating him with the category of a slave. Suetonius also reports the charge of Antony's brother that, after having had sex with his uncle, Octavian sold himself to Aulus Hirtius. (Hirtius was a Roman consul who initially supported Antony but then aligned himself with Octavian.) This accusation is coupled with the claim that Octavian tried to cosmetically soften the hair on his legs, thus making himself more effeminate.

Suetonius suggests that such gender mockery was perpetrated by the general public as well. He gives an account of a theatre audience applauding a line that they take as a reference to Octavian (*Aug.* 69). In the comedy, the line refers to a *gallus*, a castrated priest of the Mother goddess who is beating his timbrel, himself the picture of effeminacy. The line from the play makes use of a double wordplay that allows for a simultaneous reference to the drum-beating eunuch and the Roman ruler.

> *Videsne, ut cinaedus orbem digito temperat?*
>   See, a *cinaedus*'s finger beats/controls the drum/world! (my translation)

While the typical translation for *cinaedus* is "wanton," this fails to capture the full significance of the term. The word was not only about lust or lasciviousness; it also carried a network of associations that undercut the ideals of normative Roman masculinity. Though it was the primary term to describe a sexually penetrated man, as Craig Williams argues, it is not anchored in a specific sexual practice. Instead, the word is borrowed from the Greek κιναιδος, a term that was used to signify an effeminate dancer who used a tambourine and moved his buttocks in suggestively sexual ways. Thus, in the Roman context, the term became a "multifaceted insult." As Williams puts it, "To call a Roman man a *cinaedus* was to associate him with the East ... with dancing ... and with the effeminate sexual role of being penetrated."[18] In other words, when the audience laughs, it is because the comedy associates Octavian with a eunuch priest, puts him in the category of the effeminate eastern dancer, and designates him as a man who has been anally penetrated.

Other accounts from Suetonius and Dio Cassius suggest that Octavian was also challenged with respect to his military prowess, his courage, his strength, and his clemency. Suetonius records reports of Octavian's flight from battle at Philippi to Antony's camp, and then his ill treatment of the captives from the battle (*Aug.* 13). Dio's *Roman History* includes a speech by Antony to his troops before Actium that highlights Octavian's bodily weakness and military failures (DioCass 50.18.3). In short, his enemies challenged those aspects of his character that demonstrated his qualities as a true man. If this were the only picture that survived of Augustus, historians might wonder how he ever came to be Rome's "first man." Certainly, attacks such as these would put Octavian in a defensive position.[19]

It is apparently from just such a position that Octavian undertook to write an autobiography, perhaps his earliest attempt at presenting himself as a worthy man.[20] While this work has not survived, knowledge of its contents comes through a number of ancient authors who used the autobiography as a source for their own histories.[21] The most immediate access to Octavian's work is most likely Nicolaus of Damascus's laudatory *Life of Augustus* (*Vit. Caes*).[22] In writing his biography, Nicolaus appears to have relied heavily on Octavian's own account, though it is difficult to tell how much Nicolaus embellished it for his own panegyric.[23] Still, whatever combination of effort lies behind the flattering portrayal, Octavian certainly would have approved of its writing and dissemination.

Nicolaus's account covers the first eighteen or nineteen years of Octavian's life. He clearly wants to impress his readers with the promise and character that Octavian showed from a very early age. By his account, Octavian was a quick learner, more intelligent than his teachers, and one who worked hard to train both his body and mind (*Vit. Caes.* 6).[24] His public-speaking ability is established early when he gives the funeral oration for his deceased grand-mother. Thus, Octavian is depicted as one who shows promise of developing into a true man. Nicolaus makes special mention of Octavian's rite of passage into manhood, when he changed the purple-edged toga for the pure white one. At the same time, Octavian was enlisted into the priesthood (*Vit. Caes.* 8). This, however, presents certain complications for him. According to Nicolaus, al-though Octavian went to the temple on the prescribed days, he had to do so at night. Otherwise, he was in danger of being compromised by the many women who were overcome by his good looks and lineage. While his mother sought to protect him from the attentions of such women, Octavian apparently had the good sense to stay out of trouble all on his own (*Vit. Caes.* 12). In response to the sexual slander of his critics, such a story builds a very different picture of Octavian—attesting to his extraordinary appearance, but in particular to his sense of duty and virtue, especially his sexual restraint. Similarly, in one fragment of this work, Nicolaus relates a detail that highlights once again the young man's control over his passions. At an age when most young men are especially sexually active, Nicolaus tells his reader, Octavian abstained from sex for a whole year, "out of concern for his voice and fitness" (*Vit. Caes.* 36).[25] Clearly, Nicolaus is at pains to construct Octavian as a particularly disciplined young man.

The biography responds to other gender attacks as well. For instance, critiques of Octavian's courage were answered by the story that he rushed to Julius Caesar's side to join him in battle. According to Nicolaus's account, Octavian was left in Rome to recover from an illness with instructions to join his father once he was well. In response, Octavian attended to his body with great self-control, regained his strength, and set out to join Julius. The story has him racing toward Caesar and to war, covering a huge distance in dan-gerous wartime conditions (*Vit. Caes.* 22–23). Upon seeing Octavian, Julius praises him for his resoluteness and quickly runs the youth through an apti-tude test, which Octavian passes with flying colors (*Vit. Caes.* 24). Such a test seems out of place in the context and can only be understood as further proof of Octavian's rational intelligence.

Overall, Nicolaus provides quite a contrast to the picture of the young Octavian painted by his opponents. Far from a sexually deviant opportunist, Nicolaus (as Octavian no doubt does in his own account) presents a young man with extraordinary self-control. Moreover, he appears as brave on the battle-field, willing to risk his life out of allegiance to his uncle and Rome. In com-menting on the full effect of Octavian's early self-portrayal, Yavetz aptly states, "[Octavian's] enemies vilified his performance in war—he represented himself as a man of *virtus* [virtue]. His enemies depicted him as cruel and savage—he emphasized his *clementia* [clemency]. His enemies charged him with defiance of legal procedures—he paraded his *iustitia* [justice]."[26] In other words, while his opponents attacked Octavian's masculinity, in this early biography Nicolaus (and Augustus) paraded his manliness.[27]

In addition to this positive construction of Octavian's burgeoning masculinity, there is evidence of a gendered counterattack by him on his enemies. Along this line, Dio Cassius reports a speech that Augustus supposedly gave to his army before the Battle of Actium that turned the accusation of eastern effeminacy on Antony. According to Octavian, Antony is no longer Roman, but Egyptian.[28] Living like a woman in royal luxury, he can no longer think or act like a man. His body is weakened like a woman, he acts like a woman, and has become a κίναιδος (DioCass 50.27.1–6).

While Dio's speech is as much a reflection of the third century historian's own gender ideology as of the first-century figures of which he writes, it accurately reflects the gender ideology of Augustus's time as well. Indeed, certain actions that Octavian reportedly took with respect to Antony also contributed to this gendered attack. For example, Octavian illegally made public Antony's will, which included a request to be buried with his family in Alexandria. He used this as further proof that Antony had become an Egyptian (with all the connotations of effeminacy that accompanied such a charge) and intended to move the capital of the empire to Alexandria.

Not only did Octavian make the will public, but as Kraft has argued convincingly, Octavian's building of the Mausoleum displayed in monumental proportions his own "Romanness" against the "Egyptianness" of Antony. This large monument, built early in Augustus's career between the Tiber River and the Via Flaminia, was designed to feature his own rootedness in Italian soil against the eastern proclivities of Antony.[29] He and his family would be buried in Rome, in contrast to Antony.[30] The reports of Octavian and his enemies engaged in such gendered vitriol show the extent to which masculinity (or lack thereof) was central to public perception and crucial to popular support. Of course, Octavian won not just this battle of gendered rhetoric, but also the Battle of Actium in 31 B.C.E. Thus began the Roman Empire and the construction of Roman imperial masculinity in the person of Augustus.[31]

Caesar Augustus, Son of the Deified Julius

Besides defending his manliness through accounts of his sexual restraint and military courage, Octavian used another strategy to bolster his masculine status. He sought early on to establish his links with divine ancestry. Initially,

Octavian calls attention to his divine associations in the wake of the assassination of his adoptive father, Julius Caesar, in 44 B.C.E. Following the Senate's deification of Julius, Octavian quickly publicizes his new position as *divi filius* (son of god). The title was visually illustrated on coins that depicted *divus Iulius* on one side and *Caesar Divi filius* on the other.

The appearance of a comet during the Secular Games that Octavian had dedicated to Julius furthered his cause (Pliny, *Nat.* 2.93–94). Octavian reportedly interpreted the comet as an omen of Julius's apotheosis, and he adopted a star as a central symbol for Julian's divinity. Accordingly, a star was placed on all of Caesar's statues and was used more generally on coins, rings, and seals as a sign of hope in a new age. Eventually, Octavian's own helmet was decorated with a star.[32] Octavian also constructed a temple in the Forum for worship of Caesar, the newly established god, and altars were set up in cities across Italy. These actions both demonstrated Octavian's allegiance to his adoptive father and made him an immediate relative to a god. This association with Julius also emphasized Octavian's place in the divine lineage of the Julian family, which claimed descent from Aeneas and thereby Venus.

Other traditions grew around the figure of Augustus that emphasized his relationship with yet another god, Apollo, along with his destiny to be ruler of the empire. One such tradition, reported by Suetonius, links Apollo to the conception of Augustus. According to this account, while spending the night in Apollo's temple, Augustus's mother is approached by a snake. Upon waking, she purifies herself as if she has had sexual intercourse, at which point marks like the colors of the snake appear on her body. Ten months later, when Augustus is born, he is regarded as son of Apollo (*Aug.* 94.4). Another tradition relates a portent observed at Rome, warning that "nature was pregnant with a king for the Roman people." As a result, the Senate decreed that no male child born that year should be reared. However, those senators with pregnant wives saw to it that the decree was never officially filed, because, according to Suetonius, they each took the portent as a reference to their own family (*Aug.* 94.3).

Several stories of Octavian in his infancy and youth further illustrate his extraordinary traits. One tells of his disappearance as an infant only to be found in a high tower with his face toward the rising sun. Another story relates Octavian's dealings with some noisy frogs. Following his command for silence, frogs never again croaked in that place. Suetonius also reports several dreams of high-ranking Roman men that tell of Jupiter's appointment of Augustus to be savior of the country (*Aug.* 94.8–9). The origin of these accounts is unclear, as is when they first circulated. But given the early promotion of Octavian as son of the deified Julius, it is easy to conceive of Augustus and his supporters developing such traditions at a fairly early stage.

In any case, by 27 C.E., Octavian had defeated his opponents, both bringing an end to civil war and achieving sole power over the empire. While many senators were worried about the latter result, they honored the former by conferring on him the name Augustus. Several ancient authors report a discussion about giving the name Romulus to Octavian, as the second founder of Rome. The version given by Florus suggests that Augustus was chosen over Romulus because of its associations with the sacred. He writes, "It was also discussed in the Senate whether he should not be called Romulus, because he had established the empire; but the name of Augustus was deemed more holy and venerable, in order that, while he still dwelt upon earth, he might be given a name and title which raised him to the rank of a deity" (Florus, *Rom.* 2.34.66; see also Suetonius, *Aug.* 7.2; DioCass 53.16.6–8). This association with the sacred can be seen at two levels. On the one hand, the title accents the emperor's respect for and attention to the gods, that is, his *pietas*. On the other hand, "augustus" designated something in which divine power resided. As Ramage puts it, "On a more general level, the emperor could be termed *augustus* because he was the source and place of residence of his Genius that was the object of formal worship. There was no temple for this cult; the emperor was himself its *templum augustum*."[33]

In this post-Actium period, an image of the newly named Augustus begins to take shape. If the young Octavian was concerned to defend his masculinity by highlighting his prodigious intelligence, courage, strength, military prowess, and self-control, the mature Caesar Augustus sought to model it through expressions of his classical beauty, beneficence, humility, and above all, piety. If he spent the early part of his career defending his masculinity and securing his position as first man of the empire, he spent his later years defining and modeling what Roman masculinity should be.

Perhaps the best access to this Roman imperial masculinity is through Augustus's *Res Gestae Divi Augustus* (Deeds of the Deified Augustus). This was an account written by Augustus toward the end of his reign with instructions for it to be cast in bronze and displayed at the entrance to the Mausoleum.[34] It begins, as one would expect, with a detailing of his military successes and, in effect, his conquering of the world, so that he has control of everything (*Res ges. divi Aug.* 1–3). In this way, Augustus accents the universal character of his achievements. Still, he also indicates a shift in the *Res Gestae*, when he recalls that he removed eighty silver statues of himself either standing or on horseback, and he used the money to dedicate "golden offerings" in the Temple of Apollo (*Res ges. divi Aug.* 24). Even more explicitly, he establishes himself as an example, stating, "I myself set precedents in many things for posterity to imitate" (8). Others recognized his role as model as well, as is clear from the comments of Velleius: "For the best of emperors teaches his citizens to do right by doing it, and though he is greatest among us in authority, he is still greater in the example which he sets" (Vell. Pat. 2.126.4).

What example did he set as sole ruler of the empire? First, while he admits to his military successes, Augustus stresses his clemency and moderation in dealing with his enemies. He says, "As victor I spared all the citizens who sought pardon. As for foreign nations, those which I was able to safely forgive, I preferred to preserve than to destroy" (*Res ges. divi Aug.* 3). Second, in contrast to the early military statues that decorated Rome, the later images of Augustus frequently depicted him in his priestly role, veiled and offering sacrifice to the gods. The famous relief on the Ars Pacis is the most prominent among them. Here Augustus is presented in a sacrificial procession with his family. Bowersock has argued that this famous scene depicts the inauguration of Augustus as the Pontifex Maximus. Whether or not he is right on this point, he is certainly correct in seeing the priestly office as centrally important to Augustus. As Bowersock puts it, "It was in the majesty of the pontificate that Augustus presented himself as the conqueror who bought peace."[35] Furthermore, it is in this priestly role that he most clearly models his *pietas* for others to follow. In the *Res Gestae*, Augustus notes his role as priest in multiple priestly colleges, including some that he revived, and his eventual acceptance of the title Pontifex Maximus (*Res ges. divi Aug.* 7, 10). As further display of his *pietas*, Augustus lists his extensive building program, in which he built or restored multiple temples across Rome (*Res ges. divi Aug.* 19–21).

In addition to displaying his clemency as a conqueror and piety as a priest, Augustus also uses the *Res Gestae* to portray himself as a generous, beneficent ruler, caring for his citizens and soldiers like a father for his children. Indeed, he is the *euergetes* par excellence. Thus, Augustus lists in detail the sums of money paid out to soldiers and plebs, recalls how he bought grain and made food distributions, and distributed from his inheritance to the military treasury (*Res ges. divi Aug.* 5). The apex of the *Res Gestae* comes in the last chapter, where Augustus recounts how the Senate, the equestrians, and the entire Roman people awarded him the title *patrem patriae*, father of the country.[36] Suetonius recounts how Augustus accepted this honor with tears, saying he had attained his "highest hope" (*Aug.* 58).

This report of tears is in keeping with the overall tone of the *Res Gestae*. Although Augustus reports on all his achievements, he does so from a position of humility. Several times Augustus emphasizes his refusal of various honors and titles, particularly any position that was "contrary to the traditions of the ancestors" (*Res ges. divi Aug.* 6). He carefully avoids use of the word *potestas* to describe his own power, speaking instead only of his tribunal power, or of his

auctoritas. The former term had a very specific connotation of holding a particular political office. *Auctoritas,* on the other hand, implies personal authority
that accrued to individuals who achieved success in working for the republic.
As Grant puts it, "Every office, every power, and every success—the constitu-
ents of *dignitas*—enhanced the inherited *auctoritas* of Augustus until it became
his unique and personal attribute or characteristic, enabling him to act (in a
way not permitted to mere men) without *potestas* or *imperium.*[37] Thus, the term
was more of a public recognition of success than a claim to power.[38]

Historians have long puzzled over the purpose of the *Res Gestae.*[39] Given
Augustus's instructions for its public display at the Mausoleum, one might
argue that it was his final appeal to the Roman public regarding his character.
However, as Yavetz argues, it is a lengthy text to read in detail while picnicking
in the park around the Mausoleum.[40] Among the other reasons given for its
composition, two are particularly interesting for this study. The first is that the
Res Gestae was primarily intended for instructional purposes, especially for
the next generation. In keeping with the Roman tradition of educating the
young men through example, the *Res Gestae* can be viewed as Augustus's
attempt to provide a lasting model of masculinity for young Roman boys.[41] The
second idea is that the *Res Gestae* is an argument or justification for the emperor's divinization. Of course, there need be no single reason behind
the project. As Brian Bosworth argues, on one level, the *Res Gestae* is no doubt
a record of achievement. On another level, it is justification of Augustus's
divine status.[42] Both ideas are intricately linked to the ideology of masculinity.
On the earthly level, Augustus is concerned to set the next generation of boys
on the proper course to manliness though the example of his ideal leadership.
On a heavenly level, his own ideal masculinity has earned him a place with the
gods.

The Imperial Male Body or the Body Beautiful

Suetonius tells us that Augustus was exceedingly beautiful and graceful in
every period of his life, with a well-proportioned, symmetrical figure (*Aug.* 79).
This description is accompanied by a more graphic depiction that paints a
picture of Augustus as short of stature, with bad teeth, unsightly skin, a weak
left leg, an occasional limp, and a slightly bent nose. We should be careful not
to apply our twenty-first-century ideals of beauty to the first century. Even so,
the physical description afforded by Suetonius seems not entirely cohesive. In
fact, it provides a perfect example of the difference between the public imperial
image, which indeed was always exceedingly beautiful, and the very human
reality of the man Augustus. Many scholars have noted that although Augustus

lived until he was seventy-seven, there are no surviving statues or portraits of him as an elderly man. Instead, the portrait type that was copied throughout the empire showed always a youthful, handsome man.[43]

As mentioned earlier, the most well-known of the statues of Augustus is the Prima Porta statue. Much has been written about the significance of this statue, especially its ornate cuirass signifying, as we have seen, Augustus's victories as part of the cosmic order and the divine favor bestowed on Rome through him. As McEwen aptly notes, "Imbricated into the 'flesh' of this cuirass . . . is the entire natural order deployed in a highly charged cosmic-imperial narrative which—and this is the overriding point of the representation—owes its perfect coherence to the wearer's body into which it has been written."[44] And what a body! The apparently skin-tight cuirass reveals the fine musculature of Augustus's torso. Even his navel is revealed, as though one is seeing Augustus in the flesh, rather than wearing a breastplate. The point of this revealing cuirass is that the lofty ideas of victory, peace, security, and order are all worn on what was considered to be the ideal male figure. Scholars have long recognized the influence of the Greek sculptor Polyclitus on the Prima Porta statue, especially his famous Doryphoros (spear-bearer). Polyclitus was revered in his own time as a sculptor, and by the early centuries c.e., his work was widely lauded as the ideal of beauty as represented by the male form. Thus, Quintilian notes, the Doryphoros was the appropriate model when trying to represent a man who was *sanctus et grave* (*Inst.* 5.12.20). In modeling the cuirassed statue of Augustus on the Doryphoros, the sculptor chose a model famous for signifying "masculine purity, moral strength and ideal graceful beauty."[45] At the same time, as discussed earlier, the Prima Porta statue alludes to the divine status of Augustus. His unclad feet suggest a god, as does the presence of the Cupid at his side. As a descendent of Aeneas, Augustus is a son of Venus, as Cupid is. Thus, in all its detail, the statue declares, "Here is Augustus—*theios aner*, bringer of peace, savior of the world."

Divus *Augustus*

Finally, in addition to the portents that Suetonius records regarding the conception and birth of Augustus, he also relates omens of death and divinity. One story tells of lightning striking a statue of Augustus and melting away the "C" in "Caesar." This is taken to mean that he has only one hundred days to live and that he would be counted among the gods, because "aesar" was the Etruscan word for "god." (*Aug.* 97.2). Of course, Augustus was counted among the gods in a very public way after his death. Following in a tradition of state divinization that Augustus promoted with respect to his adoptive father, the apotheosis of Augustus was celebrated throughout the empire with coins, statues, poetry, temples, and sacrificial rites.

There will be occasion to return to the idea of apotheosis and the imperial masculinity of Augustus and its legacy throughout the study. For now, the words of another elite man written several decades after the death of Augustus provide an apt conclusion to the discussion:

> This is Caesar, who calmed the storms which were raging in every
> direction, who healed the common diseases which were afflicting
> both Greeks and barbarians, who descended from the south and from
> the east, and ran on and penetrated as far as the north and the
> west, in such a way as to fill all the neighbouring districts and wa-
> ters with unexpected miseries. This is he who did not only loosen
> but utterly abolish the bonds in which the whole of the habitable
> world was previously bound and weighed down. This is he who de-
> stroyed both the evident and the unseen wars which arose from the
> attacks of robbers.... This is he who gave freedom to every city,
> who brought disorder into order, who civilized and made obedient
> and harmonious, nations which before his time were unsociable,
> hostile, and brutal.... [T]he guardian of peace, the distributor to every
> man of what was suited to him, the man who proffered to all the
> citizens favours with the most ungrudging liberality, who never once
> in his whole life concealed or reserved for himself any thing that was
> good or excellent. (*Legat.* 21.147–149)

These are the words of Philo—Alexandrian provincial elite, Jewish philosopher, and ambassador to Rome. To be sure, he writes with such exuberance about Augustus to make his case against divine honors for Gaius, at least from the Jewish community. He argues that if such an extraordinary emperor as Augustus neither demanded nor elicited worship from the Jews, neither should Caligula. Nevertheless, Philo's words demonstrate the far-reaching effects of the Augustan political agenda, with Philo's complete familiarity with and use of imperial rhetoric. Thus, it comes as no surprise to find further use of the ideology of Greco-Roman masculinity in his own philosophical principles, biblical commentary, and especially the portrayal of his own divine man, Moses.

Moses and Masculinity according to Philo of Alexandria

The diverse writings of Philo make possible a nuanced and multilayered examination of his gender ideology, especially because his philosophical treatises and biblical commentaries frequently make explicit use of gender categories.[46] Throughout his writings, one finds Philo knitting together metaphorical, physical, and spiritual aspects of gender so closely that at times they are indistinguishable. Examining Philo's use of gender categories in general will help make sense of his gendered construction of Moses.

Moving Up and Down Philo's Gender Gradient

As previously discussed, Greco-Roman sex/gender identity was inherently unstable. One could never be certain that one's gender status, especially as a man, was secure. For this reason, Caesar Augustus had an entire political agenda devoted to securing his masculine ruling status across the empire, especially in light of challenges to his manliness. Philo, too, seems keenly aware of sex/gender fluidity and potential threats to one's masculinity. For him, the threat is more than one of social status. As we have seen, it also involves the state of one's soul. Thus, Philo frets over the threat of θήλεια νόσος, the "female disease" that can infect a man's body and soul and turn him into an ἀνδρόγυνος (an effeminate or "girly man") (*Contempl.* 60; also *Spec.* 3.37–38, *Abr.* 135–136). The onslaught of this disease, according to Philo, occurs when men assume the passive role in sexual intercourse. Becoming "womanish" not only softens the body but also produces a degenerate soul.[47]

There are other rewards to be gained from masculine reason and perils to face from unmanly behavior, in Philo's view. His discussion of Noah suggests that even the children one begets are a product of one's gender conduct. Because Noah "follows the right, the perfect and truly masculine reason," he begets sons (*Gig.* 1.5). On the other hand, "the spiritual offspring of the unjust is never in any case male: the offspring of men whose thoughts are unmanly, nerveless and emasculate by nature are female" (*Gig.* 1.4). Such reflections show Philo's easy slide between spiritual allegory and lived experience when it comes to gender categories. While he speaks of "spiritual offspring," he is also explaining why Noah had sons rather than daughters. For Philo, these sons were not only allegories. In any case, the idea of effeminate men producing daughters is not new to Philo. According to the physiognomic code, a "masculine" woman could be recognized by her tendency to bear male children, whereas men and women of the feminine type would bear female children.[48] So far from producing some speculative allegorical reading, Philo is adapting common cultural assumptions of gender to his reading of scripture.

But if passive or irrational behavior results in emasculation, degeneration, or (worse yet) female offspring, Philo can also conceive of gender transformations with positive implications. The possibility of movement up the gender gradient from female to male status enables progression in piety. This link between masculinity and progress of the soul is most apparent in the passage:

> For progress is indeed nothing else than giving up of the female genus by changing into the male, since the female gender is maternal, passive, corporeal and sense-perceptible while the male is active, rational, incorporeal and more akin to mind and thought. (*QE* 1.8)

Note again the way the divine/human hierarchy is intricately connected to the gender gradient. A more pious soul indicates a more masculine status, or vice versa. Becoming more pious and becoming more masculine are one and the same. Both result in a move up the cosmic hierarchy toward the divine realm. Given the earlier discussion about the body in masculine ideology, what Philo and others had in mind when they spoke of changing from male to female was likely not an anatomical transformation.[49] Instead, giving up the female genus and changing into a male would mean exhibiting particular virtues and leaving behind certain vices.[50] Thus, for Philo, a man must avoid anything that could move him in the direction of the female, not just irrational thoughts or succumbing to passion, but also wearing women's clothing! As he argues:

> So earnestly and carefully does the law desire to train and exercise the soul to manly courage [ἀνδρείας] ... that it strictly forbids a man to assume a woman's garb, in order that no trace, no merest shadow of the female, should attach to him to spoil his masculinity. (*Virt.* 18)

Again, Philo seemingly speaks metaphorically, designating that which is corporeal and sense-perceptible as "female," but when it comes to training the soul, the very literal issue of wearing women's clothing comes into play. Also notable is Philo's assumption regarding the law's earnest desire to form courageous or "manly" souls. Following the law within Judaism was commonly understood as the way to bring one closer to God. For Philo, this movement toward God through obedience to the law would necessarily involve the training of the soul in manly conduct.

Closely related to the notion of the fluidity of sex/gender is the relativity of gender identity. Both ideas are found in Philo's various discussions of the masculine nature of the feminine virtues. Consider Philo's discussion of the masculinity of Sophia:

> While Wisdom's name is feminine, her nature is masculine. For all the virtues have women's titles, but powers and activities of perfect

men [ἀνδρῶν τελειοτάτων]. For that which comes after God, even if it were chiefest of all other things, occupies a second place, and therefore was termed feminine to express its contrast with the Maker of the Universe, who is masculine, and its affinity to everything else. For the feminine always falls short and is inferior to the masculine, which has priority. (*Fug.* 51–52)

Here Philo assumes that feminine and masculine are relative to one's position in the hierarchical structure of the cosmos. In the case of Sophia, it is clear that taken on its own, the feminine name has no relevance to gender identity, because Sophia's "powers and activities" are masculine. In other words, Sophia is generative and active—key characteristics of masculinity. Philo makes a similar move with ἀρετή, explaining how in spite of the noun's feminine form, "virtue is male, since it causes movement and affects conditions and suggests noble conceptions of noble deeds and words" (*Abr.* 99–102). Yet, once Sophia and Arete are viewed in the context of the cosmic hierarchy, their masculine status becomes relativized. As the quote above shows, with respect to God, Sophia comes second; she is further down the hierarchy and thus feminine. Notice also how God is necessarily masculine in this scheme. The title Philo uses for God, τὸ τὰ ὅλα ποιοῦν (the creator of all things), emphasizes his masculine generativity.

Further indication of the relativity of gender categories can be found in texts that feature the notion of divine impregnation.[51] In this case, the virtues are understood in terms of the passive female receiving the seed from the masculine God. For as Philo puts it, God "is the father of all things, for He begat them, and the husband of Wisdom, dropping the seed of happiness for the race of mortals into good and virgin soil" (*Cher.* 49). This statement comes at the end of a section in which Philo explains that the wives of the patriarchs are in fact virtues impregnated by God (*Cher.* 43–47). The following summary statement by Jean Laporte nicely illustrates the relative aspect of gender in Philo:

Wisdom is made pregnant by God, and impregnates man while herself remaining a virgin. Feminine in regard to God, Wisdom becomes masculine with regard to man, who is made masculine by her, and begets, but who should not affirm his fatherhood of this offspring which is the work of God in him. The defilement of virtue in a soul is remedied by intercourse with wisdom, which restores the pristine condition of virginity to deflowered virtue.[52]

From Laporte's statement, one sees that not only the hypostatized virtues fluctuate between male and female, but also the men who relate to these virtues. In texts where God or God's agents are depicted as impregnating the soul, thereby taking the active male role, the man, in receiving the seed, plays the passive female role. So in *QG* 4.99 we find the man who

> has the courage to think it impious to sow the corrupt seeds of sensual pleasure in the mind, and, instead, receives the unadulterated seeds of divinity which the Father of all is wont to sow in us from above, (namely) those that are incorporeal and intelligible.

Still, as Richard Baer makes clear, for Philo it is only when a man is put in relation to a power greater than he, and therefore more masculine, that passivity is acceptable. Elsewhere, in relation to other human beings, passivity is consistently derided (*Spec.* 1.325, 3.37–42; *Somn.* 1.126; *Contempl.* 60; *Her.* 274).[53]

In sum, in terms of his construction of gender categories, Philo appears fully consistent with his cultural context. If he offers something different, it is not his conception of masculinity and femininity, but his consistent linkage between these social categories and the state of one's soul, although even this can sometimes be found in the Hellenistic philosophers. But what is most significant here is that for Philo, masculinity is not only a category within his philosophical/theological system; it is also a gender identity that is ideally embodied in his hero, Moses.

Moses: Philo's Manly Man

When Philo begins his account of the life of Moses, he introduces his reader to the "greatest and most perfect of men" (ἀνδρὸς τὰ πάντα μεγίστον καὶ τελειοτάτου) (*Mos.* 1.1). Certainly Philo is interested in showing Moses as surpassing any Greek philosopher. He is also certainly interested in drawing a distinguished portrait of Moses as the model of a Hellenistic king.[54] But in drawing this portrait, what becomes equally clear is that Philo is envisioning Moses in just the way he says, as the greatest and most perfect man. Recalling the discussion of masculinity in chapter 2, the use of τέλος is notable. Among men, Moses is the most complete, the "hottest" of men, as it were.

The depiction of Moses's early life repeatedly emphasizes his noble and beautiful appearance (*Mos.* 1.9, 15, 18). But Philo goes a step further. Because Philo connects masculinity with the state of one's soul, he makes clear that from the time of his birth, Moses's handsome appearance is also an indication of his noble soul. This, in turn, indicates the promise of a proper manly appearance as Moses matures. This promise comes to fruition. Later, when his future father-in-law first sees Moses, he is "at once struck with admiration of his face, and soon afterwards of his disposition, for great natures are transparent and need no length of time to be recognized" (*Mos.* 1.59).

As would be expected, the road to achieving this great nature was one of strict self-discipline, according to Philo. First, as the young boy matured to adolescence, he kept a tight rein over his passions. He "tamed and assuaged and reduced them to mildness; and if they did but gently stir or flutter he provided from them heavier chastisement than any rebuke of words could give" (*Mos.* 1.26). Indeed, with respect to self-mastery, Philo's Moses clearly excelled. Not only did he tame his impulses, he managed to forget all about the pleasures of sex. It only entered his mind in the context of the "lawful begetting of children" (*Mos.* 1.28).

A further indication of Moses's superior self-mastery is his avoidance of luxury (*Mos.* 1.29). As seen in the previous chapter, luxury in Hellenistic discourse functioned as a code word for all things that would lead to softness. As Daniel Garrison puts it, "Luxury at its worst is a sexual offense, making a man effeminate."[55] Elsewhere such a perspective leads Philo to speak of the Sodomites "emasculating their bodies by luxury" (*Abr.* 136). But as for Moses, Philo points out that he made "a special practice of frugal contentment, and had an unparalleled scorn for a life of luxury" (*Mos.* 1.29, see also 1.152–153).

With respect to voice and effective speech Moses also excelled. To be sure, Philo must honor the biblical tradition that has Moses protest over his ineloquence (*Mos.* 1.83). But Philo explains this protest in terms of Moses's perception of human eloquence compared to God's, as well as being an example of the admirable trait of modesty. Philo does not admit to the possibility that Moses was not an accomplished public speaker. Instead, Moses is described on a number of occasions as having comforting and effective speech (*Mos.* 1.173–175).

Finally, Moses is himself depicted as knowing what makes a man. He tells the enslaved Israelites to "bear their condition bravely" and to "display a manly spirit" (*Mos.* 1.40). Conversely, he chastises the shepherds who try to steal water from young girls as "masses of long hair and lumps of flesh, not men . . . who go daintily like girls." As Moses continues to berate the bully shepherds, they become submissive and do his bidding (*Mos.* 1.51–57). In this way, Philo's Moses engages in the same sort of gendered attacks that were apparent with Augustus and his opponents.

In sum, not only does Moses exhibit all the desirable qualities of a truly masculine man, he knows what it means to be a man and instructs the Israelites accordingly. None of this is meant to dismiss all the other ways in which Philo describes Moses—king, priest, prophet, and so on. Instead, his exemplary masculinity makes him a highly qualified candidate for all of those roles.

But even more, because he climbs higher on the gender gradient than any other person Philo discusses, he earns a special status vis-à-vis God.

Masculinity and Divinity in Philo's Moses

According to Philo, it is precisely because of qualities such as Moses's remarkable self-restraint that people first begin to consider his divine status. They wonder whether his mind was "human or divine or a mixture of both so utterly unlike was it to the majority, soaring above them and exalted to a greater height" (*Mos.* 1.27).

Philo goes on to speaks of the reward that God, who is "lover of virtue and honor" (φιλαρέτου καὶ φιλοκάλου), granted Moses for his virtuous conduct. On the top of the list of virtues is Moses's "repeated exhibition of self-restraint" (*Mos.* 1.154), but also included are "endurance of toil and hardships, contempt of pleasures, justice, advocacy of excellence." For such conduct, God gave Moses

> the wealth of the whole earth and sea and rivers, and of all the other elements and the combinations which they form. For since God judged him worthy to appear as a partner of His own possessions, He gave into his hands the whole earth as a portion well filled for His heir. (*Mos.* 1.155)

In short, as a reward for being "the greatest and most perfect of men" (*Mos.* 1.1), God granted Moses "the greatest and most perfect wealth" (*Mos.* 1.155). While being God's heir and copossessor of the whole creation may not necessarily imply divine status, it certainly suggests an elevated one.

But there is more. When Philo evokes Exodus 7:1 in his discussion of Moses, he goes a step further toward deification of Moses[56]:

> Again, was not the job of his partnership with the Father and Maker of all magnified also by the honour of sharing the same title? For he was named god and king of the whole nation, and entered, we are told, into the darkness where God was, that is into the unseen, invisible, incorporeal and archetypal essence of existing things. (*Mos.* 1.158)

Finally, at the end of the work, Philo writes of Moses's apotheosis, describing his pilgrimage from earth to heaven, from mortality to immortality, as one of unification. He is summoned by the Father who "resolved his twofold nature of soul and body into a single unity, transforming his whole being into mind, pure as the sunlight" (*Mos.* 2.288). This unified and incorporeal state is the ultimate in masculine achievement.

In drawing on the tradition of Greco-Roman apotheosis, Philo puts Moses in the category of the divinized emperors who went before him. The description of his moments "at the barrier" contains elements familiar to the Greco-Roman traditions, including the prophecy of future events by the divinized ruler and the creation of a special monument erected on his behalf[57]:

> When he was already being exalted and stood at the very barrier, ready at the signal to direct his upward flight to heaven, the divine spirit fell upon him and he prophesied with discernment while still alive the story of his own death; told how the end came; told how he was buried with none present, surely by no mortal hands but by immortal powers; how also he was not laid to rest in the tomb of his forefather but was given a monument of special dignity which no man has ever seen; how the whole nation wept and mourned for him a whole month and made open display, private and public, of their sorrow in memory of his vast benevolence and watchful care for each one of them and for all. (*Mos.* 2.291–292)

Wendy Cotter suggests that the shift from tomb to monument described in this passage reflects a familiar pattern of Roman imperial apotheosis. As she puts it:

> By moving from the idea of tomb to that of monument, Philo shifts away from the testimony to the burial of the actual corpse to the memorial raised to a hero's status. This repeats the same movement that we see in the Roman state, where the state elevated a huge monument to the *apotheosized* emperors, while the relatives discreetly visited the buried ashes in the family tomb. That is, for the Roman state, there was always tension between the *apotheosized* emperor's monument and his tomb.[58]

So, too, Philo's focus on a burial by immortal hands in a dignified monument deals with the tension between the tradition of Moses's death and burial in a tomb, and his existence with God, as "god and king of the whole nation."

Moreover, Philo's allusion to Exodus 7:1 provides a telling example of how closely Philo connects Moses's superb display of masculine characteristics with his divine status. As Moses climbs up the gender hierarchy, he simultaneously draws nearer to God. In so doing, he also becomes more godlike. Once again, one can see how Philo maps the cultural gender gradient onto the divine/human cosmic hierarchy. Both operate on the same vertical axis. Moreover, the divine/human scale has the same features as the gender gradient. It is both fluid and relative, with the exception that for Philo, God would never move down the scale.

In light of this, for Moses to excel beyond all others in achieving the ideal of masculinity would *necessarily* mean that he moves beyond any other human in achieving divinity. In some real sense, Moses moves up the cosmic and gender hierarchy simultaneously, both proving his ideal masculinity and achieving a heightened state of divinity. Of course, such divinity is always relative. Moses does not, in the end, become equal to the one God, who is, for Philo, the ultimate in masculine perfection. At this point, Gradel's notion of relative divinity versus absolute divinity is useful. The focus on divine status rather than divine essence that Gradel sees in the Roman understandings of divinity also enters Philo's conception of Moses in relation to God. Philo does have a concept of absolute divinity, and only God can be so understood. But Philo, like everyone else in the hierarchical Greco-Roman culture, also conceives of a relative divinity based on status, with Moses as a prime example.

One objection to linking masculinity with divinity in Philo's work is that in some cases Philo speaks of an asexual realm. At times, Philo's description of God as τὰ ὄν suggests a genderless conception of the deity (see *Contempl.* 2). In this sense, as one reached the top of the cosmic gender hierarchy, one would enter a realm beyond gender polarities. Along this line, Baer argues that:

> Neither God, nor the Logos, nor the rational soul is involved in the
> sphere of male and female. . . . The male-female polarity in Philo's
> writings is part of the mortal sphere of the created world. It does not
> function on a cosmic scale, particularly in the drama of creation, as it
> does in many of the Gnostic systems.[59]

To be sure, Philo conceives of an undifferentiated and incorporeal God. But Philo also makes clear that he understands God to be masculine.[60] This masculinity has tended to be read metaphorically, as a code word for superiority, but not connected to men or the male gender in any significant way. But, as discussed earlier, biological maleness was not the primary means of defining masculinity in the ancient world. Instead, traits such as generativity, action, self-mastery, and mastery over others were what mattered, even for real men with real bodies. On the basis of these traits, it is clear that God would be understood as the epitome of masculinity, as Philo himself suggests. That God is incorporeal would not hinder Philo's conception of God as masculine. Rather, it would reinforce the idea. Likewise, it would not make the notion of masculinity a purely functional, abstract category. In the "one-sex" model, beyond differentiation is the ideal—the perfected masculine ideal. As Mattila puts it, "the transcendent God may even be said to be more 'male' than 'male,' or 'ultramale.'"[61] Or, to put it another way, when elevated to the transcendent realm, one participates in asexual masculinity.

This, in fact, is how Philo describes the first man. As Annewies van den Hoek has noted, Philo makes a remarkable reversal when he comments on Genesis 1:27 and rereads the LXX ἄσεν καὶ θῆλυ (male and female) as "*neither male nor* female."[62] Philo would likely support his negation of the Genesis text by arguing that "male and female" indicates a unified being, which may be more clearly expressed as "neither male nor female." However, in using this phrase, Philo is not thinking of the absence of bodily distinctions between male and female. The point is that this initial human is undifferentiated, created in the image of the perfect unity that is God. For Philo, the "neither male nor female" means "not divided into male and female, but united as completely masculine." Or, once again, he means an asexual masculinity. While this may seem oxymoronic, it would make perfect rational sense to Philo. Indeed, he readily associates unity with masculinity in his allegory on the joining of Noah and his sons with their wives after the flood. He remarks that the time comes when it is right to bring divided elements together:

> Not that the masculine thoughts may be made womanish, and re-
> laxed by softness, but that the female element, the senses, may be
> made manly by following masculine thoughts and by receiving from
> them seed for procreation. (QG 2:49)

Thus, to return again to the language Philo uses of Moses's apotheosis, when God "resolved his twofold nature of soul and body into a single unity, trans-forming his whole being into mind, pure as the sunlight" (*Mos.* 2.288), it is a way of indicating the perfect masculinity that Moses achieves. During his life, he was a virtuous, manly man. In his immortal existence, he resides with God in a state of masculine perfection.

An Alternative Masculinity? Philostratus's Apollonius of Tyana

This last case study covers well-trodden ground with respect to New Testament Christology. Examination of Apollonius in relation to Jesus is nothing new. Nor is it risk free, given the assessment of Koskenniemi, whose studies demonstrate, according to him, "that Apollonius and the work of Philostratus, for reasons of chronology, have little if anything whatsoever to do with critical research on the New Testament."[63] With this conclusion, Koskenniemi joins in the critique of the history-of-religions school, which understood Apollonius of Tyana as the prime example of a θειος ἀνηρ (God-man), a category that was also applied to Jesus of Nazareth. Here, however, the focus will not be on how the miracles of the real Apollonius might compare to the real Jesus, or on how a generic category of "divine man" that is largely based on Philostratus's Apollonius was employed in the service of early Christology. For the purposes of this study, the focus will be on the gendered construction of a divine man, Apollonius, by a third-century C.E. author who was born in the Greek east and educated in Athens, with close ties to the imperial court.[64]

The relatively late dating of the traditions about Apollonius is not a problem. Rather, this dating is precisely what makes this figure useful as evidence for the way a particular ideology of masculinity persists over time. Also important is the different type of character encountered in Apollonius. He is not a ruler like Augustus; nor is he a philosopher-king like Philo's Moses. Instead, he is a wandering, long-haired, barefoot, vegan, wonder-working sage with Pythagorean leanings. Quite a different image of masculinity from that portrayed by the Prima Porta!

Given this, one might expect that the masculine traits on display in the manly rulers would not necessarily be found in Apollonius, and vice versa. Insofar as his Pythagorean tendencies are considered, this is certainly the case. For example, Apollonius's critique of animal sacrifice is hardly in keeping with the standard image of Roman *pietas*, at least within the first-century context in which Apollonius is situated.[65] Nevertheless, under Philostratus's hand, Apollonius will exhibit many of the same "manly" traits as Augustus and Moses. Furthermore, Philostratus is explicit in his desire that his work be read from a position of masculinity. He claims that those who do not read his account in a womanly or effeminate way will understand that a true man will never change or be servile (*Vit. Apoll.* 6.35.2).[66]

The Making of a Divine Man

In speaking of the early life of Apollonius, Philostratus relates the prerequisites of a true man in the making.[67] Like other extraordinary men, Apollonius has stories associated with his birth, appearance, and education that place him in the category of an ideal man, one who shares a close association with the gods. Before his birth, his mother has a vision of Proteus, the Egyptian sea-god, who claims that the child she bears will be the god himself. Philostratus uses this story to suggest to the reader that Apollonius's skills as a prognosticator surpass those of Proteus. Also like Proteus, Apollonius was able to escape many difficult situations (*Vit. Apoll.* 1.4).

The story of Apollonius's birth includes an appearance of swans surrounding his mother and raising their wings, the sound of which brings about the birth of Apollonius. At this point, a lightning bolt is said to have flashed and hung poised above the earth before disappearing upward. Philostratus interprets this lightning as a divine sign: "No doubt the gods were giving a signal and an omen of his brilliance, his exaltation above earthly things, his closeness to heaven, and all the man's other qualities" (*Vit. Apoll.* 1.5).

Also, as Philo writes in his account of Moses, Philostratus writes explicitly about Apollonius's education. When he was old enough to study literature, he demonstrated a strong memory and great skill in his exercises. He spoke in Attic Greek with no regional accent (1.7). At the age of fourteen, he was sent to Tarsus to study with Euthydeumus, a good orator. From here, at his request, he moved to Aegeae, away from the corruption of the city and into the company of others who studied philosophy. At fifteen, he adopted the Pythagorean lifestyle: abstaining from meat, refusing to wear clothes made from animal products, growing his hair long, and living in the sanctuary.

Not only in intellect, but also in appearance, Apollonius stood out from an early age. Rumors of his budding manhood reached the ears of a ruler in Cilicia who immediately dropped what he was doing, purportedly to seek help from Asclepius but in fact to search for the attractive Apollonius. When the two met, the delicate and lascivious ruler wanted to pray to Apollonius, "the beautiful," that he share his beauty and not begrudge the ruler his youthful charms (*Vit. Apoll.* 1.12.1). Already revealing his self-restraint, Apollonius boldly puts the ruler in his place, replying, "You're a madman, you trash!" (*Vit. Apoll.* 1.12.2).

Philostratus builds on this account with a statement of Apollonius's extraordinary self-control. Even more impressive than Augustus or Philo's Moses, Apollonius refrains from *all* sexual activity, completely controlling his desire. Indeed, Philostratus compares him to Sophocles, who claimed that he finally escaped from a "raging, wild master in his old age." Apollonius goes one better, so that "on account of his virtue and self-mastery," he was never defeated by this master. Instead, "even as a youth, he ruled over and mastered its rage" (*Vit. Apoll.* 1.13.3). In short, as Apollonius moves into his manhood, he demonstrates many of the qualifications of a real man—strong intellect, good looks, and extraordinary self-control.

In the Company of Men?

Having established the promising signs of ideal manhood in Apollonius, Philostratus's account has Apollonius seeking company with men like himself. According to Philostratus, in looking for conversation partners, Apollonius "declared that it was not people, he needed, but men" (οὐκ ἀνθρώπων ἑαυτῷ δεῖν ἀλλ᾽ ἀνδρῶν) (*Vit. Apoll.* 1.16.3). Such a statement confirms the deliberate construction of the manliness of Apollonius from the opening chapters of the

Vita, a project that will continue through the narrative. Notably, in searching for the company of men, Apollonius looks for them in holy places and temples (*Vit. Apoll.* 1.16.3). Once again, the notions of manliness and divinity are closely linked.

Much of the first half of Philostratus's narrative concerns Apollonius's travels through exotic lands. As he encounters various rulers and wise men in his travels, his desire for an audience of true men persists. As Apollonius moves into "barbarian" country (an undertaking that itself shows great courage or manliness, as Philostratus reminds the reader, *Vit. Apoll.* 1.20), he encounters a royal guard post. The governor of the post, upon seeing the unkempt Apollonius, shouts out "like a frightened woman." Given this reaction, one might suppose that travels have taken a toll on Apollonius's youthful beauty. But the point is to highlight Apollonius's otherworldly appearance. The guard covers his eyes and addresses him as one "questioning a daemon," asking from where he was sent. Apollonius replies, "I sent myself, in case somehow you might become men, even if unwillingly" (*Vit. Apoll.* 1.21.1). In this way, the traveling philosopher's first exchange with a "barbarian" emphasizes the gendered distinction between them. The true man, Apollonius, will teach the barbarians the ways of civilized masculinity. As the tension increases and the governor threatens to torture Apollonius for withholding his identity, the latter presses the point even further, stating, "Would that you be tortured in the same way, having laid hands on a real man" (*Vit. Apoll.* 1.21.2).

When Apollonius eventually gets to the city of Babylon, the king's gate-keepers and officials soon recognize him as "not just some person" (*Vit. Apoll.* 1.28.1) but as "a godsend," saying that "some god led this man here" (*Vit. Apoll.* 1.28.3). They decide that such a clearly good man will improve their own king, making him much more self-controlled and pleasant, so they "announce the good news everywhere that a man standing at the king's door was wise, a Greek, and a good counselor" (*Vit. Apoll.* 1.28.3).

Upon entering the palace, Apollonius is welcomed by the king as one whom respectable men honor and worship. When the king asks Apollonius to join him in sacrifice, Apollonius eschews the impending horse sacrifice and offers his own sacrifice of incense instead. In so doing, he addresses Helios, asking the sun god to let him come to know good men (*Vit. Apoll.* 1.31.1). Apparently his sacrifice is efficacious. Soon afterward, Apollonius tells the king that he had heard he was a true man, and now sees it for himself (*Vit. Apoll.* 1.32.1).[68]

Apollonius also critiques those who act in unmanly ways, engaging in the same sort of gendered attacks evident with Augustus and Philo's Moses. This is especially the case in his reaction to the celebration of Dionysia in Athens.

He particularly objects to the dancing, which he suggests is not like the war dance of the Spartans, but instead reckless dancing that hastens effeminacy. Similarly, the Athenians' colorful clothing makes them appear "more delicate than Xerxes's harem." Whereas the Athenians used to swear to take up weapons to defend the city, now they will likely carry a Bacchic wand while dressed in womanly disguise (*Vit. Apoll.* 4.21.1–3).[69]

Apollonius has a similar critique of the Spartan ambassadors whom he encounters in Olympia. Looking nothing like Spartans, he finds them more delicate than Lydians, with shaved legs and faces, oiled hair, and soft clothing. At his recommendation, hair removers are banned from bathhouses, a measure that apparently solves the problem and returns everything to ancient ways. Wrestling schools are rejuvenated, along with virtuous pursuits and common meals, so that "Sparta became like itself" (4.27). As a result, Apollonius sent them a letter saying, "True men do not fail, but noble men at least perceive their failures" (Ἀνδρῶν μὲν τὸ μὴ ἁμαρτάνειν, γενναίων δὲ τὸ καὶ ἁμαρτάνοτας αἰσθέσθαι).[70]

Apollonius and the Emperors

In addition to depicting Apollonius as a wandering sage, Philostratus also links him closely to imperial power, either advising those emperors he considers virtuous or harshly critiquing those he does not. Vespasian falls into the first category. Upon meeting Apollonius in Egypt, he prays to the sage to "make me emperor" (*Vit. Apoll.* 5.28). Vespasian proceeds to contrast his virtuous, manly behavior with that of his opponent Vitellius. He paints a picture of the latter as one completely out of control, partaking in heavy drinking, heavy perfume in his baths, gambling, and illicit sex (*Vit. Apoll.* 5.29.4). And this, according to Vespasian, is not even the worst of Vitellius's behavior. Vespasian, on the other hand, claims that he is eager to work for the salvation of all people (*Vit. Apoll.* 5.32.1). Apollonius gives Vespasian his full support and defends him against those who would dissuade him from his pursuit of power. Most tellingly, Vespasian asks Apollonius to teach him as much as possible about how a good emperor should act. Later Apollonius also advises Titus, who seeks his wisdom regarding ruling and kingship (*Vit. Apoll.* 6.31). Thus, while Apollonius himself is no ruler, he is a close advisor to future emperors.

Not all of Apollonius's dealings with emperors are so positive. When Nero bans philosophers from Rome, Apollonius sets his course toward the city. Whereas Apollonius's role of advisor to virtuous rulers displays his wisdom and good judgment, facing up to a "tyrant" shows his courage and conviction. On the way, Apollonius and his followers encounter a philosopher fleeing

Rome, who frightens many of them into making their escape from both Nero and philosophy (*Vit. Apoll.* 4.37.2). Consequently, the group shrinks from thirty-four disciples to eight, whom Apollonius praises for "being men like me" (ἄνδρες ἐστὲ ἐμοὶ ὅμοιοι) (*Vit. Apoll.* 4.38.1). Eventually Apollonius is brought to the Roman court on the charge of impiety against Nero and comes before Tigellinus, the prefect of the Praetorian Guard. After questioning Apollonius, Tigellinus releases him, "as if one chary of fighting against a god." Indeed, he tells Apollonius that Apollonius is too strong for him to rule over (*Vit. Apoll.* 4.44.4).

The last two books of Philostratus's work are devoted, in large part, to another journey to Rome, this time for Apollonius to defend himself against the accusations of the emperor Domitian. Philostratus prepares for Apollonius's confrontation with Domitian by discussing in what respect any philosopher has appeared more manly than another. Of course, the point is that Apollonius surpasses all other philosophers in his resistance to Domitian. Compared to other wise men such as Zeno or Diogenes, Apollonius did not merely stand up to the ruler of an island or country, but he stood against the ruler of the whole earth and sea (*Vit. Apoll.* 7.3.3).

As the narrative continues, once more many of Apollonius's disciples desert him. They are afraid to travel with him to Rome. Apollonius goes on with a select group—those who are willing to risk their lives for the cause. Apollonius himself makes clear that he is willing to give his life on behalf of the victims of Domitian. When he is once more threatened with torture, Apollonius responds that he is willing to submit to anything that may be done to his body, until he has defended "those men," that is, the philosophers who have been oppressed by Domitian. Later, Apollonius demonstrates the extent to which this submission is truly a choice made by Apollonius. When he is shackled by the imperial guard, he privately shows Damis that he can easily free himself from the chains (*Vit. Apoll.* 7.38.2). In this way, he demonstrates his freedom and makes clear that his submission is truly an active and therefore manly choice. He chooses to remain in chains so that he can bravely confront the emperor on behalf of those who have been persecuted.

While in prison, Apollonius finds opportunity to continue his teaching of what it takes to be a man. Specifically, he helps a handsome youth whom the emperor is reserving for his sexual pleasure. The youth blames his father for his predicament, because he was not willing to provide the boy with a Greek education but instead sent him to Rome to study law. Once in Rome, as he was extraordinarily handsome, he came to the attention of the emperor. By framing the boy's predicament in this manner, Philostratus turns him into a quite literal object lesson about the risk of emasculation when Greek *paideia* is withheld. Still, Apollonius helps the boy to see that he can be the master of his own body. Thus, the boy decides to offer his neck for the emperor's sword rather than have his body be emasculated by the emperor's sexual advances. In recognition of his decision, Apollonius states, "You *are* an Arcadian, I see" (*Vit. Apoll.* 7.42.5). The story has a happy ending. Philostratus informs the reader that the boy is not executed, but instead admired for his strength and released.

Apollonius, too, escapes the tyranny of Domitian—not through the clemency of the emperor but through a dramatic disappearance from the courtroom. His parting words are from the *Iliad.* Quoting his namesake, Apollo, he tells Domitian, "You can not kill me, since I am indeed not destined to die" (*Vit. Apoll.* 8.5.3). The sage thereby hints at his own immortality, something he shares with the gods. Indeed, although Philostratus shares the view that it is honorable to die on behalf of one's beliefs (*Vit. Apoll.* 7.14.2), as he closes his *Vita*, he implies that Apollonius may have escaped death altogether.

Along this line, in his final paragraphs, Philostratus relates multiple versions of Apollonius's death with the caveat, "if he did die" (*Vit. Apoll.* 8.29). Moreover, he notes that none of the accounts of this death come from his (purportedly) most reliable source, the disciple Damis. Both the insertion of the conditional phrase and the absence of an account of death from Apollonius's most loyal disciple indicate that he achieved immortality. To this end, the most dramatic version of his (non)death tells of Apollonius's imprisonment under suspicion of sorcery for being able to enter a temple in the middle of the night that was guarded by savage dogs. Apollonius frees himself from his chains, gains the attention of his guards, and then runs once more to the temple. The doors fly open to welcome him as the air fills with the sound of girls singing "Proceed from earth! Proceed to heaven! Proceed!" or, as Philostratus interprets it, "Ascend from the earth" (*Vit. Apoll.* 8.30). In this way, Apollonius also shares in the apotheosis of the Roman emperors. And that is not all he shares. The last line of the biography notes that there is a temple in Tyana to Apollonius, completed at imperial expense, "since emperors have not denied to him what has been conferred on themselves."[71] As with Augustus, the narrative suggests that Apollonius not only found his place among the gods; he was deemed worthy of worship and sacrifice as well.

Conclusion

As stated at the beginning of this chapter, the three manly figures examined here illustrate how ideologies of masculinity play a part in the representations of esteemed men across the empire. There are several key observations to make by way of conclusion. The first concerns the diverse ways that masculine ideology finds expression in each of these figures. With Augustus, we have evidence of a lifelong project of first defending his masculinity against attacks from opponents, and then carefully constructing the image of the ideal man—courageous, militarily successful, devoted to the gods, benevolent, just, beautiful, and so on. Clearly, in promoting himself, Augustus tapped into a long history of the ideal virtuous ruler. Philo, too, is aware of this tradition, and he draws on it to construct his own image of the ideal ruler in Moses. But in Philo's work one can also see how gendered philosophical categories are transferred to ideas of men and women, and especially how the ideal man is found in the person of Moses. Philostratus's depiction of Apollonius is quite different from both of these. He is not portraying a ruler but a philosopher and advisor to the rulers. Philostratus is interested in showing Apollonius as representative of the civilized Greek man, vis-à-vis the barbarian "unmen" he encounters on his travels. Moreover, Apollonius is shown to be a man willing to sacrifice himself for the cause of philosophy and for the benefit of others who are unjustly oppressed. In this way, Apollonius represents a still different articulation of masculinity.

But what links the founder of the Roman Empire, the heroic figure from Israel's past, and the wonder-working Pythagorean sage is the way their gendered construction is combined with a notion of divinity. In the case of Augustus, his divinization comes by way of Senate action. His ideal conduct in life merits divine honors at his death. With Moses, it is God himself who recognizes and rewards Moses's extraordinary virtue with a place alongside him in the heavens. Apollonius conveys the aura of the divine, or at least the supernatural, throughout his life and into his death. The various traditions about his death (or lack thereof) evoke the notion of apotheosis along the lines of the other great men discussed here.

The final observation concerns the portrayals of Apollonius and Moses in particular. Both of these non-Roman figures reflect a degree of resistance to imperial rule. With Apollonius, the resistance is twofold. First, he elevates Greek education, language, and culture above all others, including those of Rome. Second, he takes a bold stance against "tyranny," meaning emperors who would suppress philosophy. In the case of Philo's Moses, Philo expresses a resistance to Roman rule through his construction of Moses as the ideal, divinely designated copossessor of all of God's creation. But in both of these instances, resistance to Roman rule does not equal resistance to hegemonic masculinity. Rather, the construction of these figures as ideal men, based on Greek and Roman cultural ideals, is crucial to the articulation of Roman resistance. This mix of Roman resistance alongside the assimilation of Greco-Roman masculinity will be evident in certain depictions of Jesus in the New Testament.

Once again, none of these three figures is intended as background for the New Testament presentations of Jesus. Rather, they serve as examples to place alongside the early depictions of Jesus. As New Testament writings are explored in the following chapters, the individual representations of Jesus should be understood as contributions to this broader cultural discourse. In a sense, each New Testament author presents yet another case study of how the ideology of masculinity finds its way into the portrayal of an esteemed man. Thus, each contributes to the complex cultural gender discourse of the Greco-Roman period. It is to these contributions that we now turn.

4

The Unmanned Christ
and the Manly Christian in
the Pauline Tradition

It was before your eyes that Jesus Christ was vividly portrayed as crucified.

—Galatians 3:1 (my translation)

In the ancient context, a crucified body was a violated or penetrated body. It was a body subjected to the power of others, and thus an emasculated body. While none of the literate men of the first century dwelled long on the distasteful topic, Cicero addresses it briefly in his Verrine orations. There he describes crucifixion as the "most savage, most disgraceful punishment" (*crudelissimi taeterrimique supplicii*) (*Verr.* 2.5.64). Cicero goes on to state: "To bind a Roman citizen is a crime, to flog him an abomination, to slay him is almost an act of murder, to crucify him is—what? There is not a fitting word that can possibly describe so horrible a deed (*Verr.* 2.5.64). So horrible a deed, in fact, that elsewhere Cicero argues that "the very word 'cross' should be far removed not only from the person of a Roman citizen but from his thoughts, his eyes and his ears" (*Rab Perd.* 5.16).

Paul, of course, does not keep the idea of the cross "far removed" from the thoughts, eyes, and ears of his audience. As the opening epitaph suggests, the crucifixion was made evident to the Galatians in some graphic way. Similarly, Paul reminds the Corinthians that "I decided to know nothing among you, but Jesus Christ and him crucified" (1 Corinthians 2:2). The fact that he made a decision (ἔκρινά) to focus on Jesus Christ as one crucified suggests that there were other options.

In fact, Paul's letters suggest that at other times he decides not to focus on Christ crucified. As we will see, there is great variety in the way Paul speaks of the significance of Jesus, at times focusing on his death, at other times giving more attention to the resurrection, still other times speaking in terms of Christ as an ideal type. Moreover, he writes in diverse ways about each of these aspects, confounding attempts to develop a systematic understanding of his Christology. But this is not the aim here, in any case. Rather, this chapter explores how various aspects of Paul's presentations of Christ relate to broader cultural gender constructions in general. It attends especially to the disjunction between Paul's assimilation of Greco-Roman hegemonic masculinity and his proclaiming of Christ crucified. In so doing, this chapter will reveal how Paul's own masculine status was integrally linked to his proclamation of Christ, especially with respect to the rhetoric of the cross and crucifixion.

Christ against Culture in Paul?

There is a long and rich history of reading Paul "against" various cultural dynamics. Beginning with Martin Luther's "theology of the cross" and continuing through the most recent work on Paul in his political context, scholars have accented the apostle's countercultural tendencies. Although the Lutheran legacy of reading Paul against Judaism has been strongly challenged,[1] scholars have consistently seen in Paul a broader cultural critique. With the introduction of social scientific and rhetorical criticism of the New Testament, Paul's evocation of the cross is read as a challenge to the traditional status categories of the Greco-Roman world.[2] Most recently, scholars have begun to read Paul as one engaged more specifically in a critique of the Roman Empire.[3]

But the relationship of hegemonic masculinity and Paul's Christology is more complex than this, as is the question of whether he is pro- or anti-Roman or countercultural. As seen in the previous chapter, resistance to Roman tyranny does not necessarily equal resistance to a dominant masculine ideology. Even if Paul preaches Christ as one who defeats the "rulers of this world," his utilization and basic acceptance of the values associated with masculinity are nevertheless readily apparent. Along this line, Jennifer Knust's discussion of "the elite" as a category in Greco-Roman antiquity is helpful. Rather than seeing Paul as overturning the values of the elite, she rightly points to the Pauline reconstruction of the category. She notes, "The category 'elite'—when understood as not only, or even primarily, a socioeconomic designation but as a discursive production—is subject to constant renegotiation."[4] The same can be said for masculinity as a cultural category, especially because being a "true man" was intricately connected to having superior social status. With Paul, one finds basic acceptance of masculinity as something that would be (and should be) desired by the addressees of his letters. One also sees Paul engaging a range of cultural discourses on masculinity that would convince his audience of its attainability through a life in Christ.

The extent to which Paul lived and breathed the ideology of masculinity is seen most clearly in his paraenesis. Like the moral philosophers that populated his world, Paul draws frequently on athletic and martial metaphors, both with reference to believers and to himself. Believers are runners competing for the prize, as is Paul (1 Corinthians 9:24; Philippians 3:14). Paul is in rigorous training, pummeling his body into submission. Athletes exercise self-control, and so must Paul and his followers (1 Corinthians 9:25, 7:9). Epaphroditus (Philippians 2:25) and Archippus (Philemon 2) are his "co-soldiers" (συστρατιώτης). Believers are to wear breastplates and helmets (1 Thessalonians 5:8), and they should bear weapons and wear armor (2 Corinthians 6:7, 10:4; Romans 13:12). To be sure, Paul uses these terms in a metaphorical sense. He is not speaking, after all, of instruments of a typical war, but rather of breastplates of righteousness, faith, and love, helmets of hope, and weapons of light. Still, Paul's rhetoric is shaped by the cultural metaphors of masculinity, a masculinity that he applies to himself and to believing Christians.

Moreover, when Paul is on the defensive, he responds like other men in his context: he undermines his opponents' masculinity. As was the case with all three of the divine men of chapter 3, Paul turns to gender attacks when he is confronted with opposition. To this end, Paul can be violently explicit, as in his wish that his opponents in Galatia would castrate themselves (Galatians 5:12). In his letter to the Philippians, Paul insinuates the effeminacy of his opponents by pointing to their immoral lifestyle; their god is the belly, and their glory is their shame (3:19). Similarly, Paul taunts the Corinthians about their acceptance of emasculating treatment. "You bear it if someone makes slaves of you, devours you, seizes you, puts on airs, strikes you in the face" (2 Corinthians 11:20, my translation). Notably, he follows this attack with the sarcastic "To my shame I must say, we were too *weak* for that" (2 Corinthians 11:21).

As for that mainstay of manliness, self-control, Paul lists it among the fruits of the spirit (ἐγκράτεια, Galatians 5:23). The Thessalonians are urged to be sober (νήφω) (1 Thessalonians 5:6, 8), and the Corinthians are warned against temptation due to their lack of self-control (ἀκρασία, 1 Corinthians 7:5). Additionally, as Stanley Stowers has convincingly argued, self-mastery is central to the promise offered by Paul to the Gentiles in Rome, as will be discussed further below.[5]

In spite of all these ways that Paul is consistent with the dominant form of Greco-Roman masculinity, he also accentuates his weakness, asserts his dishonor, refers to himself as becoming the scum of the world—hardly badges of masculinity. This is the crux of the matter, so to speak. If Paul seems so often in line with the ideals of hegemonic masculinity, how is it that he successfully preaches an "unmanned" Christ as a way of salvation? And why does he draw attention to his own weakness in his letters?

The Vicarious Death of Christ as a Manly Death

For one will hardly die for a righteous person—though perhaps for
a good person one might actually dare to die.

—Romans 5:7 (my translation)

The first thing to note about Paul's reflections on Jesus' death is that direct references to the cross are not as ubiquitous as the strong hermeneutical tradition of his "theology of the cross" would suggest.[6] In fact, language of the cross and crucifixion is largely concentrated in the Corinthian correspondence and the letter to the Galatians. Apart from these letters, there are only two references to the cross in Philippians (2:8, 3:18) and one oblique reference (Romans 6:6, "our old self was co-crucified with him," my translation) in the undisputed epistles.[7] The absence of cross language in Romans is especially striking given the frequency with which Paul speaks of death and dying in this, his longest letter.

In fact, speaking of the death of Christ is central to Paul's mission. Nevertheless, he often does so without reference to the cross. In many cases, Paul uses the so-called dying formula in reference to this death. This formula (typically some variation of ἀποθνῄσκειν ὑπέρ..., but sometimes with περὶ...) can indicate giving one's life "for" some cause, or giving one's life "instead of" an individual or community. Both include the idea of dying "for the benefit of...."[8] Paul uses this phrase or a variation of it throughout his letters, painting a picture of Christ dying on behalf of "us" (1 Thessalonians 5:10), "the ungodly" (Romans 5:6), the "weak believers" (1 Corinthians 8:11), or as one who has died for "our sins" (1 Corinthians 15:3) or "for all" (2 Corinthians 5:14–15).[9]

While Paul makes heavy use of this formula, he did not introduce it to early Christian interpretation of Jesus' death. It is clear from 1 Corinthians 15:3 that the notion of "dying for" was already a part of the tradition.[10] It is at this point that the question of broader cultural gender ideology enters in. Although there is a long history of situating Paul's understanding of the death of Jesus in the context of the Jewish sacrificial cult,[11] more recent work has focused on ideas of a noble voluntary death in the broader cultural milieu.[12] As we have already seen and will detail further below, such a noble death was a sure way of displaying one's masculinity.

First, when Paul speaks in terms of the vicarious death of Jesus, he draws primarily on a well-known *topos* in Greco-Roman literature. Recall that Philostratus's Apollonius spoke readily of the wise man dying for his beliefs. Elsewhere he refers to the inclination to give one's life for family, friends, or lovers (*Vita Appol.* 7.14.1). In so doing, Philostratus is in line with a tradition of a noble, vicarious death for others that is firmly grounded in Greek tradition. The Peloponnesian War especially elicited the idea of a noble death on behalf of a cause. Pericles's famous funeral oration, as related by Thucydides, recasts the large loss of life and Athenian military humiliations as courageous, noble death on behalf of the Athenian democratic ideal. Similarly, Euripides, also writing in the midst of the Peloponnesian War, encouraged patriotic self-sacrifice through his dramatic adaptation of ancient sagas.[13] The playwright's retelling of the sacrifice of Iphigenia, for example, presents her as a willing victim, giving her body to be sacrificed for her country (*Iphigenia at Aulis*, 1553–55). On a more intimate level, the play *Alcestis* features a noble wife of that same name who is willing to give her life as a substitute for the life of her husband. Other Euripidean characters eager for self-sacrifice on behalf of others include Creon's son, Menoceus, in the *Phoenician Women*, and Macaria, the daughter of Heracles, in the *Heraclidae*.

Clearly, the idea of a noble vicarious death was not limited to men—in fact, the majority of Euripides's characters who die noble, vicarious deaths are women. Still, their most featured characteristic is that of courage, expressed as ἀνδρεία (manliness). In other words, these women are manlike in their willingness to offer their lives on behalf of others. Moreover, the notion of a woman demonstrating "manly" conduct is hardly unique to Euripides. Under the right conditions, women could become "honorary men" if they displayed manly virtues through practice of womanly ones, namely service and loyalty to the men in their lives.[14] There is strong evidence for this idea in the early empire and beyond. As Anderson and Moore note, "The literary and philosophical topos of the subject who is anatomically female but morally masculine is an exceptionally far-flung one, found in early Christian texts, and even in early Buddhist texts, as well as in ancient Jewish texts and pagan Greek and Roman texts."[15]

It is especially apparent in the martyrdom texts of the first and second centuries. For example, 4 Maccabees is a celebration of reason over the passions that praises the mother of seven gruesomely martyred sons as one who is "more manly than men" in her endurance (4 Maccabees 15:30; see also 16:14).[16] Similarly, the martyred Christian Perpetua tells of her own gender shift in her brush with death. Relating a vision she has while in prison, she is stripped of her clothing to face her opponent in the arena and "becomes a man."[17] In some sense, language of the crucifixion signals the reverse for Jesus. Although not anatomically a woman, he dies an unmanly death. The humiliation of being stripped before his crucifixion would serve to emasculate him, rather than reveal his masculinity. For this reason, to retell the nature of his death as a vicarious one is to turn Jesus from an unman to true man in the eyes of potential followers.[18]

The Jewish Hellenistic text of 4 Maccabees (or the Jewish Stoic text, to be more exact) is especially significant because several scholars have seen it as a link to the dying formulas used by early Christians. Notably, this text, which is essentially a manual of masculinity,[19] also makes heavy use of the notion of vicarious death. The seven brothers and their mother die "on behalf of virtue" (1:8 see 4:22) and "on behalf of the beautiful and good" (ὑπὲρ τῆς καλοσκἀγαθίας, 1.10, my translations), and for the sake of the law (διὰ τόν νόμον, 6.27, 30). Because the dating for 4 Maccabees is uncertain, one cannot argue for any direct influence from this text on the dying formulas in the Pauline epistles. But, more importantly, what both the Pauline material and 4 Maccabees confirm is the general picture suggested by Henk Versnel: by the first century, "the notion of 'dying for' became an attractive option to be admired, reflected on, and considered for application."[20]

Or at least to be drummed into young schoolboys. Recall Seneca's comment regarding his recitation of past heroic deaths. We learned from him the common view that "those stories have been droned to death in all the schools" (Ep. 24.6). But Seneca also apparently believes that one cannot get enough instruction on the notion of dying well. Musonius Rufus is also concerned with death that benefits others. One fragment attributed to him reads: "One who by living is of use to many has not the right to choose to die unless by dying he may be of use to more" (frag. 29, Lutz).[21] Similarly, "Choose to die well while it is possible, lest shortly it may become necessary for you to die, but it will no longer be possible to die well" (frag. 28, Lutz).

All this is to say that, from a gender-critical perspective, when Jesus is portrayed as one who willingly dies for the good of others, his death becomes a noble, courageous, and thereby manly act. As Carlin Barton argues, one of the characteristics of manliness in the Roman world was the notion of expendability: "the willingness, on behalf of the collectivity to lose everything, to become nothing."[22] Or, as Paul might say, "to empty oneself" (cf. Philippians 2:7). It is the "willingness" that is crucial. Making the death an act of one's will rather than a submission to the power of others turns it into a masculine rather than feminine event. Recall how Apollonius displayed his manly courage by his willingness to be imprisoned and face persecution from Domitian on behalf of Domitian's victims. Similarly, as Jeffrey Sumney puts it, "when the martyr chooses to die, it is honorable no matter what degradations she or he must endure." The martyr is "no passive victim but one who acts with purpose to benefit others."[23] In this context, the seemingly passive and emasculating death of Jesus could become the heroic self-sacrifice of a true man. The extent to which Paul understands Jesus' death in terms of a heroic self-sacrifice shines through in the passage that opened this section, Romans 5:7–8. There Paul addresses the possibility of dying for a good person, and he emphasizes the extent of God's love vis-à-vis that idea. While it is conceivable that someone might willingly die for a good person, Christ died on behalf of sinners.

Significantly, when Paul uses the dying formula, he often does so apart from references to the cross or crucifixion. Here one can perceive the tension between noble death traditions that affirm masculinity and rhetoric of the crucifixion that threatens it. The earliest reference in Thessalonians to "dying for us" (1 Thessalonians 5:10) makes no mention of the cross. In fact, there is no mention of either cross or crucifixion in the Thessalonian correspondence. As mentioned earlier, Romans contains only one brief reference to the believers being "co-crucified" with Christ, and no mention at all of the cross (Romans 6:6). Rather than focusing on the humiliation of the cross, these letters highlight the vicarious, noble death of Jesus.

To be sure, Paul did not always keep these two ideas separate. There are a few places where the image of crucifixion and the dying formula overlap. For example, Paul asks the Corinthians, "Was Paul crucified for you?" (1 Corinthians 1:13). Elsewhere, he speaks of Christ becoming a curse "for us" (Galatians 3:13). However, these instances are the exception rather than the rule. This is because the concept of the noble, manly death and the emasculating crucifixion are not ideas that are easily held together in the gendered ideology of the first century. The gendered implications of both images are like similar poles of a magnet, repelling rather than attracting one another.

Crucifixion, Weakness, Hardships—A New Masculinity?

He humbled himself, becoming obedient to death, even death on a cross.

—Philippians 2:8

Yet Paul does preach Christ crucified. The heavy concentration of cross discourse in the letters to the Corinthians and the Galatians suggests that the
occasions for these letters in particular evoked Paul's use of cross imagery.[24]
With respect to the Corinthian correspondence, the circumstances of Paul's
writing included responding to threats from his opponents regarding his own
masculine status. Early in 1 Corinthians, Paul reminds the community of how
he came "in weakness and in fear and in much trembling," without persuasive
wisdom (1 Corinthians 2:3–4). Paul seemingly has no choice but to confront
this fact, because the rest of his correspondence suggests that he was not
viewed as particularly strong within the community.

Though Paul rhetorically shrugs off their opinion ("it is a very small thing
that I should be judged by you or by any human court," 1 Corinthians 4:3), his
extended self-defense suggests that the accusations of the Corinthians have
hit home. Paul's burst of sarcasm in 1 Corinthians 4:10 gives the impression
that it is precisely his masculinity that is under threat[25]: "We are fools for
Christ, but you are wise in Christ! We are weak, but you are strong! You are
esteemed. We are dishonored!" (my translation). In 2 Corinthians, Paul quotes
the specific charges leveled against him, as in "I who am weak when face to
face with you" (2 Corinthians 10:1, my translation) or similarly, "his letters
are weighty and strong, but his bodily presence is weak, and his speech
contemptible" (2 Corinthians 10:10). In the ancient context, accusations of
weakness and poor speech are challenges to one's masculinity. Finally, Paul
admits to having been beaten by both Jewish and Roman authorities, under-
going the same sort of bodily violation as Jesus (2 Corinthians 11:23–25). In
short, if Paul is already viewed as weak by the community, he may have little
choice other than to deliberately accent that weakness and claim it as a means
to power.

That this is a particular strategy addressing the situation in Corinth is
confirmed by the lack of emphasis on weakness in Paul's other letters. When
Paul speaks of "the weak" elsewhere, he generally is not referring to himself,
but to those who are weaker in faith than he is. So he exhorts the Thessalonians
to help the weak (1 Thessalonians 5:14) and encourages the Romans to put up
with "the weak" (15:1). But in Corinth, where Paul's masculinity is particularly
challenged, Paul speaks both of the cross and of weakness.

Yet when he speaks of both, it is to make the paradoxical claim that this seeming weakness, reflected both in the cross and in his own body, is actually strength. The logic behind this paradox lies in the fact that Paul understands his weakness in relation to the weakness displayed in the crucifixion, which he defines as a divine weakness. Indeed, Paul speaks provocatively of the crucifixion as "God's weakness," but this is only to make clear that God's weakness is far stronger than any human strength. That the gods are stronger than humans, so that even their weakness surpasses human strength, is a point on which all ancients would agree. This paradoxical notion of divine weakness explains why Paul's references to his own weakness are quickly followed by language of strength or power. His most extended discourse on his weakness is his spirited defense in 2 Corinthians 11–12, which includes the declaration "when I am weak, then I am strong." Similarly, Paul's reference to his weakness in Christ in 2 Corinthians 13:4 is followed by a reference to the *power* of God. In 1 Corinthians 4, Paul paints himself as a spectacle: dishonorable, hungry, thirsty, poorly clothed, beaten, homeless—in a word, trash. But even here, Paul follows this litany with a challenge to the power of his opponents, reminding the Corinthians that the kingdom of God depends "not on talk but on power." He then displays some power of his own, threatening to come to them "with a stick" (1 Corinthians 4:20–21).

This close association between weakness and power make it difficult to claim that Paul is simply overturning Greco-Roman imperial values. A statement along those lines would sound more like, "When I am weak, then I am a true man," or, "I don't care about being strong, powerful, or manly. I am more interested in my feminine side." Facetiousness aside, this is not what Paul says. He does not celebrate his weakness as an end in itself or even as a virtue, but showcases it as a means of achieving strength.

The same is true when Paul speaks of the hardships he endures. Like Christ, Paul is tortured, or at least he catalogues his experience of suffering. In this, too, he joins his contemporaries, especially the moral philosophers, in lifting up hardships as a sign of virtue (and, in Paul's case, apostleship). In one sense, doing so is "countercultural" insofar as one cultural perspective clearly views such public displays of bodily vulnerability as emasculating. In this view, public beatings are understood as a grave insult to one's *dignitas*.[26] Like crucifixion, only a slave could be subject to such public humiliation. On the other hand, like the idea of a noble death, in the first and second centuries c.e., the idea of bearing pain—even pain inflicted in humiliating circumstances—could also be seen as the mark of a true man.

The use of hardship catalogs in Hellenistic literature underscored the connection between hardship, pain, and manliness, especially in the Stoic literature. As Catharine Edwards puts it, "In facing pain the Stoic wise man turned his body into a battlefield on which he too might show his *virtus*, prove himself a *vir fortis*."[27] So Seneca can speak of his body as an arena "in which bravery can be exercised, displayed, and observed."[28] Similarly, for Epictetus facing hardships is equivalent to Olympic training. "When a difficulty befalls, remember that God, like a physical trainer, has matched you with a rugged young man. What for? someone says. So that you may become an Olympic victor; but that cannot be done without sweat." In short, as Epictetus puts it, "It is hardships that reveal men" (αἱ περιστάσεις εἰσὶν αἱ τοὺς ἄνδρας δεικνύουσαι, *Diatr.* 1.24.1, my translation).

By situating one's endurance of personal difficulties in the same sphere as public displays of prowess and courage, the philosopher finds an alternative means of participating in the broader cultural construction of ideal masculinity. So does Paul. By turning his own body into an arena, by becoming a spectacle, he pits his own display of masculinity against that of his opponents: "Are they servants of Christ?" he asks, and responds, "I am a better one, with far greater labors, far more imprisonments, with countless floggings, and often near death. Five times I have received from the Jews the forty lashes minus one. Three times I was beaten with rods. Once I received a stoning," and so on (2 Corinthians 11:23–25). For Paul, this "weakness," this body turned battlefield, is actually a display of endurance, fortitude, conviction, manliness. Indeed, according to Paul, sufferings produce endurance, and endurance produces worth, or character (Romans 5:3–4).

With this emphasis on endurance, Paul joins multiple voices in the first century c.e. and beyond that, as Brent Shaw has shown, represent a revised perspective of the value of weakness and endurance. Just as Paul speaks of weakness as a means to achieve power, this perspective, seen in philosophical texts as well as Jewish and Christian martyrdom texts, points to the power of endurance. Shaw suggests that this focus on endurance is an "explicit cooptation of passivity in resistance as a fully legitimized male quality—a choice that could be made by thinking, reasoning and logical men."[29] He points also to the parallels drawn with the success of a well-trained athlete. If one holds out long enough, victory is achieved. In this way, "the victim of torture then acquires the greatest value attributed to persons of high social status in the world: they are ennobled, imbued with an aura of aristocratic demeanor—the type of excellence reserved by nature of the ruling elite, but one which could be acquired by a victorious athlete through the exercise of the body."[30] Such can be seen in the reflections of the Stoic philosopher Musonius Rufus, who draws on the image of cockfighting to make his point. Gamecocks, he observes, "with no understanding of virtue . . . nevertheless fight against each other and even when maimed stand up and endure until death so as not to submit the one to the other." Submission, of course, would imply a loss of the masculine status, at least from Musonius's perspective. He continues:

> How much more fitting then, it is that we stand firm and endure, when we know that we are suffering for some good purpose, either to help our friends or to benefit our city, or to defend our wives and children, or, best and most imperative, to become good and just and self-controlled, a state which no man achieves without hard-ships.[31]

Thus, not only does endurance display one's masculinity; it may also help one achieve it.

While Shaw points to this shift to passive endurance as a "moral revolu-tion," in light of the abundance of active and aggressive values normally as-sociated with manliness, I suggest that by the first century the revolution seems very nearly complete, and not limited to Jewish-Christian martyrdom texts. That is to say, within the broader culture, under Stoic influence, *andreia* (courage/manliness) was becoming "a quieter virtue; a virtue of endurance and of self-control rather than of perseverance in action."[32] Thus, when Paul draws on the rhetoric of endurance and hardship to bolster his reputation, he draws on an already well-established masculine discourse that entered the culture through Stoic responses to tyrannical rule.[33] To be sure, it is a paradoxical discourse. As Helen Cullyer argues, "Stoic *andreia* is at once opposed to and congruent with heroic *andreia*. It is opposed in that the Stoics do not view physical strength, nor even objective success as goods. . . . Yet Stoic *andreia* is heroic in its embracing of death and danger for the sake of the noble and honorable."[34] Thus, in some paradoxical sense, heroic action was still at the center of the rhetoric of endurance. For this reason, in their emphasis on endurance under trial, Paul's hardship catalogs might better be understood as claims to masculine status rather than challenges to the status quo.

In fact, from this perspective, Paul's letters contribute to the general pic-ture of alternative constructions of masculinity that were promoted through the Greek and Roman moral philosophers, as well as by Hellenistic Jewish and Christian texts. That such alternatives were possible indicates both the at-tractiveness and the malleability of masculine ideology. Even men clearly op-posed to the "rulers of this earth," such as Paul, found an alternative way of achieving and displaying masculine status and thus, paradoxically, of partici-pating in one of the ideological foundations of imperial rule. As was the case with Philo's Moses and Philostratus's Apollonius, here one can see a tension between resistance toward rulers and an attraction toward a gendered ideology that under girded ruling power. Paul's letters should be placed alongside the depictions of divine men such as Augustus, Apollonius, and Philo's Moses as another example of how one might negotiate masculine ideology under imperial rule.

Salvation as a Means of Masculinity

Finally, the extent of Paul's attraction and assimilation of masculine ideology can be seen in the ways that he connects it to his soteriology. As already mentioned, Stowers has pointed to the focus on self-mastery that is at the heart of Paul's letter to the Romans.[35] As Stowers argues:

> The rhetoric of Romans pushes the theme of self-mastery, or the lack of it, into the foreground in three ways. First, Romans tells the story of sin and salvation, problem and solution, punishment and rewards at its most basic level as a story of the loss and recovery of self-control. Second, the letter represents the readers as characters in this basic story that concerns self-mastery. Third, Romans relates this story of loss to the story of God's righteous action through Jesus Christ so that Christ becomes an enabler of the restored and disciplined self.[36]

Although Stowers speaks only marginally of gender in his rereading of Romans, Moore takes Stowers's argument to its logical conclusion. If Christ is the enabler of mastery over self, and if Christ "makes righteous" the one who has faith (Romans 3:26), it is also the case that

> *righteousness in Romans is essentially a masculine trait*; it is, in fact, the very mark of masculinity. What then is unrighteousness, sin, with its cunning accomplice, "the flesh"? What else but loss of self-mastery, lack of masculinity—in a word, femininity. *Sinfulness, therefore, is essentially a feminine trait in Romans.*[37]

In other words, when Paul speaks of salvation, he speaks, in part, of that which enables ideal masculinity.

Can the same interests be seen in other Pauline letters as well? What of Paul's dealings with the Galatians, in which Paul obsesses about the potential lack of Galatian foreskins? First, as Brigitte Kahl has shown, the gender dynamics of Galatians are quite complex. On the one hand, the letter is infused with language regarding male anatomy—including the remarkable phrases "gospel of the foreskin"/"gospel of the circumcision" (τὸεὐαγγέλιον τῆς ἀκροβυστίας / τῆς περιτομῆς, 2:7).[38] It is also the letter in which Paul includes the baptismal formula, with its negation of the gender binary: "There is no longer male and female" (3:28).

Putting aside for the moment what Paul intends with this formula, note that the point of the baptism is to become one in Christ, to be "of Christ," and if the Galatians are "of Christ," then they are also Abraham's σπέρμα (seed). Significantly, Paul goes on to illustrate the transition that the Galatians have undergone with analogies that stress a shift to higher status. Before they were of Christ, the Galatians were like minor children under a manager and slaves in the household. In fact, the Galatians were enslaved to the weak and worthless στοιχεῖα (elements) but have become like the child of the free woman (4:8–31). They are no longer "unmen," but have become free men.

Notably, when Paul uses the language of the cross and crucifixion in this context, his words are concerned precisely with the idea of mastery over the flesh. Those "of Christ" have crucified the flesh with its passions and desires. The works of the flesh include those things that are equated with behaviors that are out of control, while life in the spirit includes, among other civilized and manly behaviors, self-control (5:19–24). As with his Gospel to the Romans, the new life in Christ that Paul describes for the Galatians includes an increase in masculine status by virtue of increased freedom and self-control over bodily passions. Or, as Knust aptly puts it, "To Paul ... the only men truly capable of mastering desire were those 'in Christ.'"[39]

With this, we arrive once again at Galatians 3:28. For the past decades this text has been widely interpreted as promoting equality between men and women. Dale Martin identifies the work of Krister Stendahl and Elisabeth Schüssler Fiorenza as particularly influential in moving Galatians 3:28 to the center of discussions on gender equality.[40] Both of these scholars have vigorously promoted the idea of egalitarianism between men and women in the Christian community, drawing in particular on Galatians 3:28.[41]

In contrast to this focus on equality, Wayne Meeks argues that Galatians should be read in the context of ancient androgyny.[42] He rightly notes that ancient androgyny does not necessarily imply male and female equality. But, as Martin points out, Meeks still interprets Galatians 3:28 as a statement on equality.

Much as I support the idea of gender equality, in both the church and the broader society, I would argue that this ancient baptismal formula is not about egalitarianism between "males" and "females." Instead, the passage draws on ancient ideas about an ideal state of unity or oneness in which there is "no male and female" because there is only the masculine. In the ancient world, androgyny was not the blending of female and male with an equal mix of the two. Instead, both Christian and non-Christian texts speak of a transformation to a higher state as a leaving behind of the female for the masculine. As Martin puts it:

> What we see as soteriological androgyny in ancient texts is only misleadingly called "androgyny" that is male combined with female. It is actually the subsuming of the weaker female into the stronger male, the masculinization of the female body, the supply of male "presence" (heat, for instance) for the former experience of female "absence" (cold, understood as lack of fire). In this system, which is the overwhelmingly predominant kind of "androgyny" in the ancient world, it would be a mistake to portray androgyny as implying any equality at all between male and female.[43]

Thus, in Galatians 3:28, although in Christ there is "no male and female," there is masculinity, that is, a life commensurate with ideal masculine deportment. Paul does not change the Septuagint wording as Philo does, but he does share Philo's emphasis on unity ("all are one in Christ"). He would also agree with Philo on the concept underlying the *neither male nor female* formulation. To have no sexual distinction is to arrive at perfect masculinity.

Resurrection and Ruler Ideology in Paul

For this reason Christ died and lived again, so that he might rule over both the dead and the living.

> —Romans 14:9 (my translation)

In focusing on the language of death, suffering, and sacrifice that constitutes so much of Paul's language, one could easily overlook another major component of his Christology: the resurrection. But the idea of Christ being raised from the dead was certainly as significant to Paul as Jesus' death, if not more so. References to the resurrection accompany the earliest Pauline reference to the death of Christ (1 Thessalonians 1:10) and open Romans, his last surviving letter (Romans 1:4). Romans 14:9, as quoted above, suggests that it was his death and resurrection together that brought about the ruling power of Christ. In other words, although Paul understands the death of Christ to have saving significance apart from the resurrection, it is doubtful that he would have developed such a position apart from his conviction that God raised Jesus from the dead. This claim of resurrection brings Jesus into the arena of ruling power and divine status.

To consider language of being raised from the dead in the context of the first century c.e. necessarily evokes the idea of apotheosis. If presentations of ideal men such as Caesar Augustus, Philo's Moses, and Philostratus's Apollonius all include some language of apotheosis, it is no wonder that early Christian presentations of Jesus would do the same. As later chapters will show, the Gospels have their own versions of the apotheosis of Jesus. In Paul, the clearest image of the exalted and deified Jesus is found in Philippians 2:6–11.

Most scholars view this text as an early Christian hymn that Paul has incorporated into his argument.[44] While this is likely the case, it is equally likely that Paul accepted the Christological convictions expressed by the hymn. The text presents Jesus as one who, because of his obedience, was exalted by God, given a new name, and worshipped by every being in the cosmos. Moreover, as Donald Walker emphasizes, the hymn suggests that Jesus *earned* a new name by his extraordinary conduct, as rulers often did. (Recall, for instance, the conferral of "Augustus" on Octavian). As Walker puts it, "By discharging dutifully a horrific labor, Christ was elevated to divine status, given divine honors, and entrusted with divine rule; he became a κύριος at the head of a βασιλεία of universal scope."[45] As Walker also notes, further evidence of the ruler connotations of the hymn are found in the closing acclamation ritual (Philippians 2:10–11). The use of public acclamations was wide-ranging in the Greco-Roman world, but they were most commonly used to honor rulers.[46]

Philippians is not the only letter that links the resurrection to ruling power. The same is true for Romans 1:4. Here Jesus Christ is declared to be υἱοῦ θεοῦ ἐν δυνάμει by means of resurrection from the dead. Again, the closest cultural association for such language would be apotheosis. The opening of Romans places less emphasis on the salvific death of Jesus than on the divine status he acquired through resurrection from the dead. Walker traces this ruler imagery throughout the letters of Paul, noting especially the functions of the good king that Christ exhibits. The main goal of Walker's work is to explain Paul's appeal in 2 Corinthians 10:1 that he offers διὰ τῆς πραΰτηος καὶ ἐπιεκείας τοῦ χριστοῦ. The NRSV translates the verse as follows: "I myself, Paul, appeal to you by the meekness and gentleness of Christ." To speak of the meekness and gentleness of Christ would seem to suggest an alternative masculinity, because nowhere else have we uncovered a call for meekness or gentleness as part of ideal masculine deportment.

But "meekness and gentleness" is likely a misleading translation of these terms. Following a detailed semantic analysis of both terms, Walker makes the case that such language is thoroughly at home in "good king" rhetoric of Greco-Roman antiquity, connoting the treatment an ideal ruler is expected to display toward his conquered subjects. Such traits were commonly upheld as kingly virtues, because they were yet another example of self-restraint. We saw this idea reflected, for example, in Augustus's *Res Gestae*, when he wrote of his moderation in dealing with his captives. In doing so, he followed a well-established tradition that is reflected in the work of Cicero, who recommends kindness as the best means to secure and maintain power. "Of all motives, none is better adapted to secure influence and hold it fast than love; nothing is more foreign to that end than fear. The most suitable means to win and maintain power is love, the most unsuitable is fear" (*Off.* 2.23).[47] Even more to the point is Seneca's definition of *clementia* as "restraining the mind from vengeance when it has the power to take it, or the leniency of a superior towards an inferior in fixing punishment" (*Clem.* 2.3.1). Finally, the idea of leniency or kindness as a trait of masculinity is evident in Marcus Aurelius's reflections on fits of anger. From this ruler's perspective, that which is "lenient and gentle is more human and thus more manly" (ἀλλὰ τὸ πρᾷον καὶ ἥμερον ὥσπερ ἀνθρωπικώτερον οὕτως καὶ ἀρρενικώτερον, *Med* 11.18). So, when Paul appeals to the Corinthians διὰ τῆς πραΰτητος καὶ ἐπιεκείας τοῦ χριστοῦ, it would be better understood as "through the leniency and clemency of Christ."[48] Such a phrase evokes the language of the ideal male leader, and Paul uses it to defend himself against accusations that he is servile (ταπεινός) when with the Corinthians, and courageous only when he is apart from them (2 Corinthians 10:1). Rather than servility, he shows self-restraint when among them but stands ready to punish when the time comes (2 Corinthians 2:6). Still, the fact that the rest of Paul's text is replete with images of weaponry and warfare suggests he means to convey his authority and strength, even while he exhibits his leniency.

One last point regarding Walker's work: he notes that when Paul appeals to the philosophical *topos* of the good king, he taps into a countercultural strand of thought. But by the first century C.E., that strand is firmly embedded in the culture and conveyed through the educational system. Socrates might have been countercultural in his time, but, as we have seen, narratives about dying on behalf of a cause were standard school curriculum in Paul's time. So, too, holding up hardships as a badge of honor was a common *topos*. Indeed, Stoic philosophy had been so thoroughly mainstreamed into imperial ideology by the first century that to adopt such ideas could hardly be seen as countercultural. In short, while Paul may have been anti-empire, it does not follow that he was countercultural or that he subverted basic gender ideologies of his time. In fact, it seems that the language he uses for the death and resurrection of Christ was largely in keeping with an ideal masculinity.

The Cosmic Christ of the Deutero-Pauline Epistles

The Pauline tradition does not end with the undisputed epistles but finds expression also in the disputed Pauline epistles such as Colossians, Ephesians, and the so-called Pastoral epistles.[49] In this section, the focus will be on the deutero-Pauline epistles, with special emphasis on the letter to the Colossians.

As discussed above, in the undisputed letters, one gets occasional glimpses of the exalted Christ reigning in the heavens with God. In the deutero-Pauline epistles, the exalted Christ takes center stage, and the suffering crucified Christ recedes into the background or disappears completely. For example, 2 Thessalonians is principally concerned with the return of Christ. The author presents "the Lord Jesus Christ" in ways far more similar to Revelation than to Paul. The Christological portrait is drawn in strongly apocalyptic strokes; believers will be relieved of their suffering "when the Lord Jesus is revealed from heaven with his mighty angels in flaming fire, inflicting vengeance on those who do not know God and on those who do not obey the gospel of our Lord Jesus" (2 Thessalonians 1:7–8). He will consume the lawless one with the breath of his mouth (2 Thessalonians 2:8). At the same time, this Lord Jesus Christ will gather together the faithful (2 Thessalonians 2:1). They will be the first fruits of salvation and obtain the glory of the Lord Jesus Christ (2 Thessalonians 2:13–14). More attention will be given to this apocalyptic Christ in chapter 9. For now, it is enough to note that while apocalypticism is often linked primarily to Jewish origin, in many ways this triumphant, vengeful, and at the same time saving figure is closer to imperial masculinity than Paul's dying and rising Christ.

In Colossians and Ephesians, the exalted cosmic Christ is found writ large across the pages. At times, the authors use traditional expressions to convey this, such as depicting the risen and exalted Christ, seated at the right hand of God (Colossians 3:1; Ephesians 1:20). At other times, these letters present quite new notions of the cosmic Christ. The author of Colossians envisions Christ as a cosmic body through which all is created and in which all is held together (Colossians 1:16–17). As such, Christ is the εἰκων τοῦ θεοῦ τοῦ ἀοράτου, the icon of the invisible God.

As van Kooten discusses, the idea of a cosmic body held together by bonds was a well-known concept in Stoic and Middle Platonist thought.[50] Such a cosmic principle seems far removed from the language of gender, especially since the Stoics conceived of the fundamental cosmic elements as fire and water.[51] But as we have already seen, the gender gradient worked at a cosmic level as well as an earthly one. Philo defined the masculine principle as "active, rational, incorporeal and more akin to mind and thought" (*QE* 1.7). The Stoics spoke of the same idea in terms of νοῦς, or mind, the ordering principle of the universe. Drawing on Cicero's account of Stoic physics, van Kooten summarizes the relationship of God to the cosmos: "God is the world itself, and the universal pervasiveness of its mind. . . . He is the world's own commanding faculty, since he is located in intellect and reason; that is the common nature of things, universal and all-embracing."[52] With this description, we are indeed in the realm of the masculine.

In this sense, the cosmic Christ of Colossians is the most perfectly masculine of all—an active, creative, coherent principle, responsible for the creation and coherence of the whole created order. All things were created in him, "whether thrones, dominions, rulers or powers" (1:16). Moreover, the Colossian Christ is the "head of every ruler and authority," and he (or God?) has "stripped them and made a public spectacle of them, triumphing over them" (Colossians 2:15, my translation). While this reference to rulers and authorities should be understood at the cosmic level, rather than the earthly one (see Ephesians 6:11), this does not lessen the rhetoric of emasculation. Whether one reads ἀπεκδυσάμενος τὰς ἀρχὰς καὶ τὰς ἐξουσίας as stripping of the armor of the rulers and authorities (as in the NRSV's "disarming") or as a more literal stripping and humiliating public display, the point is the same. Christ's victory involves the subjugation of, and thereby emasculation of, all other powers beneath him.

It is in this same context that the language of the cross appears, but in a different way than in Paul's undisputed letters. The Colossian author speaks in a decidedly metaphorical way about the cross, noting that God (or Christ; the pronominal reference is unclear) "wiped away the written decree that opposed us and set it aside, nailing it to the cross" (Colossians 2:14). It is not Christ but a legal document convicting the believer that is the crucified victim. Similarly, there is one reference to "the blood of his cross," but this, too, takes on cosmic dimensions that seem far removed from the violence and humiliation of the cross. Instead, it becomes the means by which God "makes peace" and thereby reconciles himself to all things on earth and in heaven (Colossians 1:20). That the author is not focused on the image of a crucified Christ, in spite of this reference to the cross, is confirmed by the lack of attention to Christ's suffering. As Sumney notes:

> Nothing in the letter's comments about the death of Jesus suggests that suffering was crucial to its meaning or efficacy. It is the power and exaltation that come through and even during the crucifixion that are vital for the effectiveness of the work of Christ. Nowhere does

Colossians state explicitly that Christ suffers for the readers, except in 1:24.[53]

Thus, as the Pauline tradition develops in this letter, the unmanly crucifixion no longer plays a central role. It is left behind in favor of the masculine cosmic Christ.

This emphasis on the exalted cosmic Christ makes the effects of his salvific power look different as well. That is to say, believers also participate in some type of cosmic, incorporeal existence. With Christ, they have "died to the elemental spirits of the universe" and have already been raised with him (Colossians 2:20). But in ways similar to the language of Romans 6, they should therefore put to death earthly things—sexual deviance, impurity, passion, and evil desires (πορνείαν, ἀκαθαρσίαν, πάθος, ἐπιθυμίαν κακήν, 3:5). Likewise, they must rid themselves of anger, overwhelming passion, evil, slander, and obscene language (ὀργήν, θυμόν, κακίαν, βλασφημίαν, αἰσχρο λογίαν ἐκ τοῦ στόματος ὑμῶν, 3:8). That is, they are to put off those behaviors that would call into question their masculine status, seeking "the things that are above."

Given this, it is notable that believers have "stripped themselves" (3:9), recalling the same language used for the rulers and authorities. But rather than standing in humiliation as a public spectacle, believers have clothed themselves with a new self. The author describes this renewed life as a unified one, using a version of the baptismal formulas found in Paul's letters. The formula does not include the gendered phrase "no male or female." In addition, as the household code that follows soon reveals, the categories of slave and free are most certainly part of this renewed life. Perhaps this is why believers are further urged to clothe themselves with compassion, kindness, modesty, leniency, and forbearance (σπλάγχνα, οἰκτιρμοῦ, χρηστότητα, ταπεινοφροσύνην, πραΰτητα, μακροθυμίαν, 3:12). Such traits are "in the image of the creator," according to the author, but they are also promoted by cultural elites as qualities of an ideal man/ruler/master.

To be sure, the author adds a particularly Pauline element, holding up love as that which binds everything together (3:14). Elevating love as a defining trait of the renewed self is a distinctive addition to the general cultural discourse regarding masculine deportment. Still, the moment is fleeting, as the author quickly situates love neatly into a broader scheme of household relations. Wives, children, and slaves are to be submissive and obedient. Husbands/ fathers/masters (ἄνδρες /πάτερες /κύριοι)—that is, those in control of others—are to demonstrate their self-restraint. They are to love their wives and not embitter them, not provoke their children, and be fair and just to their slaves. In short, a renewed life in the image of the creator produces an ideal husband/father/master.[54]

The Civilized Masculinity of the Pastoral Epistles

The Pastoral Epistles, 1 and 2 Timothy and Titus, take the reader beyond the early Pauline tradition into the second-century appropriation of that tradition. The letters take the form of instructions from Paul to Timothy and Titus on proper leadership and conduct in the Christian community. In this sense, as Mary Rose D'Angelo notes, the letters are essentially "man-to-man counsel." This counsel is based on the normative household codes of the Greco-Roman elite, in which man, women, children, and slaves all have their proper place. By advocating for this household structure, the "Paul" of these letters defines a masculinity that affirms Roman family values.[55] Not only that, but the author makes clear that the benefits of salvation include a Christian *paideia*, or education in proper masculine deportment. The saving grace of God, according to the author, "teaches us [παιδεύουσα ἡμᾶς] to renounce impiety and worldly passions, that we may live self-controlled, just and pious lives in the present age" (Titus 2:12, my translation). Thus, in these later letters there is a continuation of the idea that belief in God through Christ enables one to achieve a virtuous, manly status.

The Pastoral Epistles are not simply manuals for masculinity. As Jennifer Glancy has rightly noted, the author strikes a defensive posture throughout the letters, probably in response to "gender-baiting" by early opponents to Christianity.[56] For example, she points to the gendered attacks reflected in Origen's refutation of Celsus. Celsus claims that Jesus was born of an adulterous union, was driven out of the home by his father, and became an apprentice to magicians (*Cels.* 1.28). In response, Origen "attempts to convert the tale of Jesus' lowly and shameful origins to a triumphant narrative of masculine self-fashioning, turning on Jesus' successful achievement of a masterful speaking style."[57] Origen's defensive posture is illustrative of the position of "the pastor," as Glancy refers to the author of these Pauline letters. As Glancy argues, the pastor, too, may have felt the sting of gendered attacks against Christians and responded with pastoral advice that would ensure conformity to cultural standards of masculine deportment.[58]

The Christology of these letters adds to this impression. While there are some familiar Pauline themes to be found, others have gone missing in these later letters. What is present, for instance, is the notion of vicarious death. Christ is called a ransom for all (1 Timothy 2:6) who "gave himself for us" (Titus 2:14). Christ also appears as one who is merciful and patient, much like the Christ who shows clemency in Corinthians (1 Timothy 1:13–16). The virtue of endurance is evident as well. The author urges his reader to be a "co-sufferer" like a good soldier of Christ (2 Timothy 2:3). Those who live in Christ are guaranteed persecution (2 Timothy 3:12), but they are also promised that endurance will bring the reward of ruling with Christ (2 Timothy 2:11, 4:8).

What is missing, however, in spite of the emphasis on suffering, are references to the cross or crucifixion. It is as though the author, in his earnestness to both promote proper gender deportment and defend against gender attacks, wants to avoid the complicated issue of Christ's death. In fact, shame seems to be on the author's mind throughout the letters, including the acknowledgment of the possible shame involved in following Christ. If the Paul of Romans declares that he "is not ashamed of the gospel," the Paul of the pastorals urges Timothy not to be ashamed "of the testimony about our Lord" (2 Timothy 1:8). He further insists that he is not ashamed of his own suffering, suggesting that the treatment he has received would be viewed by others as emasculating (2 Timothy 1:12). By the second century, this concern about looking shameful is understandable in light of the opposition that was voiced by opponents such as Celsus. Thus, in the Pastoral Epistles one finds traditions of Jesus' vicarious self-sacrifice interwoven with assertions against the shamefulness of Christ or his followers and detailed exhortations to conform to normative gender scripts as closely as possible.

Conclusion

The undisputed letters of Paul reveal the early impetus to transform the humiliating death of Jesus' crucifixion into the manly death of a hero. Paul's rhetorical strategies illustrate several ways of effecting this transformation. In so doing, Paul's letters also provide insight into the multiple discourses regarding the attainment of masculinity that were available in the culture. At those places where one's masculinity seems challenged beyond one's control, at those places where one might be perceived as vulnerable, defeated, and emasculated, the ideology of masculinity was able to accommodate alternative strategies for achieving the goal. Thus, from a Christian perspective, if Jesus appeared defeated and emasculated in death, it was only because his vicarious, noble death for others had not been understood. If Jesus (and Paul) seem weak, it is because both have chosen to take on hardships for the benefit of others. In this way, the weakness of both is actually manly courage.

To be sure, the transformation from weakness to strength of which Paul speaks is not accomplished on his own—Paul is not a self-made man. As Paul describes in 2 Corinthians 12:9, the Lord revealed to him that "power made perfect in weakness." It is not Paul's own power but the "power of Christ" that dwells in him. But could this notion be an adaptation of a similar idea in the broader culture? In the first century c.e., it was the "power of the emperor" that "dwelled" in the local elites and shored up their own masculine status in their communities, even while their own power was diminished vis-à-vis the emperor. Similarly, Paul looks to Christ as the one who both empowers him with strength and authority and the one to whom he readily submits. In Paul's view, even Christ ultimately submits to God, who is above all (1 Corinthians 15:28).[59]

Paul also looks to Christ and urges other to look to him as the one who enables "righteousness" in the believer. As we have seen, this righteousness is essentially a masculine trait; it is that which enables manly conduct, such as self-control. By emphasizing the attainment of righteousness through belief in Christ, Paul offers another means of gaining status in the broader culture.

Later deutero-Pauline tradition also conveys a link between salvation and manly status, but it leaves behind the spectacle of the crucifixion. In Colossians, masculine deportment is linked to a cosmic incorporeal ruling identity. This cosmic identity includes the familiar demand to exhibit self-mastery, as well as an alignment with traditional cultural codes of conduct for the family. The Pauline tradition reflected in the second-century Pastoral Epistles reveals an ongoing concern about the unmanly nature of the crucifixion coupled with the pressing desire for followers of this crucified one to conform to the expectations of manly deportment.

5

The Markan Jesus
as Manly Martyr?

Jesus is never the man we expect. . . . Christology, which is attempting to fathom the character of Christ as the representation of
God, is and remains a riddle in Mark.

—Graham Ward, "Mimesis: The Measure
of Mark's Christology"

If Christology is a riddle in Mark, so also is the gender identity of the
Markan Jesus. The few studies that have explored the masculinity of
this Jesus have unearthed contradictions, ambiguity, and ambivalence.[1] Given the dating of this Gospel, this should come as no surprise. If Mark's Gospel was written just after the destruction of
the Jerusalem temple in 70 c.e., as most scholars contend, then the
narrative took shape during a particularly violent show of Roman
force. Whether or not the author was directly associated with these
events, the story he tells ripples with the reverberations of this cata-
strophic event. So does the gendered portrayal of Jesus. The Markan
Jesus is a divinely appointed strong man, critic of Roman "great ones,"
noble martyr, but also a passive, emasculated victim who suffers a
humiliating death. As such, the Christology of the Gospel shows
evidence of adaptation, accommodation, resistance, and perhaps
resignation to hegemonic Greco-Roman masculinity. But this should
not surprise. Because the ideology of masculinity was so closely integrated with the Roman imperial project, the literary products of
those under Roman power would understandably be ambivalent. This

chapter will explore how the Markan Jesus embodies the dissonance between the desire to resist Roman aggression and the lived experience of Roman might. This dissonance produces a character whose masculinity is shaped in large part by a major strand of Roman masculine ideology even while it reveals the underside of such ideology.

The Markan Jesus as Strong Man:
Resistance through Accommodation (Mark 1–8)

Mark begins at the beginning, with the introduction of Jesus Christ, the Son of God (Mark 1:1). As discussed in chapter 1, a primary source for information about Jesus has been the titles that are attributed to him. The Gospel of Mark opens with two such titles. Jesus is identified as Ἰησοῦ χριστοῦ υἱοῦ θεοῦ, "Jesus Christ, the Son of God" (1:1).[2] Here, χριστός seems more proper name than title, and its use in the Gospel this way is confirmed in 9:41. But in other places χριστός stands in apposition with "Son of the Blessed One" (14:61) and "King of Israel" (15:32), suggesting that the author clearly understood "Christ" as a title as well. As such, χριστός would connote the granting of God's special favor and the conferral of divine authority and power. Likewise, in the context of a first century c.e. Mediterranean audience, the most immediate cultural reference for Son of God would be to a Roman ruler as *divi filius*.[3] Thus, the titles that are attributed to Jesus in the first line of the Gospel suggest the ruling authority and the divine status of Jesus. They also suggest accommodation to masculine military figures in Hebrew and Hellenistic traditions.

Once past this titular introduction of Jesus, the Gospel narrative takes a different course from the typical portrayals of ideal men. There is no record of the extraordinary birth or childhood of the Markan Jesus. And while the ideal men of chapter 3 are all noted for their extraordinary physical appearance, neither the narrator nor John the Baptist, who announces the coming of Jesus, provides such a description of Jesus.[4] Nevertheless, there is much to suggest the superiority of Jesus in these opening verses. First, the announcement of John includes words that come close to a physical description. Using a comparative term, John affirms that Jesus is ὁ ἰσχυρότερός, the "stronger" or "mightier" one, a term that implies both physical strength and superior rank. John accentuates the point by indicating his unworthiness with respect to Jesus. He is lower than a slave or woman (those who typically would remove a man's sandal in the ancient Mediterranean) compared to Jesus (1:7).

The baptismal scene further emphasizes the status and power of Jesus. Like the extraordinary events that accompany the birth of Augustus or

Apollonius, this inauguration of Jesus is marked by the tearing apart of the heavens and the descent of the Spirit on him. As Boring notes, "The coming of the Spirit is not a soft, warm-fuzzy image (despite the analogy of the dove). 'Spirit' connotes power, eschatological power, as in Isaiah 11:1–5."[5] The voice of the divine God/Father speaking directly to Jesus (and to the audience) makes clear Jesus' filial link to the divine and his status as one loved by and pleasing to God.

Such divine favor apparently does not preclude a test of strength, however. After receiving these words, Jesus is immediately "driven out" (ἐκβαλλω) to the desert, seemingly by the very Spirit that has just been conferred on him. The verb implies forceful, if not violent, action. The author uses it most typically to describe Jesus' actions against demons (1:34, 39; 3:15, 22; 6:13; 7:26).[6] In this sense, Jesus is acted upon rather than active, a condition to which he will return in the passion narrative. Here is the first indication that all is not what it seems with the masculine power of Jesus.

The test itself is not described, but there is no indication that it involves the sort of moral temptations meted out by Satan in Matthew's and Luke's versions. Instead, πειράζω may be better understood here as a "contest of opposing forces."[7] That is, Jesus, having been endowed with divine power, is now driven out to the desert to struggle against Satan. The outcome of the conflict goes unstated, though the presence of the angels waiting on Jesus suggests divine assistance in the struggle (while the "wild beasts" likely are on the side of Satan).[8] The overall impression from this introduction is one of Jesus as a man endowed with high status. He is the bearer of both divine approval and power, but as such he is driven by forces that are beyond him.

This impression continues as the narrative progresses, though as Jesus launches into his traveling ministry, the initiative appears to come from him.[9] He calls a team of men around him (Simon, Andrew, James, and John), speaks publicly, heals, and casts out unclean spirits—all within the first chapter. These activities continue at a rapid pace in the early part of the narrative, so that soon Jesus has "cured many." As a result, he attracts such huge crowds that he is worried that he will be crushed (3:9–10).

In this initial part of the Gospel, stories of Jesus' healings are combined with stories of conflict with authorities from Jerusalem (2:1–12; 3:1–6; 3:22–29). It is at this point that hints of Roman resistance first surface. In fact, both the healing stories and the resulting conflict can be seen as instances of subversion of imperial power structures. As we will see, especially in the case of the controversy stories, these scenes are also occasions for gender displays.[10]

With respect to the miracle stories, scholars have long recognized the theological implication of the healings and exorcisms as signs of the in-breaking kingdom of God that Jesus announced in 1:15.[11] In the Roman imperial setting, such theological implications would be directly related to political structures. Proclaiming the coming of an alternative kingdom is a clearly subversive move. Reinforcing such an announcement with the working of miracles further undercuts the existing structures of authority.

Such miraculous confirmations of emerging and subversive authority were not limited to early Christianity. G. W. Bowersock has shown that the exhibition of miracles was a typical part of the mechanism of imperial subversion.[12] Among the most interesting examples are those of healing miracles wrought by Vespasian upon his arrival in Alexandria. There he is approached by a blind man and a man with a withered hand who have sought him out at the bidding of Serapis. After consulting doctors who assure him that the healings would be effective if Serapis wishes them to be, the healings take place. Then Vespasian enters the temple and receives a favorable portent regarding his ascension to the throne (Tac. *Hist.* 4.81.1–3; Suet., *Vesp.* 7.2; DioCass 64.9.1).

In both Matthew and Luke, a similar link is made between miracles and ruling authority when Jesus lists the works he has performed in reply to the question, "Are you the one who is to come, or should we wait for another?" (Matthew 11:3; Luke 7:18–23). In the Gospel of Mark, the connection between ruling authority and miracles is made by the crowd. They identify Jesus' first exorcism as "a new teaching with authority" (1:27). The specific reference to ἐχουσία suggests that teaching "with authority" is not something to which the crowd is accustomed. In fact, the narrator has already made the point explicitly by drawing a contrast between Jesus and the scribes precisely with respect to their authority (1:22).

That Mark represents these scribes as coming from Jerusalem suggests that they represent the local ruling elite. Past interpretations of Mark have often assumed that the conflict with the scribes is purely a religious one. In this view, the scribes, Pharisees, and priests represent the legalistic "experts" on the written and oral religious tradition of Judaism whom Jesus challenges in the interest of a more spiritual and humane interpretation of tradition. More recently, New Testament scholars have begun to recognize Jesus' conflicts with authorities as also political in nature.[13] This perspective stems from the Roman imperial structures of authority that operated primarily through local elite men. In other words, once Rome secured its vast empire, it could hardly rely on military strength to keep its subjects under control. Instead, the Roman system relied on local leaders, a "retainer class" who benefited from cooperating with Rome.[14] These were typically men of privilege who supported the imperial system and in return were permitted to remain in their positions of power. This is how the scribes would have been viewed at the end of the

Second Temple period, during which most were "either Temple personnel or employed in the government administration."[15] Even after the destruction of the Temple, the collective memory of the early Christian communities likely associated the Jerusalem scribes and priests with Roman authority. Thus, when the Markan Jesus surpasses the scribes in his demonstration of authority through miracles, he engages the same sort of subversive mechanism seen in the story of Vespasian.

This theme of subversion through authority and strength appears in another conflict between Jesus and the scribes. The scribes from Jerusalem claim that Jesus' power comes from "the ruler of demons" (3:22). In response, the Markan Jesus argues that if his power came from Satan he would not be casting out demons, because a house divided against itself cannot stand. Introducing the idea of strength once again, Jesus continues, "No one can enter the house of a strong man and plunder his belongings without first tying up the strong man. Then his house can be plundered" (3:27, my translation).[16] The description of the "strong man" recalls the opening of the Gospel. There John the Baptist pronounced that one was coming who was stronger than he was. This was followed by a testing narrative scene in which Jesus was forced to struggle with Satan. Now Jesus suggests that he is even stronger than Satan, who is himself "a strong one."[17]

Given the case studies in chapter 3, if this conflict with the scribes has political connotations, it is likely that gender ideologies are at work as well. To be a man included besting one's competitor, whether on the battlefield, in the sports arena, or in verbal jousting. Over the course of the narrative, the author uses several designations for Jesus' competition, but the most common are references to the scribes, and in the Jerusalem setting, the chief priests. References to the Pharisees are about half as frequent, and the "Herodians" appear only twice (3:6, 12:13). Mark's focus on the scribes is particularly interesting given the association between literacy and masculinity as outlined in chapter 2 and illustrated in the superior intellect exhibited by Augustus, Moses, and Apollonius.

In Mark's Gospel, Jesus is not depicted as reading or writing, though teaching in the synagogue could well imply reading. Nevertheless, his superiority over the scribes suggests an intellect superior to that of those who were viewed as the educated leaders in the community. The scribes in Palestine typically came from affluent, priestly families,[18] which may explain the frequent pairing of the scribes with the chief priests in the narrative (e.g., 3:22, 7:1, 11:27, 14:43). The narrative suggests that the role of the scribes involves interpretation of scriptural and religious traditions (9:11, 12:32–33), but Jesus warns his followers to beware of the scribes, painting a picture of them as men who love public recognition and prestige but who are vicious toward the disadvantaged (12:38). He also indicates that forgiveness will be denied the scribes from Jerusalem who blasphemed against the source of his power, the Holy Spirit. The scribes are guilty of sin forever (3:29), perhaps the most severe pronouncement of the Gospel, unless the prediction regarding the destruction of the scribes and chief priests in 12:9 is worse. Coming from the perspective of those under Roman occupation, one can understand both images of condemnation applied to those who represent Roman authority in the local communities.

This perspective can be seen beyond the conflict with the scribes, in passages containing more pointed allusions to Roman control. Most striking is the thinly veiled "exorcism" of Roman military occupation in the story of the Gerasene demoniac (5:1–20). The story involves Jesus arriving by boat in "the region of the Gerasenes" and encountering a demon-possessed man living among the tombs. Although this is one of a series of exorcisms, this one is distinctive in that Jesus demands to know the name of the demon. The response, "My name is Legion," is the first indication that this exorcism is more than a healing story (5:9). As many have noted, the Latinism "Legion" is the term for a Roman cohort of soldiers.[19] Derrett has pointed to other allusions to the military, such as the term ἀγέλη. The word is typically translated "herd," because it refers to the group of pigs (even though pigs do not gather in herds), but the term was also used for a group of military recruits. Also, ἐπέτρεψεν (he permitted) and ὥρμησεν (they charged) are both verbs frequently used in a military context. The first is used of a military order, and the second frequently refers to rushing into battle.[20] Upon hearing the story of Jesus encountering a "Legion," casting them out, and ordering them to enter a herd of swine that then charges into the sea, an audience would likely perceive the multiple allusions to a Roman army and its comic demise.

Note also that in this story of political resistance, Jesus' strength once more is thematized. The narrator emphasizes that no one could restrain the possessed man, and no one had the strength to subdue him (5:3–4)—no one, that is, except Jesus. In fact, the way the story is narrated suggests that the Markan Jesus hardly has to use his strength. In this text filled with military language, Jesus is presented as the military conqueror, the divine prince (Son of the Most High God) in charge of the defeated and captured enemies. Indeed, so anxious is the narrator to relate the man's supplication and plea for clemency that he allows the story to run ahead of itself. Only after the man pleads with Jesus to "Swear to God that you won't torture me!" (5:7 NIV) (a plea that a captured war prisoner might well make to the conqueror) does the audience hear that Jesus had commanded the unclean spirit to come out of him. While

Jesus takes no such oath, he does grant the request of the demons to be allowed to enter the pigs. Of course, this leads to their destruction in any case (assuming that the demons were destroyed along with the pigs, 5:13).

To summarize the depiction so far: the Markan Jesus of the first part of the Gospel is a man powered by a divine spirit that descended on him at baptism. He is thus bearer of divine authority, strength, and power. He betters his opponents in various conflicts and competitions, including those opponents who represent the elite leaders in the community. Moreover, he single-handedly (albeit symbolically) defeats an entire Roman legion. What better indicators might there be for depicting an ideal man for a people who are ruled by Roman power and part of a broader culture that promotes a masculinity based on Greco-Roman models? In this way, the depiction of the Markan Jesus draws on the standards of hegemonic masculinity to express resistance to Roman domination.

Notably, while Jesus is portrayed as a "strong man" throughout the first part of the Gospel, he is not one who seeks honor or fame. As Elisabeth Struthers Malbon notes, Jesus exhibits a certain reticence about his work in this Gospel.[21] The Markan Jesus wants to be alone, away from the crowd, and invites his disciples to do the same (1:35, 6:31). He (at times) does not want to draw attention to the healings he performs (1:44, 5:43, 7:33–36, 8:26) and points to "the Lord" as the one responsible (5:19). He urges both demons and followers to keep quiet about his identity (3:11, 8:30, 9:9). Whether these aspects of the text amount to a grand scheme on the part of the author, they are significant to the presentation of the Markan Jesus.[22]

With respect to gender implications, the notion of the reticence of the Markan Jesus is helpful. Malbon's point is to distinguish between the narrator's point of view, from which the identity and significance of Jesus are openly stated (Mark 1:1), and the point of view of the Markan Jesus, from which attention to his power and identity is continually deflected. As she puts it, "A Jesus who talked like the narrator could hardly be a Jesus who came not to be served, but to serve (10:45)."[23] Instead, because of his reticence, the Markan Jesus appears modest about his power and appropriately aware of its origins.

This, too, is what one would expect of the ideal man/ruler in the Greco-Roman world. Certainly Augustus exhibited a careful degree of modesty in his Res Gestae, reluctant to claim potestas, but demonstrating his auctoritas. Augustus was also extremely attentive to piety. His devotion to the gods (as a model for all Roman citizens to follow) was central to the ideology of Roman power. Similarly, Jesus refrains from taking credit for his own power but deflects attention to its source. The narrative is careful to show Jesus' devotion to God as he seeks a deserted place for prayer (1:35, 6:46, also 14:32–39), indicates the power of prayer, and encourages it among his disciples (9:29, 11:24). As with Augustus, however, the reticence and deflection of the Markan Jesus do little to turn attention from Jesus in the narrative. Those who are saved by him cannot contain their enthusiasm. The demons who are threatened by him recognize his authority and bow down before him.

The Markan Jesus as Noble Martyr (Mark 8–10)

Although the first half of the narrative is intent on showing the Markan Jesus as a strong and powerful man, in the second half, the Markan Jesus punctuates his teaching on the way to Jerusalem with three predictions of his own suffering and death. Each of these passion predictions are followed by a disturbance of some sort involving Jesus' disciples, which in turn calls for a teaching moment from Jesus. Thus, in this section the audience learns of the fate of Jesus and the costs and benefits of being one of his followers. What does this teaching section suggest about the gendered identity of Jesus and his followers?

First, the predictions of the Markan Jesus concerning his death are in keeping with the rhetoric of the noble death that was already established in the broader culture and was already associated with the death of Jesus, as seen in Paul's letters. To be sure, the Gospel narrative does not evoke the image of the noble death as frequently as Paul does. However, the two statements in the Gospel of Mark that relate most closely to the noble-death tradition are offered by the Markan Jesus himself, lending weight to their significance. With his first passion prediction and the scenes that follow, Jesus addresses any doubt regarding the nature of his death and its implications for his masculine honor.

At 8:31, Jesus offers his first teaching regarding his abundant suffering, rejection, and death. He proclaims that the Son of Man must suffer (a lot, πολλὰ παθεῖν) and be killed. There is divine necessity (δεῖ) in what he will endure. This recalls the divine will that lay behind the suffering that Paul endured and through which he displayed his masculine virtue. Similarly, the Markan Jesus teaches his disciples that "the Son of Man came not to be served but to serve, and to give his life a ransom for many" (καὶ δοῦναι τὴν ψυχὴν αὐτου λύτρον ἀντι πολλῶν, 10:45). Although the saying does not use the typical dying formula, nor is it evident to whom the ransom must be given, it is clear that Jesus' death will benefit many. Moreover, the Markan Jesus soon evokes the dying formula as he tells his disciples that his blood, the blood of the new covenant, will be poured out on behalf of many (τὸ ἐκκυννόμενον ὑπερ πολλῶν, 14:24). Thus, both of Jesus' statements about his death fit the category of a noble, vicarious, manly death.

But, as if the Markan Jesus is not himself convinced of his manly death, soon after this passion prediction he addresses an alternative possibility—that his suffering and death will be seen as shameful. He pronounces (defensively?), "For whoever is ashamed of me and of my words in this adulterous and sinful generation, so the Son of Man will be ashamed of him" (8:38, my translation). The warning admits the reality of how death by crucifixion would be viewed. But perhaps the reference to shame is also an unwitting recognition of the unmanly way that Jesus will die in this Gospel: with a loud cry and abandoned by all. If so, the Markan Jesus strongly affirms his masculinity while he still has the chance. He explicitly threatens anyone who might feel shame about him by drawing on gendered terminology for disloyalty or treachery. Jesus speaks of an adulterous (μοιχαλίς) generation. As discussed earlier, in the Greco-Roman rhetoric of hegemonic masculinity, adultery was regarded as effeminate behavior. Furthermore, this threat of humiliation is wrapped in an image of the Son of Man coming in the glory of his father with the holy angels.[24] This, Jesus states, will mark the kingdom of God coming with power (8:38). As with the rhetoric of Paul's letters, the language of suffering is interlaced with the rhetoric of power. The Markan Jesus conjures the specter of an unmanly death only to exorcise it with the image of an exalted heavenly Jesus coming in power.

Not only that, but the scene that follows offers a few chosen men a private preview of Jesus in his glory (9:2–8). The Markan Jesus leads Peter, James, and John up a high mountain by themselves. Then, he transforms before them, so they see him arrayed in dazzling white clothes, flanked by the esteemed figures of Moses and Elijah, who talk with Jesus (9:3–4). While the three men are terrified and confused by the vision, from the perspective of the audience it would surely be understood as a confirmation that an exalted Jesus will indeed "come in power" as he claimed. But to dispel all doubt, before the vision fades, the men hear a voice from heaven confirming the divine status of Jesus: "This is my beloved son," the voice says, and it commands them to "Listen to him!" (9:7). The conclusion of the scene has Jesus cautioning the disciples to remain quiet about this vision until after the Son of Man has risen from the dead.

Not surprisingly, it is this idea of resurrection that stays with the disciples as they make their way down the mountain (9:10). Although Jesus will go on to teach two more times about his suffering and death, the dazzlingly bright light of glory and power has already been seared into the minds of the disciples, at least James and John (10:35–37; see also 9:33–34). By juxtaposing Jesus' prediction of his suffering and death with the scene of this glorious apparition, the Gospel suggests that (at least for Jesus) suffering and dying for the sake of many will be rewarded with transcendent glory. If we recall the close link between masculinity and divinity that was evident with the divine men of chapter 3, Jesus' reward also suggests his status as an ideal man. Indeed, such heavenly transcendence means movement up the gender gradient into the realm of ideal masculinity.

There is more than one passion prediction, of course, and the other two are building blocks for further teaching. These teaching opportunities allow Jesus to make clear that the suffering of which he speaks is not limited to him alone. Listening in on this teaching, the audience learns that to be a disciple of Jesus means to lose one's life (8:34–35), to be a servant to all (πάντων διάκονος, 9:35), to give up possessions and family (10:21, 28–29), and to be slave of all (πάντων δοῦλος, 10:44). From the perspective of masculine identity in the ancient world, the implication of such teaching is that to be a disciple of Jesus means to give up any claim to masculine status. Or so it would seem. The other part of the lesson includes the rewards gained by discipleship. While Jesus is to receive an exalted heavenly status on account of his vicarious death, followers of Jesus receive other types of rewards for their suffering. These rewards include life (8:35), bountiful family and possessions (10:30), and to be first (10:31). Finally, like the brothers of 4 Maccabees who offer their lives for the sake of the law, these followers of Jesus also have a noble cause for which to die. Whereas Jesus gives his life as a ransom for many, they are to give theirs for his sake and the sake of the good news (8:35, 10:28).[25]

One curious aspect of the mention of family is the exclusion of fathers. Believers are promised that those who leave behind brothers, sisters, mothers, and fathers will receive mothers, brothers, and sisters, but not fathers (10:29–30). From a feminist perspective, the omission of fathers has often been viewed as an anti-hierarchical statement. That is to say, insofar as God is father of all and all are subject to him, then all humans are on the same footing. Typical of this perspective is Johanna Dewey's comment that the missing human father, "the symbol of authority and hierarchy," points to God's community as "a replacement egalitarian kinship group."[26] Dewey points also to 3:31–35, a text that also omits reference to a father, as additional evidence of this replacement kinship group. But however important the notion of egalitarianism is for the twenty-first century, it is doubtful that the concept played a role in the narrative of Mark's first-century Gospel.

On the one hand, the absence of fathers likely does concern the notion of God the Father. In 3:31–35, this seems clearly to be the case. The description of Jesus' family as "his mother, brothers and sisters" reinforces the claim that the narrator has made from the beginning of the Gospel, namely that God is Jesus' father. Still, in the Roman world, there was already an understanding that there was one father of all. Recall Augustus's pride at being given the title of *patrem patriae*, father of the country. But this did not put citizens on equal footing; instead it positioned them along a hierarchy vis-à-vis the emperor at the top.

Still, the final instructions from the Markan Jesus do present a call for a particular way of being among the disciples and a challenge to imperial structures of authority. The disciples are not to "rule over" (καταεξουσία) each other as οἱ μεγάλοι, "the great ones," rule over their subjects. Instead, as mentioned above, those who want to be great must serve, and those who want to be first are to be slaves. Here then is the most open sign of resistance to οἱ μεγάλοι, "the great ones" of the empire. The conduct that Jesus calls for in his own followers sounds like the language of submission, and of course, being servile was commonly associated with being effeminate. What may be easily overlooked is that Jesus addresses those among his disciples who want to be great and those who want to be first. In other words, the lesson concerns those who want to win the masculinity contest of the Greco-Roman world and win supremacy over others. These are the ones whom he urges to adopt a position of servility. In so doing, the Markan Jesus joins other discourses on leadership, or kingship, found in the broader imperial culture.[27] After all, the imperial rhetoric did not hold up tyranny as the ruling ideal, but quite the opposite. Indeed, there is ample evidence of the rhetoric of service and slavery used even with respect to kingship. Dio Chrysostom's orations on kingship, especially the following concerning the emperor Trajan, aptly illustrate the notion of the ideal humane ruler:

> The care bestowed on his subjects he does not consider an incidental thing or mere drudgery, when weighed down, let us say, by cares, but as his own work and profession. . . . It is only when he helps men that he thinks he is doing his duty, having been appointed to this work by the greatest god, whom it is not right for him to disobey in anything, or to feel aggrieved, believing as he does, that these tasks are his duty. (*Or* 3.55)

Seneca has a similar description of rulers in the "golden age":

> They kept their hands under control, and protected the weaker from the stronger. They gave advice, both to do and not to do; they showed what was useful and what was useless. Their forethought provided that their subjects should lack nothing; their bravery warded off dangers; their kindness enriched and adorned their subjects. For them ruling was a service, not an exercise of royalty. (*Ep.* 90.5)

The idea of a humane ruler can also be seen in the maxims such as "kingship is an honorable slavery" or "a noble slave service."[28]

Given such a description of a ruler, Jesus' reference to the great ones who rule over the Gentiles as a critique of leadership is based on the terms established by the rhetoric of the literate elite within the empire itself. In itself, this can be an effective means of resistance to the dominant ruling powers. As Anuradha Needham argues, critiquing the colonizers on their own terms renders them vulnerable by exposing the gap between their ideology and the reality of their rule.[29] Jesus' statement appears to do just this by calling attention to the failure to live up to imperial ideals. Still, in so doing, it hardly inverts the Roman ideology of leadership. If anything, what Mark presents is not an alternative ideology of imperial rule but a presentation of Jesus as a leader who embodies that ideology and who calls those who will lead under him to do the same. Thus, while Jesus' teaching may be seen as a critique of the reality of Roman rule, it may be too much to claim it as ideological subversion. One sees no attempt to redefine the ideal masculine ruler. Rather, in Jesus' teaching to those who would be "great" or "first," one finds the call for conduct befitting the ideal king.

The Markan Jesus as Emasculated Victim (Mark 14–16)

It remains to speak of the death of Jesus in the Gospel of Mark. To do so complicates the picture of the manly Markan Jesus. Given the words of Jesus earlier in the Gospel, one would expect the narration of a heroic and noble death.[30] But the depiction of the death of the Markan Jesus is ambiguous—or, perhaps more accurately, ambivalent. At points, it is as if the author, while knowing and approving of the tradition of the vicarious, noble death applied to Jesus, cannot fully dismiss the ignominy of the crucifixion.

For instance, nothing in the Gospel prepares the audience for the Gethsemane scene. If one was expecting Jesus to face his death with a noble martyr's speech along the lines of the Maccabean brothers, it is not found in the garden. Whereas the brothers ask their torturer with one voice, "Why do you delay?" (4 Maccabees 9:1), Jesus asks that God "remove this cup from me" (14:36). While a willingness to die for a cause may transform otherwise humiliating defeat into a noble death, Jesus indicates that his pending death is decidedly not his will. The Markan Jesus teaches that he must suffer and die, but the scene in the garden makes clear that he really would rather not. As Thurman argues, "Here at Gethsemane... Jesus' sure-footed stride to Golgotha stutter-steps onto the path of a different desire."[31] Similarly, Krause notes that in the garden, "Jesus unmasks the Father's will as distinct from his and resists it—even as he submits to it."[32] For in the end, Jesus does submit to God's will (ἀλλ' οὐ τί ἐγὼ θέλω ἀλλὰ τί σύ, 14:36c) and thus is presented as the epitome of obedience. If there is a masculine aspect to this scene, it would be found in the "heroic overcoming of the passions" and the display of Jesus' supreme self-mastery.[33] But it is questionable whether such a submissive posture, even if it involves self-restraint, would be understood by a man in the Greco-Roman world as masculine deportment.

Instead, this is another instance in which the relativity of the ancient gender gradient is relevant. Up to this point, Jesus has been portrayed as a strong man as he contends with Satan, the demons, and the authorities from Judea. But in Gethsemane, he is dealing with God. In fact, this is a time in the narrative when Jesus directly addresses God, and when he does he calls him father (Αββα, ὁ πατήρ).[34] In relation to this ultimate masculine figure, Jesus cannot be shown to the stronger one. He must obediently submit to paternal will. He must position himself beneath God on the gender gradient. This is the culturally correct posture for the son in relation to the father, especially the divine father.

Once this submissive posture is assumed, the Markan Jesus maintains it, not just in relation to the Father, but throughout much of the arrest and trial scene. The narrative reports the repeated "handing over" (παραδίδωμι) (or manhandling?) of Jesus by Judas, the chief priests, Pilate, and the Roman soldiers (14:44, 15:1, 15:15). As the Markan Jesus is passed around, he is spit upon, stripped, mocked, beaten, and whipped. In this way, as Thurman notes, the narrative traces "the increasing passivity and hence 'feminizing' of Jesus."[35] What is required by God, it seems, is not just submission to God's will, but submission to the will of Jesus' opponents.

Even in this feminizing of Jesus, there are moments of ambivalence. For instance, the narrator stresses Jesus' silence in the face of his accusers (14:61, 15:5). Is this a sign of feminizing passivity or defiant, "active" resistance?[36] Later interpreters of Jesus' passion certainly read his silence of as a sign of his courage. So Origen, for example, argues that Jesus "manifested a courage and patience superior to any of the Greeks who spoke while enduring torture" (*Contra Cel* 7.55). Moreover, Jesus does respond to two crucial questions about his identity. His reply to the chief priest's question, "Are you the Messiah, the Son of the Blessed One?" is the most open declaration of his identity in the Gospel. Jesus' statement, "I am. And you will see the Son of Man seated at the right hand of the Power and coming with the clouds of heaven," is surely intended as a dramatic high point in the narrative (14:62). Similarly, when Pilate asks him, "Are you the king of the Jews?" (15:2), Jesus' reply, "You say so," suggests a degree of defiance before the Roman ruler.[37] During the trial scenes, Jesus remains passively silent in response to the charges brought against him, but responsive to questions about his identity. Thus, the image of Jesus as passive victim is complicated.

On the other hand, the depiction of the death of Jesus does little to preserve the masculine dignity of Jesus or the notion of an honorable death. Boring puts it bluntly: "It is not a triumphal death."[38] In fact, at this point, any earlier ambivalence regarding the manly or unmanly death of Jesus is resolved in favor of the latter. As Best rightly observes of the scene, "It would be highly inappropriate in any form of the Passion story which was used for apologetic, evangelistic or liturgical purposes. It interferes with any presentation of Jesus as the Righteous Sufferer, the martyr, or the true model for Christian living."[39] It is also highly inappropriate if the goal is to portray Jesus as facing his death in a manly way.

Especially at issue are Jesus' loud cries from the cross. He first calls loudly to God, not with conviction regarding his sacrifice, but in anguish about his abandonment. "My God, my God, why have you forsaken me?" (Mark 15:34). The Markan Jesus cries out loudly once again just before dying, seemingly a wordless shout. Although these final cries bring the themes of suffering and abandonment to a dramatic climax, they may not present Jesus as one who bears his hardships like a man. Cicero discusses at some length whether it is acceptable for a man to cry out in pain. "Sometimes, though seldom," he notes, "it is allowable for a man to groan aloud." But he seems quite ill-disposed toward such a scene, going on to make clear that the brave, wise man never groans aloud, "unless perhaps to make an intense effort for steadfastness [or strength, *firmitatem*] in the way runners shout on the race-course as loudly as they can" (*Tusc.* 2.22.55). Some commentators on Mark understand Jesus' cry in just this way. Robert Gundry, for instance, argues that the author emphasizes the loudness of Jesus' shout to show "that he did not die in fleshly weakness, did not lapse into unconsciousness," but rather displayed "strength at the moment of expiration."[40] Thus, for Gundry, Jesus' final cry from the cross is one more presentation of the strong man. Such a reading relieves the narrative tension between the strong-man Jesus and the anguished body on the cross. The Markan Jesus is a strong man from beginning to end. But surely there are more straightforward ways to display manliness, strength, and courage in a death scene.

Compare this scene to the martyred Maccabean brothers. Far from crying out in anguish or simply shouting out loudly, they each give reasoned speeches about dying for the sake of the law. The parting words of the eldest brother, for instance, are a plea to his brothers to fight on after he is gone:

Although the ligaments joining his bones were already severed, the courageous youth, worthy of Abraham, did not groan, but as though transformed by fire into immortality, he nobly endured the rackings. "Imitate me, brothers," he said. "Do not leave your post in my struggle or renounce our courageous family ties. Fight the sacred and noble battle for religion. (4 Maccabees 9:21–24)

As we have seen, some have pointed out that because Jesus' final words are a quote from Psalm 22, they should be understood as a prayer.[41] This may be the case, and if so, one could see in his words Jesus' ongoing devotion to God even in his anguish. But the brothers pray as well, and their prayers highlight their courage. Here are the eldest brother's dying words:

You know, O God, that though I might have saved myself, I am dying in burning torments for the sake of the law. Be merciful to your people, and let our punishment suffice for them. Make my blood their purification, and take my life in exchange for theirs. After he said this, the holy man died nobly in this torture; even in the tortures of death he resisted, by virtue of reason, for the sake of the law. (6:27–30)

The brother's prayer is an appeal to God for the vicarious efficacy of his death. The narrator then affirms the brother's noble, virtuous death that he dies for the sake of the law. None of this is made explicit in the crucifixion scene in Mark. While the Markan Jesus was reticent in the earlier part of the narrative, where the narrator displayed his glory, here the narrator joins Jesus in his reticence.

There is one parallel between this Maccabean prayer and the Markan crucifixion scene. Both texts include acknowledgment of the possibility of the sufferer being able to save himself. In the Maccabean narrative, the eldest brother draws attention to his own steadfastness: he could have given in to his torturer and lived, but he resisted. In Mark's Gospel, the notion of Jesus' saving himself comes in the form of a taunt from the bystanders: "He saved others; he cannot save himself" (15:31). This statement, certainly an ironic moment in the Gospel, is true on a number of levels. First, it recalls Jesus' admission that by divine will, he *must* die and in that sense cannot save himself. It also recognizes the finality of the death sentence; there is no offer of life made by the Jewish or Roman authorities in exchange for Jesus' submission to their demands. This also complicates the interpretation of Jesus' death as a willful act. On yet another level, the taunt recalls Jesus' own paradoxical teaching on life and death (8:35). To "save himself," according to his own teaching, would be to lose his life. On the other hand, to lose his life will be (paradoxically) to save it. This brings us to the puzzling conclusion of the Gospel.

Although the Gospel has earlier revealed a transfigured Jesus, there is no reappearance of this figure after the death of Jesus. Mark's conclusion features an empty tomb, a man in white who predicts a reunion with Jesus in Galilee, and, famously, women who run away from the messenger and the tomb, frightened into silence. The disciples are still nowhere to be found. The scribal traditions reflect dissatisfaction with this ending from an early date, and at least two attempts at more acceptable conclusions were made.

Because Jesus is present in this closing scene only in absence, it is difficult to determine the implications for his gendered status at the Gospel's end. If the crucifixion scene left him decidedly unmanned, does the empty tomb scene restore his status? There is no vision of the resurrected Jesus, and the audience does not ever see "the Son of Man coming on clouds of glory." Still, the point of the empty tomb is surely to confirm Jesus' predictions that after three days, he will rise again (8:32, 9:31, 10:34). In confirming this prediction, there is also implicit confirmation of Jesus' interpretation of his own death as a ransom for many. To be able to see Jesus in Galilee suggests that just as he taught, losing his life enabled him to gain life. Moreover, as the divine men discussed in chapter 3, the prediction of seeing Jesus again suggests that his virtuous conduct, piety, and obedience to God as expressed in his vicarious death for others have earned him immortal status.

Literary readings of the Gospel often suggest that the instructions to go to Galilee function as a pointer back to the beginning of the story. Considering the gender identity of Jesus in this Gospel, this also means returning to the Markan Jesus of strength and power. Perhaps the audience is to view this strength and power only through the lens of the weakened and crucified messiah. This is a common understanding of the Christology of Mark; that is, his identity as Messiah can only be understood once it is clear that the Messiah must suffer. Yet from a gender perspective, another point could be that enduring a humiliating and unmanly death, if it is a matter of divine will and for the benefit of others, returns one to (or enables one to achieve) a position of authority, power, and strength.

Conclusion

To return to the words of Graham Ward that opened this chapter, it is not that Jesus is *never* the man we expect. For much of the Gospel, Jesus is very much what one would expect of an ideal man. Following him on his journeys in

Galilee, the audience comes to know the strong-man Jesus who resists both Satan and those representing Roman authority. Consistent with this strong masculine image, Jesus teaches of his impending death in terms of a noble martyr's death, including the predictions of his pending honorable sacrifice for others.

Given all this, when the time of Jesus' death arrives, it happens in both expected and unexpected ways. Although the narrative prepares the reader for Jesus' suffering and death, it also suggests that it will be a vicarious, noble death. But this noble martyr's story takes an unexpected turn when Jesus asks for relief from death and then cries out in anguish as he dies. It is as though the author knows that a vicarious death is a manly death, but when standing on the other side of a violent and deadly show of force by Rome, perhaps he does not quite believe it. Or, to put it another way, the author knows the demands of this particular version of masculine deportment, but he shows its underside as well.

Significantly, while the Markan Jesus provides an explanation for this death earlier in the Gospel, at the time of the crucifixion there is no accompanying interpretation or affirmation of this death as the scene unfolds. Instead, the narrator who declared Jesus to be the Messiah in the opening verse is noticeably detached from the scene. Events are related—the tearing of the temple curtain, the centurion's statement—but there are no interpretive asides giving insight into their meaning. The details have left generations of scholars grasping at solutions.

Drawing on postcolonial theory, Thurman suggests that the ambivalent portrayal of masculinity in Mark is a result of colonized subjectivity. For Thurman, Jesus can only be an imperfect imitation of the divine. But for much of the Gospel, there is little reason to see Jesus as imperfect. And the conclusion suggests that Jesus lives on after death—a clear indication of divinity. Given this, another way to think about the Markan crucifixion scene is as a moment of revelation in which the cultural demand for ideal masculine deportment, even in the most gruesome of circumstances, turns in on itself, to borrow Brakke's phrase. Such a turn may still be explained as the result of a colonized subjectivity, especially for those living in the aftermath of the destruction of Jerusalem. In this context, Mark's portrayal of the death of Jesus might be theoretically understood as a noble martyr's death on behalf of many. But in its telling, it is the brute reality of the Roman execution, in all its humiliating implications, that looms large.

That is to say, even while the Gospel of Mark draws on the noble-death formula and reinforces the image of Jesus as the "strong man," its relationship with hegemonic masculinity is ambiguous. In the end, the Gospel does not depict a noble death, but instead presents Jesus as crying out in anguish, exposed and vulnerable. To be sure, for many this is part of the power of the Gospel and the reason that many view it as the Gospel of the suffering Messiah. But when one views this crucifixion scene both in the broad context of hegemonic masculinity and in the immediate context of the rest of the Gospel of Mark, the picture is even more striking. This is one place in the New Testament where the masculine ideology that would call for a manly death is fully exposed (by the very subject who is supposed to be upholding it) as the grueling cultural demand that it could be. Perhaps at some unconscious level, there is genuine resistance to hegemonic masculinity to be found here, in the cry of anguish from the cross. If so, it is only a brief moment of resistance, because the narrative soon moves to the rewards of the manly death represented by the empty tomb. But in the telling of the death itself, the demands of hegemonic masculinity are revealed in the anguish of Jesus, who, after all, wanted to avoid this painful death, but had to follow the will of the father.

The Matthean Jesus

Mainstream and Marginal Masculinities

Thy fathers' sins, O Roman, thou, though guiltless, shall expiate.

—Horace, Odes 3.6

She will bear a son and you are to name him Jesus, for he will save his people from their sins.

—Matthew 1:21

He shall have the gift of divine life, Shall see heroes mingled with gods,

    And shall himself be seen by them, and shall rule the world to which his father's prowess brought peace.

—Virgil, Eclogue 4.15–17

Do not think that I have come to bring peace to the earth. I have not come to bring peace, but a sword.

—Matthew 10:34

The Matthean Jesus, though constructed in a text that makes use of almost all of the Gospel of Mark, emerges as a character quite distinct from the Markan Jesus. Because Matthew incorporates so much of the Gospel of Mark, much of what was said in the last chapter might also apply here. For instance, Matthew preserves Mark's "strong man" sayings (Matthew 3:11, 12:29), his three passion predictions (16:21–23, 17:22–23, 20:17–19), his anguished words from the cross (27:46), and his empty-tomb account (28:1–10). Given this, one might conclude that the Matthean Jesus shares the same ambivalent relationship with hegemonic masculinity as the Markan Jesus.

But Matthew's additions and revisions to Mark's Gospel, along with his use of other sources, change the depiction of Jesus in significant ways. On the one hand, Jesus' ideal masculine status is accentuated in Matthew's Gospel, as Jesus becomes the bearer of royal honorific titles, a prolific public speaker, a righteous teacher, and a bold agitator in a heightened conflict with his opponents. On the other hand, the Matthean Jesus also advocates an alternative masculinity, as seen in certain antifamily teachings (10:34–35) or in the surprising reference to those who become "eunuchs for the kingdom of heaven" (19:12). Whereas in Mark's Gospel the ambiguity around masculine deportment finds its locus in the portrayal of Jesus' death, in Matthew's Gospel the ambiguity manifests itself more in Jesus' teaching about discipleship and life in community. While some of his instructions correspond to hegemonic masculinity, other sayings will tap into more marginalized gender discourses.

The Matthean Jesus: King/Master/Householder/Son

The "Roman" of Horace's ode and the boy of whom Virgil writes in the opening epigraphs point to an imperial ideology that was replete with prophesies of an impending golden age. Virgil, in particular, celebrates one who will save the world (and Rome) from the sins of the fathers and usher in an age of peace.[1] This same one will "receive the life of gods" and mingle with heroes and gods alike. While Matthew's Gospel does not allude to Roman political mythology directly (except in his use of the "Son of God" title), the depiction of Jesus in the opening chapters deploys strategies found also in the Roman material. The author of the Gospel shares with Horace and Virgil a desire to situate the story of his hero in the founding mythology of a particular people. In this way, the impetus that lies behind Matthew's reworking of Mark's Gospel and the poets' accolades of a Roman imperial ruler are similar. All of these authors are interested in affirming the significance of their subject in ancient authoritative traditions as a fulfiller of prophesies, interpreter of ancient sacred traditions, ideal ruler, and divinely favored son who will save the world from wickedness and corruption.

Matthew builds such a picture beginning with the opening narrative of his Gospel—first with a genealogy, and then with a birth narrative. The genealogy begins with the designation Jesus Christ and adds to it the titles Son of David and Son of Abraham (Matthew 1:1). In this way, from the first line of the Gospel, Jesus is designated as heir to the royal dynasty of Israel and descendent of its founding father, Abraham. Such claims grant high status to Jesus by situating him in the ancient and revered past. Whereas Virgil writes Augustus into the Homeric myth as a descendent of Aeneas and thereby Apollo, Matthew writes Jesus into the lineage of David and thus the divinely chosen monarchy. Jesus' place in the divine lineage is emphasized throughout the narrative as multiple characters appeal to Jesus as "Son of David" (9:27, 12:23, 15:22, 20:30).

Matthew's genealogy has been of special interest to biblical scholars who note the unusual presence of four women in the line of descendents (1:3, 5, 6b). The attempt to find something in common between these four women has centered typically on their irregularity, their supposed sinfulness, or their foreignness.[2] Because Tamar, Rahab, Ruth, and Bathsheba cannot all be identified as sinners or foreigners, such interpretive efforts have faltered.[3] More recently, commentators have given up on finding similarities between the women and have pointed instead to their distinctive qualities. So, drawing in part on the first option, Daniel Harrington suggests, "In their own distinctive ways they prepare for and foreshadow the irregular birth of Jesus that will be described in Matthew 1:18–25."[4] More recently, John Nolland argues that each of the women is included because of her "unique individual potential for evoking important aspects of the story of Israel's history."[5] The presence of the women in Matthew's genealogy has been particularly significant for feminist scholars, but for different reasons.[6] Elaine Wainwright, for example, reads the women's anomalous presence as a threat or challenge to patriarchy, rather than a mere irregularity.[7] While such feminist readings are empowering and useful to women in our contemporary setting, it is doubtful that an ancient reader would understand Matthew's genealogy as a strike against patriarchy. On the contrary, a major point of the genealogy is to place Jesus within this line of honorable masculine ancestry. It is to show that Jesus, by way of his adoptive father Joseph, is part of the royal Davidic line.

Additionally, the presence of these women anticipates the shift to Mary as mother of Jesus in 1:16. The focus must be on Mary as the genealogy concludes, given the extraordinary conception that the author goes on to narrate. It is not Joseph, after all, who begets Jesus. Like Augustus, Jesus is conceived not by a mortal act but by a divine one. The audience learns first from the narrator and then from an angel that Mary has conceived a child from a holy spirit (ἐκ πνεύματος ἁγίου, 1:18, 20). While this is not the same as Augustus's mother being visited by a snake in the temple of Apollo, the reference to a divine presence who is responsible for the conception of Jesus has similar implications. Like Augustus, Jesus is a divinely conceived Son of God, an idea reinforced more than once in Matthew by a voice from heaven, as well as by multiple characters in the narrative (3:17; 4:3, 6; 8:29; 14:33; 17:5; 26:63; 27:40, 54). As Robert Mowry has convincingly argued, the use of this title in Matthew would be heard as allusions to imperial power by members of Matthew's audience.[8]

The angel also announces that Jesus is to be given a second name, Emmanuel, which is translated into Greek as "God is with us" (1:23). While the idea of God's presence among the people had a long history in the Hebrew tradition, the notion of this presence being manifest in a particular person is also at home in Greco-Roman imperial ideology. As Warren Carter notes, it was the emperor who manifested god's presence on earth. Thus can the poet Statuis refer to Domitian as a deus praesens, "that present god" (Silvae 5.2.170), and Gaius can purport to be "the new Zeus made manifest," according to Philo (Legat. 346).[9] Thus, from Carter's perspective, naming Jesus as the mediator of God's presence to the world would constitute an act of resistance against Roman domination. This is an idea to which we will return.

Other aspects of the birth narrative also correspond to the stories of extraordinary men. As a lightning bolt signaled the birth of Augustus, and a shooting star marked the divinization of his father Julian, so a rising star leads wise men from the east to the birthplace of Jesus. Davies and Allison suggest that the homage of the wise men recalls other traditions of the superiority of the Jewish hero to foreign wise men.[10] A similar idea is evident in the case of Philostratus's Apollonius, who, although he journeys to the east to find wise men, ends up imparting wisdom to the foreigners. So also in the Gospel of Matthew, as the narrative progresses, Jesus will become the dispenser of wisdom to those who have ears to hear—Jews and Gentiles alike.

The wise men in Matthew are not simply looking for wisdom, however. They tell Herod that they have come to bow down before the newborn, which in fact they do once they find Jesus (2:2, 8). The Greek verb προσκυνέω typically indicates an act of worship or veneration before a god, but is also used in the sense of prostrating before a superior (as in Matthew 18:26). Matthew uses the verb far more frequently than the other Gospel writers, probably understanding it in both senses in reference to those approaching Jesus.[11] Along with the foreign wise men, those who prostrate themselves before Jesus later in the narrative include a leper who seeks healing (8:2), a ruler appealing to Jesus to restore his daughter to life (9:18),[12] his disciples (14:33, 28:17), a Canaanite woman (15:25), the mother of two disciples (20:20), and Mary Magdalene and "the other Mary" (28:9). In several cases, this bowing down is paired with one of Matthew's favorite designations for Jesus, κυριός. On the other hand, where Mark uses προσκυνέω to describe the Roman soldiers' mockery of Jesus before his crucifixion, Matthew omits it (Mark 15:19, Matthew 27:30–31).[13] The implication is clear. Apart from his opponents, all who encounter Jesus in the Gospel recognize his superiority and bow down to him in ways befitting a master, ruler, or god.

Given this, it is not surprising that early in the narrative, the journey of the wise men attracts the jealous attention of the client king Herod. Notably, when Herod hears from the wise men that they have come to give honor to the child who has been born "king of the Jews," not only is he frightened, but also "all of Jerusalem with him." The statement is puzzling until one goes on to read that Herod called together "the chief priests and scribes of the people" for consultation (2:4). These men in positions of power are likely what the author means by "all of Jerusalem." They serve as the king's advisors in local matters and are depicted in Matthew as working closely with him. At Herod's request, these leaders dutifully inform Herod of the prophetic tradition concerning the birthplace of the Messiah, "for from you [Bethlehem] shall come a ruler who is to shepherd my people Israel" (2:6).[14] It is thus evident that the birth of Jesus has political implications and that he will present a challenge to the ruling authorities.[15]

Herod's response to the escape of Jesus and his family is tyrannical rage and the slaughter of all children in and around Bethlehem. While the story alludes to the Exodus narrative and Pharaoh's order to kill all of the Hebrew boys (Exodus 1:22), Herod's actions also recall Suetonius's report of the portent before the birth of Augustus indicating that nature was "pregnant with a king for the people." Recall that, like Herod, the threatened Roman Senate decreed the slaughter of all male children born that year.[16] Whereas the Senate did not follow through on the decree to kill the male children, the Gospel narrative presents Herod as carrying out the slaughter. In this way, he represents the tyrannical ruler who is out of control and lacks the qualities of ideal leadership and ideal masculinity. As we will see, Jesus will be presented as the opposite of Herod—the ideal ruler who embodies the virtues of an ideal man.

All this is not to suggest that the author deliberately modeled his portrayal of the birth of Jesus on the traditions of Augustus. As the narrative continues, it becomes clear that the author is far more interested in comparing Jesus to another esteemed man, Moses, than to Augustus. As already noted, Herod's "slaughter of the innocents" recalls Pharaoh's instructions to kill all the male children of the Israelites. The flight to Egypt to escape the wrath of Herod (2:13–15) also brings to mind the Moses tradition. Even more so, the setting of Jesus' sermon on a mountain, from which he delivers the law anew, evokes images of Moses and suggests Jesus as one who surpasses Moses.

Still, by the first century c.e., for a Jewish writer to compare Jesus to Moses or Augustus would amount to much the same thing in terms of gender identity. As we have seen with Philo, Moses had already been rewritten as an ideal man within the Jewish tradition on the basis of the same traits of ideal masculinity that applied to the emperors. Thus, to depict Jesus as superior to either Moses or to the Roman emperor would require much the same thing: a story of an extraordinary birth, followed by the depiction of a virtuous, kingly, ideally masculine (and hence divine) figure. In large part, this is what one finds in the Gospel of Matthew. In fact, the allusions to Moses traditions are just one example among many in the Gospel where the narrative echoes Roman imperial masculinity by means of more direct allusion to Hebrew traditions. In other words, in constructing its image of Jesus, the Gospel of Matthew draws on values of Greco-Roman masculinity ideology but articulates them through reliance on Hebrew scriptures and traditions.

Matthew's modification of Mark's baptism scene and the temptation story add further dimensions to the Matthean Jesus. Matthew's baptism story shares much in common with Mark's, but his use of Q material for the depiction of John the Baptist introduces conflict with the authorities even before the ministry of Jesus. In this tradition, John attacks the Pharisees and Sadducees who are coming for baptism as a "brood of vipers" and warns them "to bear fruit worthy of repentance." He goes on to introduce "one stronger than I" who will come with a winnowing fork to separate the wheat from the chaff (3:11–12). While this picture of Jesus as an eschatological judge is present to some degree in all the Gospels, Matthew accentuates it with traditions unique to his narrative. For instance, in 13:24–30, the Matthean Jesus tells a parable about weeds growing amidst wheat, and then goes on to "de-allegorize" it for his disciples (13:36–42). The sower of the wheat is the Son of Man, who sends his angels at the "end of the age" to punish the evildoers (the weeds) and reward the righteous. Yet another rendition of this final judgment occurs later in the narrative (25:31–46). In this version, the Son of Man executes judgment from a heavenly throne. This same figure is referred to as a king who separates the bad people (the goats) from the good ones (the sheep). The implication of this complex of images is that beginning with Matthew's baptism scene, the Son of Man is a divine, kingly figure who metes out justice from his throne.

The Gospel continues with the temptation scene. As was seen in the last chapter, the temptation scene in the Gospel of Mark is very brief. It indicates only that Jesus is compelled by the Spirit to go into the desert and struggle with Satan. In Matthew's Gospel, the tradition is revised and expanded to detail a series of tests that Jesus undergoes. First, Matthew softens the sense of compulsion in Mark's Gospel: Jesus is not "driven out" but "led" (ἀνήθη) by the Spirit into the wilderness (4:1). While the Spirit is still active, it is Jesus who goes willingly where he is led. Second, Matthew adds a forty-day fast *before* the testing scene and indicates that at the end of this period, Jesus was famished. The detail creates a sense of Jesus' vulnerability, but by that very fact, it also establishes his fortitude in withstanding Satan's tests. Overall, Matthew's version of the temptation story depicts Jesus as one who is more willing to do battle with Satan, and more in control of events as he does.

Third, in Matthew's Gospel, Jesus contends with Satan by means of scriptural quotations. As Satan entices a famished Jesus with the possibility of food (4:3), a display of divine intervention from God (4:5–6), and finally with total ruling power (4:8–9), Jesus resists his temptations by quoting scripture. The result of Matthew's modifications to the testing scene is that Jesus emerges as an authority of scripture, able to wield the word in battle against the enemy.

The Matthean Jesus as Public Speaker and Teacher

The most significant difference between the Markan Jesus who preaches, heals, exorcises, and teaches, and the Matthean Jesus who does the same things, is that the Gospel of Matthew emphasizes the teaching of Jesus. It does so in multiple ways. In Matthew's Gospel, Mark's narrative framework has been interlaced with five extended sections of discourse (5–7, 10, 13, 18, 23–25). The effect of this structure is the presentation of Jesus as an effective pubic speaker and teacher. In the Gospel of Mark, when Jesus first teaches in the synagogue, the narrator reports that people are astounded "for he taught them as one having authority, and not as the scribes" (1:22). Nevertheless, the content of Jesus' teaching goes unmentioned in Mark, and the focus immediately shifts to an exorcism, which is viewed as "a new teaching—with authority" (1:27). In Matthew, the situation is reversed. The public ministry begins with a brief summary of Jesus' activities (4:23–25) but then turns to a prolonged account of his teaching (5–7). It is after this first extended discourse ("after Jesus had finished saying these things") that the crowd in Matthew is "astounded." Moreover, rather than an exorcism, as in Mark, it is this detailed teaching that is contrasted with the teaching of "their scribes" (7:28–29). Although this is just the first of Jesus' teaching sections in the Gospel, the crowds' reactions convey how Matthew thinks all of Jesus' teachings should be received.

Indeed, the overall effect of these sayings collections is the presentation of Jesus as a public speaker who dispenses wisdom to the crowds and his disciples, along with sharply critical barbs to his opposition. Moreover, this same Jesus states that one who accepts and acts on his teaching will be like a wise man (ἀνδρὶ φρονίμῳ), and one who does not will be like a foolish man (ἀνδρὶ μωρῷ) (7:24–27). Such imagery recalls the contrast between the wise and the foolish in Proverbs and contributes to the picture of Jesus as a wisdom teacher.

From a gender-critical perspective, the role of public speaker/teacher was a decidedly masculine one in the ancient world. Jerome Neyrey, who relies on a social scientific approach to the New Testament, points to the distinction between public and private space as male and female realms respectively. He rightly argues that featuring Jesus in the role of a public speaker highlights his ideal masculine identity. In the ancient Mediterranean culture, it was typically elder men or men of high status who were permitted a public voice.[17] To be sure, Matthew does not depict Jesus as an expert in declamation. But he does emphasize Jesus as a speaker held in high acclaim by those who hear. This alone contributes to his masculine status.

Even more explicitly, the Matthean Jesus calls attention to his own high status vis-à-vis his followers. While the narrative sections highlight the elevated status of Jesus through various titles, the Messiah Jesus speaks directly of his own worth. Indeed, in his second discourse, Jesus warns anyone who loves parents or children more than him that they "are not worthy of me" (οὐκ ἔστιν μου ἄξιος). He says the same of anyone who does not take up his cross and follow him (10:37–38). The language of worthiness is distinct to Matthew in this context. Only Matthew uses the term ἄξιος, referring to the comparative value or worth of something. In Luke's version of this saying, Jesus says simply that such a one "cannot be my disciple" (Luke 14:25–27). Along the same lines, the Matthean Jesus refers to himself as οἰκοδεσπότης or "master of the house," making the point metaphorically that his disciples (who are like slaves, or other household members to the master) do not rank above him (10:24–25).

In fact, as Anderson and Moore point out, οἰκοδεσπότης "a term redolent with hegemonic assumptions about masculine destiny," appears to be a preferred term of Matthew's, appearing in his Gospel seven times compared to one occurrence in Mark and four in Luke.[18] The term is used in multiple ways in Matthew, sometimes figuratively for "the kingdom of heaven" (20:1–16) or for God (21:33–43), with the disciples in subservient roles. Other times it is the disciples—those waiting for the return of the Son of Man—who are "the householders" (24:43) or the "scribe who has been trained for the kingdom of heaven" (13:52). Thus, while the term is clearly malleable for the author, his regular use of it suggests a basic alignment with the hierarchal structures of hegemonic masculinity.

Even where the specific term "householder" is not used, these hierarchical structures are sometimes frighteningly evident in the Matthean Jesus' teachings. Consider the parable of the servant who was forgiven a debt by his master (κύριος), only to insist on payment from his own debtors. As punishment for his slave's lack of mercy, the master hands the slave over be tortured until his debt is paid off. Then comes the pronouncement, "My heavenly father will do the same thing to each of you, if you all do not forgive your brother from your hearts" (18:35, my translation). Another parable compares the kingdom of heaven to a king who ties up and casts out an unprepared guest "into the outer darkness" (22:13). In short, the men who populate the parables of the Matthean Jesus are often kings, householders, masters—men in power—who make their point vis-à-vis those under them. To be sure, characters in parables do not have a one-to-one correspondence with Jesus or God and so do not pertain directly to the characterization of Jesus. On the other hand, it is Jesus who tells such stories, and in so doing generates images that reinforce the masculine structures of the culture. Or, as Anderson and Moore put it, "The Greco-Roman master of a house, looms exceedingly large in this Gospel, and his traditional hegemonic prerogatives are nowhere explicitly called into question."[19]

Other aspects of Jesus' teaching also call attention to his high masculine status. In his role as public speaker, he positions himself as interpreter of the sacred traditions of Israel. He confirms what has already been suggested by the birth narrative: that he comes to fulfill the law and the prophets. He then proceeds to interpret the law in new and expansive ways, exerting his own authority by repeating the formula, "You have heard it said...but *I* say to you..." (ἐγὼ δὲ λέγω ὑμιν, 5:21–22, 27–28, 31–32, 33–34, 38–39, 43–44). The formulation invites speculation as to Jesus' relationship to the Torah and to the lawgiver Moses. It is clear that Jesus fulfills the Torah, but does this formula also suggest that he surpasses it in authority? Or is the audience to understand Jesus as the embodiment of Torah? All of these options are plausible, and it may not be necessary to choose among them. What is clear is that the formula reinforces Jesus' authority as the interpreter and teacher of God's law.

While the notion of Jesus as Torah may not carry particular gender connotations, it leads to another feature of Matthean Christology that may. Beginning in the Second Temple period, with writings such as Wisdom of Solomon and Sirach, Torah was identified with the figure of personified Wisdom. This figure often was imaged as feminine.

Jesus as Personified Wisdom in Matthew— A Gender Transmutation?

In the midst of the preponderance of masculine images for Jesus in Matthew's Gospel is the portrayal of Jesus as a wisdom figure.[20] The link between Jesus and Wisdom occurs on several different levels in the Gospel. As mentioned earlier, the fact that Jesus is presented as the teacher of righteousness *par excellence* already positions him as a dispenser of wisdom. But there are more explicit associations with wisdom as well. At one point, in defending himself against his critics, the Matthean Jesus alludes to himself as wisdom, claiming that "wisdom is vindicated by her deeds" (11:19). Similarly, a saying that is attributed to "the Wisdom of God" in Luke (11:49) is a direct quote from Jesus in Matthew (23:34).[21]

The most frequently cited passage regarding the evocation of personified wisdom in Matthew is 11:28–30. Here Jesus urges readers to "come to me" and "take my yoke upon you, and learn from me." Similarly, in Sirach 24:19, Wisdom exhorts, "Come to me, you who desire me," and "Draw near to me, you who are uneducated" (see also 6:24–26, 51:23). Ben Sira also urges his readers to "Put your neck under her yoke, and let your soul receive instruction; it is to be found close by" (Sirach 51:26). These parallels suggest that the figure of personified Wisdom was one of the images of divine presence that was used by the author of Matthew. What makes this one particularly interesting in this context is that Wisdom is often personified as female.

In Proverbs, Wisdom is a woman calling from the heights and crossroads for "simple ones" to heed her (Proverbs 8:1–11). In Sirach, the audience is provocatively encouraged to pursue Wisdom "like a hunter," lying in wait on her paths, peering through her windows, and listening at her doors (Sirach 14:22–23). Later Wisdom is referred to as a mother or young bride, giving food and water to those who seek her (Sirach 15:2–3). The Wisdom of Solomon portrays the speaker (purportedly Solomon) as falling in love with Wisdom, desiring her as his bride, and becoming enamored of her beauty (Wisdom 8:2). Thus, when Jesus is portrayed as God's Wisdom, he speaks in the voice of a figure that was regularly portrayed as female.[22] Should a feminine dimension be ascribed to the Matthean Jesus as well, complicating the masculine dimensions seen so far? If we consider the portrayal and function of the Wisdom figure still further, especially in light of the Matthean Jesus, the answer seems to be no.

For, although Wisdom is personified as female in the wisdom literature, this is not because she has feminine traits as understood in the ancient Mediterranean context. On the contrary, among other things, Wisdom is generative, prudent, just, and reasoned—all those things that defined an ideal man. Indeed, that is why men were encouraged to pursue her in the first place: listening to Wisdom would teach one how to become a man. Wisdom offers her followers these same benefits, teaching self-control, prudence, justice, and courage (Wisdom 8:7). Why, then, is Wisdom portrayed as female? Perhaps it is precisely because she is to be pursued by men. The language of desire, love, and pursuit that is often connected to the attainment of wisdom might impinge on the masculine identity of the pursuer if it were otherwise.[23]

Moreover, this is a phenomenon that goes beyond the Jewish Wisdom tradition. In the Greco-Roman world, virtues were often hypostasized as female but were nevertheless regarded as masculine traits. It follows that because the Matthean Jesus embodies the masculine virtues associated with God's wisdom, he can be identified *as* Wisdom. This identification does not negate his masculine status, but rather reinforces his virtuous character. Recall Philo's statement that "all the virtues have women's titles, but powers and activities of perfect men" (*Fug.* 51). Given this first-century perspective, it should not be surprising that, as Deutsch suggests, "Matthew absorbs the female figure of wisdom into the male and historical, if exalted, figure of Jesus."[24] Or, to put it a different way, instead of the virtues being hypostasized in female form, they are embodied in the male form of Jesus.

Another significant aspect of the association between Jesus and Wisdom concerns the general milieu out of which this female figure emerged. As Deutsch and others have pointed out, the context for the development of these Wisdom traditions (and apocalyptic traditions are included in this category as well) was most certainly the male learned elite—i.e., the scribal class of ancient Israel and the Second Temple period. As Deutsch puts it, "For the most part they were upper class males who expressed themselves in terms of status reversal."[25] Moreover, she points to the author of Matthew as among this male learned elite.[26] Note, for example, the uniquely Matthean expression of a scribe being "trained for the kingdom of heaven" (13:52) (the same one who is "like a householder"). Such language likely comes from one with a scribal perspective. In this way, the portrayal of Jesus as Wisdom brings both Jesus and the audience of the Gospel into the sphere of the learned male elite.

Finally, there is another dimension to at least one of the allusions to Wisdom in Matthew that should be considered. On this point, the work of Deirdre Good is helpful. Even though, as we have seen, there are allusions to Wisdom in Matthew 11:28–30, Good argues against Wisdom as the primary reference for the passage. Instead, she suggests that here, too, the image of Jesus as an ideal king is at the heart of the passage. In 11:29, Jesus claims, "I am gentle [or lenient] and humble of heart" (πραΰς εἰμι καὶ ταπεινὸς τῇ καρδίᾳ). This is language we have encountered already in Paul's reference to the "leniency and clemency of Christ" (2 Corinthians 10:1), where it referred to his kingly virtues. Good suggests that here, too, the Matthean Jesus' statement should be understood in light of the virtues that Jesus is claiming for himself, virtues that are in keeping with ideal kingship. Noting that the preceding verse (11:27) focuses on the identity of Jesus as "son," Good suggests, "The Son is *praus* and lowly of heart because the son is a king."[27] Jesus' reference to his "easy yoke" and "light burden" fit this interpretation as well, perhaps even more so than as a reference to Wisdom. Being "under the yoke" typically refers to coming under submission and service to a king (e.g., 1 Kings 12:3–4, Jeremiah 27:1–15, and 1 Maccabees 8:31). Thus, the central passage in Matthew that associates Jesus with Wisdom also categorizes Jesus as a virtuous ruler, and the second association is perhaps even stronger than the first.

The same idea is conveyed later in the narrative when Jesus enters Jerusalem on a donkey, fulfilling the scripture: "Tell the daughter of Zion, 'Look, your king is coming to you, humble [πραΰς], and mounted on a donkey'" (Matthew 21:5). The quote is from Zechariah 9:9 (LXX), which relates the victory procession of the triumphant messianic king. He has the proper demeanor that is expected of a Hellenistic king after victory in battle; namely, he is πραΰς. Not surprisingly, that Jesus is a πραΰς king links him also to Moses. Readers of the Septuagint would recognize the same attribute in Moses, as emphasized in Numbers 12:3: "The man Moses was more humble [πραΰς] than anyone else on the earth." Moreover, Good notes how well beyond the first century, the "meekness" of Moses was a virtue to be imitated.[28] So, Jesus too is seen as the ideal king, displaying his leniency as king as he enters Jerusalem in a victory procession (Matthew 21:1–9). Here again, one can see a strategy of associating Jesus with a Greco-Roman virtue by means of Jewish figures, in this case through the direct allusion to the messianic king of Zechariah, and more indirectly through associations with Moses.

Also relevant to this interpretation is the claim that occurs in Matthew 12:38–42, namely that Jesus is superior to Solomon, the king who embodied wisdom in the biblical tradition. Recalling 1 Kings 10:1–10 (also 2 Chronicles 9:1–9), Jesus predicts that "the queen of the south will rise up at the judgment with this generation and condemn it, because she came from the ends of the earth to listen to the wisdom of Solomon, and see, something greater than Solomon is here" (12:42). Jesus' words in 11:28–30 ("easy yoke" and "light burden") recall, in reverse, the accusation of Solomon as a harsh king in 1 Kings 12:3–4 ("heavy yoke" and "hard service"). Not only is Jesus superior to Solomon in wisdom, but also in his kingship. He will be a lenient and gentle king, where Solomon was not. In this way, the evocation of Wisdom along with the comparison to Solomon accentuates the masculine and kingly image of Jesus.[29]

Matthean Exhortation, Ideal Masculinity and Ideal Discipleship

Given Matthew's interest in portraying Jesus as a teacher, we should also consider the content of Jesus' teachings in light of ancient masculine ideology. In several instances, Jesus' instructions for discipleship are in keeping with the

Greco-Roman moral philosophers' understanding of proper masculine deportment. They likewise echo the teachings of Wisdom in much of the wisdom literature. Thus, although the Matthew Jesus nowhere uses terms connoting self-control, he does encourage the practice of it.[30] Brothers are not to get angry at each other or insult one another (5:21–22; see Sirach 10:18), nor are they to commit adultery or lust after a woman (5:27).[31] Note that both instructions are intended especially for men. Furthermore, both are in keeping with the idea of self-mastery.

Jesus also downplays the significance of wealth or material comforts, reflecting the anti-luxury sentiments of the moral philosophers. He tells his audience that they should have no interest in accumulating "treasures" (6:19, 6:24), nor should they worry about clothing or food. Although much of the literature on this saying puts it in the context of poverty—the Matthean community is suffering, and the saying addresses their anxiety—this is not necessarily the case. Given the reference to the Gentiles as a negative model, the Matthean Jesus seems not to refer to the destitute who are wondering where their next meal will come from. Instead, the context suggests the issue is excessive attention to material comforts, or, as the philosophers would put it, a lifestyle that leads to "softness" or effeminacy. According to the Matthean Jesus, it is the Gentiles who desire such material comforts.[32]

In addition to these teachings that overlap with aspects of hegemonic masculinity, there are some concepts that scholars often view as countercultural but may not be so radical from the perspective of gender ideology. For instance, Jesus' teaching "Do not resist an evildoer. If someone strikes you on the cheek, turn the other also" (5:39) is often viewed as a countercultural teaching on nonviolence. It likely did run counter to many people's perspectives on a proper response to an "evildoer," but this teaching can also be understood in light of the Greco-Roman emphasis on self-restraint and moderation. In this sense, it is not particularly countercultural, insofar as it is promoting an especially disciplined (and manly) response to one who offends.[33]

In this category also belongs the Matthean Jesus' statement, "Blessed are the meek" (5:5). The term that is typically translated as "meek" is from the same term, πραΰς, that was discussed in chapter 4 regarding the "leniency" of Christ. While many see the passage as honoring the weak, instead it links with the virtue of self-control. In other words, one who exhibits proper self-restraint is one who will "inherit the earth." In fact, the ethical imperatives found in the beatitudes share much in common with standard Hellenistic concepts of virtue.[34] Justice and mercy (5:6–7) are virtues that an ideal ruler should exhibit and that the emperors claimed for themselves. Similarly, Augustus, for one, understood himself both as a "peacemaker" and a "son of god" (5:9).

In other words, the teaching of the Matthean Jesus is in keeping with the exhortations that would apply to the construction of an ideal man in the Greco-Roman culture. Ultimately, Jesus urges his listeners to "Be perfect, therefore, as your heavenly Father is perfect" (5:48). Recall that the idea of "perfection" is a regular occurrence when speaking of ideal masculinity. Aristotle indicates the superior perfection of the male embryos (*Gen. an.* 775a). Philo assumes that "male is more perfect than female" (*QE* 1.7). Likewise, Galen opines: "Now just as mankind is the most perfect of all animals, so within mankind the man is more perfect than the woman" (*Usefulness of the Parts*, 2.630).[35] Here then is perhaps the most direct call in the New Testament for ideal masculinity: a call to imitate God the Father in his masculine perfection. Moreover, because the Matthean Jesus also says that no one knows the Father except the Son and anyone to whom the Son chooses to reveal him (11:27), part of what the Son reveals must be the masculine perfection of God.

The Death and Apotheosis of the Matthean Jesus

The Gospel of Matthew maintains much of the Markan tradition in the passion narrative, but it modifies the material in ways that downplay the shamefulness on display in the Gospel of Mark. This is already evident in the first passion prediction. There Jesus, as in the Gospel of Mark, teaches both of his pending death and of the Son of Man who "is to come with his angels in the glory of his Father" (16:27). But instead of speaking of those who might be ashamed of the Son of Man, as Mark did, he turns to language of judgment and recompense: "He will repay everyone for what has been done." There is no acknowledgment in this prediction that the death of Jesus might evoke shame. Instead, the focus is taken away from Jesus and put on the audience, inviting them to consider their own actions and how they will be viewed by the coming Son of Man. Far from the idea of shame, as we have seen, Jesus speaks of those who are "worthy" of him, pointing to his own honorable status.

While Matthew maintains Jesus' cries on the cross, the presence of God is overwhelmingly evident in the events that follow his death. As with Mark, the temple curtain tears, but this is accompanied by an earthquake, opening of tombs, and resurrection of "the saints." Just as the birth of Jesus is heralded by extraordinary events, so too is his death. Virgil describes a darkened sun, earthquakes, the sighting of phantoms, and other remarkable events for the death of Caesar (*Georgics* 1.475).[36] In Matthew's Gospel, it is the occurrence of these cosmic events, rather than the death of Jesus, that elicits the centurion's response, "Truly this man was God's son" (27:54).

Most significantly, Matthew's Gospel features resurrection scenes that are not present in Mark. In a far more supernatural way than in Mark's account, Matthew's narrative features an "angel of Lord" who announces that Jesus has been raised from the dead and will meet them in Galilee (28:5–7). In Matthew's Gospel, there is no need to speculate about whether Jesus truly appeared in Galilee as predicted. No sooner do the women leave the tomb than Jesus appears to them, and they worship him (28:9). Like the angel, Jesus announces his pending appearance in Galilee, and he tells the women to pass this news on to the disciples. Soon after, the Matthean Jesus does appear on a mountain in Galilee where, once again, he is worshipped by his disciples (28:17).

As Wendy Cotter has shown, these scenes should be seen in light of the Greco-Roman apotheosis traditions. Recall that all three case studies of "divine men" underwent some type of apotheosis at the end of their lives, in spite of all the ways that they differed. So, too, Jesus is portrayed as one exalted and transformed at death into another state. As Cotter puts it, "Matthew concludes his Gospel with the appearance of the hero whose body has been transformed so that it is fitting for paradise."[37] But, as she also notes, Matthew goes even further than this. Whereas the emperors were understood to rule the earth from the heavens, the Matthean Jesus claims that "all authority has been given to me in heaven and on earth" (28:18). To quote Cotter once more:

> Whether or not the listener to this Gospel would have been ready to believe the claims that Matthew makes for Jesus in the *apotheosis*, the claim itself is clear. Jesus has been divinized and given a total cosmic imperium, a directing authorization for the remaining history of the cosmos.[38]

In this way, Matthew concludes his narrative on a note that surpasses the claims for most idealized representation of imperial masculinity. Augustus was ruler of the earth, but is never said to be ruler of the heavens. This was Jupiter's role, as Ovid makes clear:

> Jupiter controls the heights of heaven and the kingdom of
>   the triformed universe;
> but the earth is under Augustus' sway. Each is both sire and ruler.
> (*Metamorphoses* 15:858–860)

Not so with the Matthean Jesus. Whereas the beginning of the Gospel predicts that a ruler will come from Bethlehem to shepherd the people of Israel, the end of the Gospel makes clear that this same ruler is Lord of heaven and earth. In this new state of ultimate authority, the apotheosized and immortal Jesus assures his followers that he "will be with them always" (28:20). In this way,

Matthew goes beyond even the imperial masculinity displayed in Augustus. In this final scene of apotheosis, the Matthean Jesus is exalted on the masculinity/ divinity gradient far beyond the level of any Roman emperor.

The Matthean Jesus and Marginal Masculinities

In spite of all the ways that the Matthean Jesus models and encourages masculine deportment, there are some ambiguous aspects to the Gospel's relationship to hegemonic masculinity. For example, Jesus' teaching regarding the practice of piety runs counter to what would be expected of the ideal man in the Roman Empire. The frequent portrayal of Augustus in his priestly sacrificial role suggests that one's piety was a virtue to be put on display. The elaborate ceremonies of the Romans with their processions, public sacrifices, and dedications make clear that one main way of gaining status in the broader culture was precisely through the public demonstration of piety and euergetism. Euergetism, a transliteration of a Greek word literally meaning "good work," denotes a practice in which wealthy representatives of Rome gained power and prestige through benefaction. But Jesus critiques just this sort of demonstration, teaching his followers to practice their piety in secret (6:1–6, 17–18). In so doing, he speaks against a major means for displaying one's manly conduct.[39]

Also, for all the images of "householder" that are evident in the Gospel, Jesus speaks of himself as not having a home. "Foxes have holes and birds of the air have nests, but the Son of Man has nowhere to lay his head" (8:20). The image suggests that Jesus has left the household, and thus, as Halvor Moxnes argues, has moved out of "male space."[40] Moreover, Jesus calls his disciples to do the same, leaving their homes, families, and work—indeed, "everything" in the words of Peter (4:18–22, 9:9, 19:27–29). When Jesus instructs the disciples on what they should not take on their missionary travels (e.g., no money, bag, extra tunic, sandals, or staff; Matthew 10:9–10//Mark 6:8–9//Luke 9:3), he engages rhetoric that would be familiar within Greco-Roman ascetic (especially Cynic) teachings.[41] Moreover, when Jesus says that he has come "to set a man against his father, and a daughter against her mother" (Matthew 10:35//Luke 12:53), he is not advocating the sort of family values that would have been promoted by the empire. Instead, this antifamily language signals a renunciation of the dominant social order represented by the household. To be sure, such ascetic impulses are not unique to Matthew's Gospel. As indicated, the author draws on both Mark and Q traditions for these sayings. Still, by incorporating these traditions, the author has constructed an image of Jesus as one without a home and as one who will himself break up households. In so doing, the Matthean Jesus stands on the margins of hegemonic masculinity. And insofar as he requires that his followers share in this renunciation, he brings them to the margins as well.

Still, however marginalized from the mainstream culture, this antifamily rhetoric is also influenced by masculinity ideology, albeit an alternative form of this ideology. Renunciation of traditional social structures is a form of asceticism, and ascetic practice was in itself a means toward ideal masculinity. In fact, one might think of asceticism as a sort of "hypermasculine" practice in that it often involves going to great lengths in the practice of self-mastery and thus becoming more manly. This is the perspective of both Josephus and Philo, who comment on ascetic communities in ways that valorize the masculine. Philo notes that the Therepeutae are more virtuous than any Greek or barbarian (*Ant.* 18.20), and Josephus notes that the Essenes make a special virtue of the control of their passions and that they disdain marriage (*BJ* 2.220).[42] Similarly, the ascetic lifestyle advocated by the Cynics was in the service of a life of virtue achieved through the gain of self-mastery. Recalling the three divine men of chapter 3, Apollonius also represents this alternative masculinity; his ascetic lifestyle went hand in hand with a life of virtue. Such a lifestyle, from Philostratus's view, moved him closer to the masculine ideal. So, too, do certain aspects of the Matthean Jesus place him in the sphere of this alternative, more marginalized strand of masculine deportment.

Finally, there is the case of the eunuch saying, which takes us even further toward the margins of gender identity in the ancient world. The saying is found only in Matthew, where it seems out of place in its context. In response to Jesus' teaching against divorce, the disciples say, "If such is the case of a man with his wife, it is better not to marry" (19:10). In other words, if they have no power to divorce, it is better not to marry in the first place. Their response suggests that they experience Jesus' teaching as a loss of power. But rather than address their complaint, the Matthean Jesus introduces the figure of the eunuch. "For there are eunuchs who have been so from birth, and there are eunuchs who have been made eunuchs by others, and there are eunuchs who have made themselves eunuchs for the sake of the kingdom of heaven. Let anyone accept this who can" (19:12). Even if one knew nothing about eunuchs in the ancient world, Jesus' closing tag indicates that the saying would be problematic to its ancient audience. As many have pointed out, if there is a figure in the ancient world that embodied a challenge to hegemonic masculinity, it was the eunuch.[43]

The challenge was not simply that the eunuch was a physically emasculated figure. Instead, the issue is that the eunuch is a thoroughly ambiguous figure. On the one hand, the eunuch represented the ultimate "unman" or "half-man" (*semiviri*), as they were sometimes called. Thus, as Peter Brown puts it, "the physical appearance and the reputed character of eunuchs acted as constant reminders that the male body was a fearsomely plastic thing."[44] On the other hand, the type of eunuch that is praised by the Matthean Jesus—the voluntarily eunuch—could suggest something quite different. Here is a man who has taken the renunciation of passions to the extreme. The eunuch's drastic deviation from hegemonic masculinity could also, as Arthur Dewey suggests, "reinforce at a deeper level the basic male fantasy of control even at enormous price."[45] Thus, in some ways, the mere presence of this ambiguous saying in the Matthean narrative undercuts the masculine imperial image of Jesus that has been projected throughout most of the narrative.[46]

At the same time, Matthew's narrative attempts to resolve the tension created by the saying. For, whatever connotations "eunuch" had for the audience, to use the saying in response to the disciples' statement "it is better not to marry" suggests that it should be interpreted as a reference to celibacy. Along this line, Jesus' indication that his teaching is not for everybody recalls a similar approach to celibacy by Paul. As a result, regardless of whatever radical effect the evocation of the eunuch might have had on the masculine construction of Jesus, the context of celibacy moves him and the disciples into the realm of less radical ascetic practices.[47] And if the evangelist is responsible for neutralizing the eunuch saying, he is the first of many others who will do likewise. Few, including the author of the Gospel, seem eager to envision Jesus or the disciples as "eunuchs for the kingdom of heaven" in any literal sort of way.[48] Nevertheless, Matthew does include the saying (assuming it came to him through tradition) and in so doing adds more to the picture of the marginalized, ascetic, hypermasculine practice discussed above.

Conclusion: The Mix of Masculinities in Matthew

The Gospel of Matthew presents a complex and multifaceted picture of Jesus from the perspective of masculine ideology. Like Paul and the author of Mark, the author engages multiple discourses of masculinity in constructing Jesus the man. For the reader of Matthew's Gospel, Jesus is the ideal masculine ruler, worshipped as divine and honored as one with high status. The story of his birth is appropriately filled with signs of the extraordinary nature of the man that Jesus will become, and the story of his death and resurrection fits well within the traditions of imperial apotheosis. Such an image competes with and challenges the image of ideal masculinity represented by the emperor and those who modeled themselves after his image.

The Gospel also presents Jesus as embodied Wisdom and authoritative teacher of righteousness. While the Wisdom traditions lying behind this image are often female, it is not a "real" woman that is at play in the identification of Jesus with Wisdom but something closer to the deified virtues of the Greco-Roman world. Many of the virtues espoused by the Jesus-Wisdom figure are standard virtues valued by the Greco-Roman man. Moreover, the evocation of wisdom puts the Matthean Jesus at the center of the male-elite interests of a scribal community.

On the other hand, this same figure is one who advocates an alternative masculinity, one who resists the standard constructions of family and household and aligns himself instead with a life of ascetic renunciation. This renunciation manifested itself in dislocation from the household and a challenge to the basic coherence of the family. To be sure, those who admired such a lifestyle, even if they did not live it themselves, saw it as a particularly masculine practice. But it was not a type of masculinity that stood at the center of the empire. Instead, in Matthew's Gospel this alternative presents itself as a hypermasculinity—an ideology that resists imperial structure by challenging the household structure that was its foundation.

The result of this mix of masculinities is a complex image of a Jesus who at times resists hegemonic masculine ideology, even while the narrative presents him in decidedly imperial masculine terms. As was the case with the Gospel of Mark, insights from postcolonial theory help make sense of such literary dynamics. With Mark, the still-raw events of the crucifixion impinged on his portrayal of the otherwise noble martyrdom of Jesus. In the case of Matthew, we should consider the postcolonial concept of mimicry. This is the term used to describe the tendency of the colonized subject to mimic the rhetoric and ideology of the dominant power even in the course of resisting such power. With Matthew's Gospel, this mimicry is seen in the portrayals of Jesus as king, son of god, householder, and so on. But the Matthean Jesus goes beyond mimicry of hegemonic masculinity by "upping the ante," so to speak. Calling on his followers to be perfect, demanding a righteousness that exceeds that of the Pharisees and scribes, modeling an ascetic lifestyle that is essentially a performance of hypermasculinity—all these acts suggest ways in which the Matthean Jesus encourages the performance of an alternative masculinity that is even "more perfect" than the ideal imperial masculinity of the empire.

7

The Lukan Jesus
and the Imperial Elite

For I also am a man set under authority . . .

———Luke 7:8

With Luke-Acts, we enter a narrative world that is completely at home within the masculine power structures of the Roman Empire. Almost anywhere we turn in this world, we find those elements that were necessary for the construction of the ideal man in the Roman world. The heroes that we encounter in this world—Jesus, Stephen, Peter, Paul—are portrayed as educated, articulate, reasonable, self-controlled, pious men, fully capable of holding their own in the upper echelons of the masculine world of the Roman Empire.

In a most basic way, the frequent occurrence of the Greek word for "man" in this Gospel already signals an interest in masculinity. Luke uses the word ἀνήρ 27 times in his Gospel, compared to the four occurrences in the Gospel of Mark. Moreover, the word occurs 100 times in Acts.[1] Of the hundred occurrences, more than twenty of them involve some form of public address, often in apposition with another vocative. Men such as Peter, Stephen, James, or Paul repeatedly address other "men," whether they are "brothers," Judeans, Israelites, or Athenians (e.g., Acts 1:16; 2:14, 22; 3:12; 7:2; 13:16; 17:22). These frequent addresses to a male audience set the emergence of Christianity in a civic forum before a male audience.[2] In a few places, both men and women are specified as members of the audience (8:3, 12; 9:2;

17:4, 12). But these few places only reinforce the primarily masculine focus of the enterprise.[3]

While this frequent use of ἀνήρ is a constant reminder of the masculine focus of Luke-Acts, there are far more indications of the concern to situate the emerging church in the context of the male elite world of the empire. This chapter will focus on three central aspects of this world—education, government, and cult—demonstrating the ways that Luke's narrative world intersects with these imperial structures. Doing so will provide another witness to the ways that masculinity in the ancient world was not simply about "men," but was deeply ingrained in the fabric of the Greco-Roman culture.

Luke-Acts and the Educated Elite

With his opening prologue, the author of Luke-Acts distinguishes himself as a member of the educated elite. He positions himself as a client of the "most excellent" (κράτιστε) Theophilus, a title that indicates someone in high social circles.[4] Whether Theophilus was a real person or a literary figure—a point of scholarly debate—does not change the effect of the address in the opening of the Gospel. The author sets the writing of his work in the context of the literate elite. As D'Angelo notes, "through the prologues, the gospel and Acts are set up as an exchange between elite males, between noble, initiated patron and literate, sophisticated narrator."[5]

This author writes with a literary sophistication beyond any of the other Gospel writers. Not only does he have better command of Greek than his source Mark, he is familiar with the rhetoric and patterns of historiography.[6] If education is a crucial part of the socialization of the elite male as discussed in chapter 2, the author of Luke-Acts surely took part in this process. Among the many aspects of his writing that stand out, the use of long speeches by various characters throughout the narrative in Acts is especially revealing. Such a writing technique reflects a background in declamation exercises, a major part of the Roman curriculum for young boys. Declamation exercises required the development of a reasoned argument in response to various cases, typically involving some sort of infringement on property. Key to the exercises was the practice of *fictio personae*. That is, the student was expected to imaginatively create a character as defined by the case and speak from that character's position. This could mean speaking from the perspective of a woman, a slave, a poor man, a rich man, and on. As Martin Bloomer argues, this "schooling in persona" was a way of managing the hegemonic identity for a class of speakers. The boy learned the position of the male elite vis-à-vis those stationed beneath him, including how to speak for the subordinate members of the culture.[7] If the author of Luke-Acts engaged in such exercises, and it seems likely that he did, it would not only explain his ability to write speeches in character but also the extent to which he was acculturated into the elite social class.[8] Recalling the discussion of education in chapter 2, it is clear that this author had progressed a good way up the path that shaped one into an elite male.[9]

Given this, it should be no surprise that Luke's work is the most explicitly concerned with showing Jesus and the leading figures of the emerging Christian community as models of masculinity. Not only does the author present himself as an educated male, he finds ways to depict all the leading figures as literate men. Some of the same strategies evident in the construction of the divine men of chapter 3 are also seen here. Like Philo's Moses, Augustus, and Apollonius, the Lukan Jesus distinguishes himself intellectually at an early age. At age twelve, he impresses the temple authorities with his precociousness, sitting in the midst of the "teachers" and showing profound understanding so that all are amazed (Luke 2:46–47). The narrative provides no further indication of the identity of these teachers. However, as will be explored further below, their location in the temple indicates that they are among the educated and elite members of Jerusalem society. Later, Jesus proves his literacy by reading from the scroll in the synagogue in Capernaum (Luke 4:16–22). In Acts, Peter and John, despite their lack of training (ἄνθρωποι ἀγράμματοί εἰσιν καὶ ἰδιῶται), surprise authorities with their public-speaking ability (παρρησία) (Acts 4:13). Most impressive is Luke's presentation of Paul. He knows both Greek and Hebrew, having been educated at the feet of Gamaliel (Acts 21:37, 21:40–22:3). He speaks in public regularly and shows evidence of rhetorical training complete with knowledge of appropriate gestures (Acts 26:1). At one point, Festus even suggests that Paul has had "too much learning" so that he is losing his mind (Acts 26:24). We will return to the portrait of Paul below. For now, it is enough to note the narrative emphasis on his education. As we have seen, to emphasize the literacy and rhetorical skill of the characters is to also assure the reader of the characters' training in masculinity. In depicting his characters as literate men skilled in public address, the author goes a long way toward constructing them on the model of the imperial masculine ideal.

The Lukan Jesus and Roman Imperial Masculinity

With the character of Jesus, this construction begins before he is born. As has long been noted, throughout the infancy narrative, Luke uses rhetoric typically reserved for the Roman emperor to speak of Jesus. For Luke, as with all the Gospels, this includes the title "Son of God" (Luke 1:35). But Luke goes even further than this in his imperial allusions. While no other Gospel writer refers to Jesus as σωτήρ, the title is used frequently in Luke-Acts (Luke 1:69, 2:11; Acts 5:31, 13:23). The language of "savior" and "salvation" can certainly be found Septuagint references to God, and this may have been Luke's scriptural basis for using it. For the majority of people living in the empire, however, a much more immediate context for such language would be the myriad images and rhetoric surrounding imperial rule. Honorary statues for the emperor frequently included the description of the emperor as "savior and benefactor" or "savior of the inhabited world."[10] The imperial ideology of *pax Romana* was equally prominent. For example, the famous Priene inscription from Asia (9 B.C.E.) marks the institution of a new calendar "for good luck and salvation" (τύχῃ ἀγαθῇ καὶ ἐπὶ σωτηρίᾳ) based on the birthday of Augustus.[11] Notably, the decree describes the work of divine Providence in producing Augustus as one:

> ὃν εἰς εὐρεγεσίαν ἀνθρώπων ἐπλήρωσεν, ἀρετῆς ὥσπερ ἡμεῖν καὶ τοῖς μεθ' ἡμᾶς σωτῆρα χαρισαμένη τὸν παύσαντα μὲν πόλεμον κοσμήσοντα δὲ εἰρήνην...[12]
>
> whom for the benefit of humankind she has filled with virtue, as if for us and for those after us she bestowed a savior, who brought an end to war and established peace...

Similarly, the Lukan Jesus is associated with salvation and described as the bringer of peace (Luke 1:77, 79; 2:14; 2:30; Acts 4:12; 10:36; 13:26, 47; see also 9:31 and 16:17). Perhaps the most striking example among these is Peter's speech in Acts wherein he claims "there is no other salvation, nor another name under heaven given among people in which we must be saved" (Acts 4:12, my translation). Given the frequency with which other powerful men were named as saviors and bearers of salvation, this statement stands out as a bold challenge to imperial authority.

An association with the emperor is also evident in the ascension scene that is unique to Luke-Acts. Even more strongly than is the case with the Gospel of Matthew, Luke's description of the bodily ascension of Jesus calls to mind the apotheosis traditions of the emperors. Not once but twice, the narrative details the carrying up of Jesus into the heavens (Luke 24:51, Acts 1:9). One can find heavenly ascension in the Hebrew scriptures and in Second Temple apocalyptic literature, but in a narrative so firmly grounded in the imperial context, a more immediate cultural reference for the scene would be the apotheosis of the Roman emperors. Building on the practice begun after the assassination of Julius Caesar, the deification of Caesar Augustus in 14 C.E. was celebrated throughout the empire. With newly minted coins, through temple dedications, and with the proliferation of cult-rites and priesthoods, as Beard and Henderson note, "Divus Augustus was permanently stamped on the Roman empire."[13] Though the ascension scenes in Luke-Acts may not be intended as rituals of deification, they certainly evoke the imperial images of apotheosis. The description of Jesus ascending bodily to the heavens would recall the images of the emperor ascending to the heavens on a chariot to take his place among the gods. In particular, Gilbert notes how the presence of eyewitnesses at Jesus' ascent in Luke-Acts closely mirrors the accounts of eyewitnesses to imperial ascents. Moreover, the response to Jesus' ascension ("and they worshipped him," Luke 24:52) points to a connection between the Roman apotheosis and the ascension scenes in Luke-Acts.[14]

Together, the allusions to the emperor in the infancy narratives and with the ascension scene frame the life of Jesus. At the beginning and end of his life, the reader is encouraged to see Jesus in light of the most prominent and powerful man in the empire. Further, in addition to these allusions to the emperor, the narrative is filled with references to and encounters with Roman officials. The earthly ministry of Jesus opens and closes with the evocation of Roman authority figures. The baptism of Jesus is temporally situated with reference to seven different ruling figures: Tiberius, the emperor; Pilate, the governor of Judea; Herod, the ruler of Galilee; Philip of Ituraea and Trachonitis; Lysanias, ruler of Abilene; and the Jewish high priests Annas and Caiaphas (Luke 3:1–2). By the end of the narrative, Jesus will come in contact with four of these men—Pilate, Herod, and the high priests—though the priests are not mentioned by name in the trial scenes (Luke 22:54–23:25). While the trial before Pilate is clearly grounded in the tradition, only Luke adds the meeting with Herod. Moreover, Herod is portrayed as one eager to meet Jesus, having heard of him already (Luke 23:8). While in the end Herod will mock Jesus, the addition of this trial scene emphasizes the status of Jesus, whom Herod knows by reputation and wants to see. Moreover, the outcome of the meetings with Pilate and Herod is notable. It has long been clear that Luke makes a special effort to have Pilate exonerate Jesus. Pilate finds nothing to accuse him of (Luke 23:4). And although Herod is disappointed in the results of his meeting, Pilate points out that Herod has not found Jesus guilty of a crime.

An even more telling interaction between the Lukan Jesus and a Roman official occurs in the midst of Jesus' ministry. Indeed, the story of the centurion and Jesus moves us into the heart of Luke's world of masculine imperial authority (Luke 7:1–10). Luke has taken this Q tradition, attesting to the faith of a Gentile, and adapted it to highlight the status and rank of the characters. Unlike Matthew's version, Luke's version of the story includes a double delegation—first the Jewish elders of Capernaum and then the friends of the centurion are sent to speak with Jesus. The addition of these delegations creates a scenario in which the centurion never speaks directly with Jesus, in spite of the use of first-person pronouns in Luke 7:6–8.

Notably, neither of these delegations focuses on the request for healing as much as they focus on the character of the centurion.[15] The Jewish elders, the men with prestige in the community, do communicate the request for healing. Even more, however, they bear witness to the worthiness of the centurion. According to their testimony, the centurion both loves the Jewish people and has built their synagogue in Capernaum (Luke 7:4–5). One could see this as euergetism, a type of benefaction that was common throughout the eastern provinces and one of which Luke is clearly aware (Luke 22:25). Thus, the centurion is depicted as an affluent and powerful man who has bestowed gifts on the Jewish community so that they honor him and consider him worthy of favor.[16] In this way, Luke's version of the story offers a snapshot into his imperial world, in which colonizing authorities work closely with the local elite to gain prestige and authority.

As the story continues, however, it takes a surprising turn. When Jesus approaches the centurion's house, the centurion denies his own worthiness to see Jesus. As we have seen, this denial happens not face to face with Jesus but through communication from the centurion's friends (Luke 7:6–7).[17] Still, even as the centurion points to his unworthiness, he emphasizes his shared experience with Jesus as "one set under authority." He knows what it is like to speak and have his soldiers or slaves obey. Moreover, he recognizes in Jesus a similar power. If Jesus commands his servant to be well, he will be well. Indeed, it is this recognition of power and authority that constitutes the centurion's statement of faith at which Jesus marvels.

This, then, is the image of Jesus that Luke wishes to construct. The Lukan Jesus is not only one who teaches with authority, as in Mark, but also one whose authority is established vis-à-vis the male elite authorities of the Roman world. In Luke's Gospel, we find explicit recognition of Jesus' commanding power by a Roman official. Moreover, the centurion's actions indicate that he views Jesus as ranked high above him, so much so that he does not find it appropriate to come into his presence.

Lukan Apostles and Roman Officials

Since Robert Tannehill's detailed work on the literary structure of Luke-Acts, it has been clear that the story of the Lukan apostles closely parallels that of Jesus in the Gospel.[18] This is no less true when it comes to the construction of mascu-linity. With the apostles, too, there are frequent encounters with Roman officials that highlight the status and virtue that accompany true masculinity. Moreover, in this second volume, these encounters drive home a second point: belief in Jesus enables one to achieve true masculinity—to become a manly man.

In many cases, this point is made through demonstration of the status that has already been achieved in the apostles, patterned after Jesus' own status that was established in the Gospel. For example, in Acts there is an appearance of another centurion. Cornelius, as he is named, is portrayed in an even more favorable light than our first centurion. He is a pious and god-fearing man, along with his whole household (εὐσεβὴς καὶ φοβούμενος τὸν θεὸς σὺν παντὶ τῷ οἴκῳ αὐτοῦ). He not only has the endorsement of local leaders but ap-parently is spoken well of by *all* the Jews (μαρτυρούμενός τε ὑπὸ ὅλου τοῦ ἔθνους τῶν Ἰουδαίων, 10:22). While Cornelius allows Peter into his house (as the angel commands him to do), he nevertheless engages in a remarkable display of deference, falling at Peter's feet and prostrating himself before Peter in front of all the close relations whom he has gathered together (Acts 10:24–25). So, like Jesus before him, Peter evokes the deference of a Roman official, even if he does not accept it (10:26).

Turning to Paul, one finds numerous encounters with the Roman estab-lishment. As with Jesus, these highlight both Paul's innocence and his elite status (e.g., Acts 25:25, 26:30–31).[19] In many cases, the Roman officials have a special desire to hear Paul. This is the case with Paul's first brief encounter with Sergius Paulus, the proconsul of Paphos, who wants to hear the word of God from Paul and Barnabas. The narrative draws a sharp contrast between Sergius Paulus, an "intelligent man" (ἀνδρὶ συνετῷ), and the Jewish magi-cian/false prophet Bar-Jesus, also called Elymas (Acts 13:7–8). Paul quickly dispenses with the magician, issuing a string of invectives and striking him blind. Thus Paul is shown to recognize and combat the magic of Bar-Jesus (13:9–11). One could read this as Paul's rejection of *superstitio* and alignment in favor of the more respectable and powerful tradition that he offers.[20] The appeal and respectability of the "teaching of the Lord" that Paul offers is established by the intelligent Roman official's ready belief.

To be sure, not every encounter between Paul and a Roman official goes so well. In Thyatira, the magistrates publicly beat and imprison Paul and Silas (Acts 16:22–23), which, as we have seen, would have been a truly emasculating experience. But even here, the story concludes with Paul working to protect their manly honor as Roman citizens. He refuses to go "in peace," as the jailer asks. Instead, Paul points to the unjustified public humiliation they received (δείραντες ἡμᾶς δημοσίᾳ ἀκατα κρίτους) and demands that the magistrates come themselves to release them. The scene concludes with a personal apology from the magistrates as well as an escort from the prison (Acts 16:37–39). In effect, Paul and his companions regain their status and end up humbling their persecutors.

Paul's trials in Jerusalem and Caesarea revolve around his identity as a Roman citizen. His announcement of his birthrights causes his interrogators to draw back in fear and elicits the protection of Roman officials. Luke reports that no fewer than 470 soldiers, cavalry, and spearmen are involved in a rescue effort to bear Paul away from an ambush into the safety of the governor's care in Caesarea—certainly extraordinary measures for a dispute over religious ideology. Housed at the governor's palace, Paul gains audiences with governors Felix, Festus, and "King" Agrippa. Moreover, Paul meets on equal terms with these men. Of special note is the pandering flattery of the attorney, Tertullus, to Felix, compared to Paul's straightforward defense (Acts 24:1–21).[21]

Later, when Felix sends for Paul to speak to him and his Jewish wife, Drusilla, we get a telling glimpse of faith in Jesus Christ as defined for a Roman ruler: it is about justice, self-control, and the coming judgment (περὶ δικαιοσύης καὶ ἐγκρατείας καὶ τοῦ κρίματος τοῦ μέλλοντος, Acts 24:25). Thus, faith in Christ concerns two quintessentially masculine virtues combined with the messianic expectations of Judaism. Belief in Jesus is what enables one to be a true man. Notably, the "unmanliness" of Felix (a nonbeliever) is soon shown with his underlying motivation for conversing with Paul—he wants a bribe (24:26).

In case the link between belief in Jesus and gaining self-control is missed, Paul's account of his conversation before Agrippa makes it all the more clear. As Lentz has shown, the image of Paul in his preconversion days is that of one completely out of control. Paul reports being so out of his mind with rage at the followers of Jesus that he even pursued them out of Jerusalem into foreign cities (τε ἐμμαινόμενος αὐτοις ἐδίωκον ἕως καὶ ἔξω πόλεις 26:11). But when Festus responds to his speech by accusing Paul of insanity, Paul assures him that he is not mad. Instead, Paul speaks truth and moderation (ἀληθείας καὶ σωφροσύνης, 26:25). The implication is, as Lentz puts it, "Before his conversion Paul was 'kicking against the goads' and hence he was ruled by madness, whereas after his conversion he speaks the truth and self-controlled wisdom."[22] Thus, "in recognizing Christ, Paul has become a man of true virtue corresponding to his natural advantages of good pedigree, wealth, and high social status, as described by Luke."[23] In short, through belief in Jesus, Paul becomes the picture of ideal masculinity.

The attention devoted to Paul's case by the Roman magistrates contributes to this picture. Paul's trial appears to be the first thing on the agenda for Festus as he begins his new appointment as governor. "King" Agrippa requests a meeting with Paul that is carried out with great ceremony and includes military commanders and the prominent men of the city (25:23). Finally, Paul's dealings with the Roman rulers in Palestine take him all the way to the top with his appeal to the emperor. The appeal itself suggests a person of high status. Despite whatever legal rights were granted Roman citizens, only those of high social status could presume that they would be brought before the emperor.[24] The narrative effect of Paul's appeal is that the emperor stands in the background of the whole latter part of the narrative as Paul travels toward Rome (25–28). On the sea voyage, despite his military escort, Paul becomes the one in command of his journey, telling the centurion and the ship's crew what must be done for them to arrive safely (27:21–26, 31). Once they do, Paul's imprisonment in Rome seems hardly that. He welcomes large numbers of visitors into his own lodging, and as the closing line of the narrative relates, speaks to them with "all boldness and without hindrance" (28:31).

Finally, the apostles' dealings with Roman officials highlight their status in yet another way. As Penner has argued, such encounters frequently illustrate the superiority of the Christians. As we saw in the case of Mark's Gospel, here too the narrative suggests that the early Christians surpass the elite members of the culture on the basis of their own values. As Penner puts it:

> Throughout Acts we . . . meet tyrants such as Herod, petty governors such as Felix, corrupt kings such as Agrippa, ineffective proconsuls such Gallio, impotent Roman legions, treacherous Jewish councils, and Jewish and Greek mobs running amok while those in power are frequently unable to establish order. It is evident that Jewish, Greek, or Roman readers would take this much away from Acts; the great civic traditions of antiquity are manifested in the narrative in the Christian community.[25]

Masculinity, the Lukan Jesus, and Cult Practice in the Empire

Thus far this study has focused on the ways that the ideals of Roman imperial masculinity are evident in the depiction of Lukan heroes. Now we turn to another major aspect of this narrative, namely its focus on the Jerusalem temple. Like the allusions to imperial power, the interest in the temple also begins in the infancy narrative and is woven through the narrative as a whole. While Lukan scholars have long been interested in the role of the temple in Luke-Acts and have also noted the imperial rhetoric, especially in the infancy narratives, few have considered the relationship between the two. In fact, given all the ways that Luke positions his narrative in the context of the Roman imperial world, the fact that he also shows great interest in the Jerusalem temple presents a scholarly puzzle. Why would a writer so clearly interested in Roman imperial power go to such lengths to portray Jesus and the emerging church in close contact with the Jerusalem temple—especially because, at the time of its writing, the temple cult no longer existed?

While the majority of answers to this question have focused on Luke's interest in the temple in terms of his relationship to Judaism, here I will explore another angle.[26] I suggest that the author of Luke-Acts was interested not only in the *Jerusalem* temple (the temple as the center of the Jewish cult) but also the Jerusalem *temple* (that is, the temple as a symbol of status and authority). In other words, in addition to its importance to Judaism, the temple, like other temples in the empire, carried more general associations with piety, imperial power, literacy, and status—all things that were central to elite male identity in the imperial world. Thus, whatever the author might have felt about the relationship between Christianity and Judaism, linking Jesus and the Christian movement with the Jerusalem temple would be another way to connect both with a sacred space that represented status and power. Moreover, putting Jesus and his apostles in close association with the temple cult would be another way to compare their own virtuous conduct with the male elites of the empire, including the emperor himself.

When considering the emperor and cult practice, New Testament scholars typically focus on the worship of the emperor and the problems that this civic duty raised for early Christians. In so doing, they tend to overlook the religious role of the emperor as priest. Yet this was a major aspect of the role of the emperor, beginning with Augustus. As part of his reform Augustus became a member of each of the four priestly colleges and was made a member of three lesser priesthoods (*Res ges. divi Aug.* 7). The importance of this priestly role can be seen in the many surviving images on altar reliefs, statues, and coins of the veiled Augustus offering sacrifice.[27] In fact, from the time of Augustus onward, "virtually no one else [besides the emperor] is depicted on a Roman public monument conducting sacrifice."[28]

Why was this image of cultic sacrifice so prominently displayed and eventually so exclusively linked to the emperor? Because a major part of Roman imperial theology involved the depiction of the emperor as a model of piety whose sacrifices benefited all of the empire. The understanding was that the emperor's exceedingly virtuous character, especially in the form of piety, gave him special access to the gods. This in turn enabled the emperor to bring peace and goodwill to the people. As we saw in chapter 2, piety as a kingly virtue had a long history in Hellenistic political ideology. To quote Fears once more:

> Through his actions [an ideal king] shows himself possessed of the noblest virtues: piety towards gods and men, wisdom, courage and prowess in battle, temperance, generosity, faithfulness, and love of truth. Such a ruler is *soter* and *euergetes* to his subjects; his power is the source of supernatural benefits.... His piety towards gods and men earns him the love and solicitation of both; he stands in the center of a double stream of affection, prayed for by his subjects and protected by the gods.... His virtues mirror the divine, and the rule of the good king is an earthly reflection of the divine order.[29]

All of this, of course, perfectly reflects the ideology of Virgil's *Aeneid* with its depiction of the virtuous "pius Aeneus," whose primary interest is in obeying fate and maintaining the good will of the gods.[30] Indeed, since Rome's favored position among the gods was central to its imperial identity, one of the emperor's most celebrated virtues had to be piety. Precisely his piety, together with his other manly virtues, made the emperor worthy of divine honors. And so we see, for example, Julius Caesar, "the imperator and pontifex maximus ... savior and benefactor of all the Greeks," honored with a statue at Pergamum because of his "piety and justice."[31] This emphasis on piety, with the emperor as the premiere example, extended to the other male elites of the empire. They, too, were expected to be models of piety for other citizens to follow.

With this in mind, when we look to the Lukan Jesus, the ties to the temple take on connotations apart from his connections to Judaism. As we saw above, allusions to the Roman emperor frame the earthly ministry of Jesus. In a similar way, references to the temple frame the Gospel as a whole, as the Gospel narrative begins and ends in the Jerusalem temple. In fact, the first character to be named is Zechariah, a priest, chosen by lot to perform the incense offering in the temple (Luke 1:5). The concluding line of the Gospel depicts the disciples in the Jerusalem temple continually blessing God (Luke 24:53). Thus, both emperor and cult provide bookends to the story of Jesus, and both add to the portrayal of his masculine imperial image.

While the author does not attempt to portray Jesus in a priestly role (like the Roman emperor), allusions to a cultic setting are found throughout the infancy narrative. As mentioned above, the opening scene is that of a sacrifice offered by the priest Zechariah. The angelic announcement of John's birth comes to him at the very moment he is offering a sacrifice of incense (1:10–12). The angelic visitation to Mary is followed by a song of praise (1:46–55). Allen

Brent notes that details such as the altar of incense and Mary's "victory song" would evoke associations with the imperial cult and Roman praise of the deified "Victoria." He states, "It is arguable that the Imperial Cult represents the real pagan backcloth for this seemingly Jewish backcloth, if *Luke* is written after A.D. 70 when the Jewish Temple rites have been abolished."[32]

While Brent is correct to see evocations of pagan cult practice (not limited, I would argue, to the imperial cult), he does not address the parallels with the Hebrew scripture that are clearly evident as well. For example, the language of Mary's song closely echoes Hannah's song (1 Samuel 2:1–10), and this, in itself, evokes a cultic setting. Hannah sings her praise song as she leaves her son Samuel to be raised by Eli in the sanctuary at Shiloh and so to grow up in the "presence of the Lord." Jesus, too, goes early in his life to the house of the Lord. The reasons for Jesus' first visit to the temple are confused, as the author condenses a number of gender-related aspects of the cultic rituals around childbirth. Circumcision of the male child on the eighth day is quickly followed by the required purification after childbirth (though here the reference to "their purification" rather than to just Mary's is odd). This purification ritual is collapsed into the required sacrifice for the redemption of the firstborn male (Luke 2:21–24; see Leviticus 12:2–8; Exodus 13:2, 12).

Even if these cultic activities do not reflect accurately the scriptural regulations, the author is clearly conscious of cultic requirements involving male children and their birth mothers, showing that all are executed with respect to Jesus. This fulfilling of the prescribed cultic rituals signals the piety of the parents, those around Jesus, and Jesus himself. Here we see another way in which the emphasis on cultic ritual and sacrifice may be linked to the notion of imperial power. Like the emperor, Jesus is depicted as the son of god, the bearer of peace and justice, the savior of the people, all in the context of cultic piety, the first duty of the emperor.

The emphasis on Jesus' piety and special access to God does not end in the infancy narrative. As the narrative continues, the temple will be a frequent location for Jesus' teaching—indeed, he will eventually teach there "daily" (Luke 19:47, 21:37, 22:53). Jesus' piety also is shown through repeated references to Jesus in prayer (e.g., 3:21; 5:16; 6:12; 9:18, 28–29, etc). Following the parting instructions of Jesus, the apostles, again modeled after the pious Jesus, will spend their days praying, healing, and teaching in the Temple (Acts 2:46, 3:1–10, 5:19–25), in spite of the authorities' attempts to stop them (Acts 5:17–18). Indeed, the speech by the Pharisee Gamaliel urging the council to let the apostles alone to let God determine the outcome provides further indication that the temple activities of the apostles are divinely approved. In spite of their arrest, flogging, and warning from the council "not to speak in the name of

Jesus," the apostles continue their teaching and preaching in the temple, demonstrating their divinely bestowed authority and power over the temple leadership (Acts 5:33–42). Finally, this episode calls attention to the fact that the temple is contested space in the Gospel and Acts. In fact, only Luke's Gospel prefaces the plot to put Jesus to death with a reference to his daily teaching in the temple and the attraction of early-morning crowds who come to hear him (Luke 21:37–22:1).

To summarize, although the story of Jesus is set in the context of the revered Jewish past, the associations with the temple also link him and his followers with imperial masculinity in the present. Especially with respect to a Gentile audience that was accustomed to the promotion of piety as a civic virtue, the picture of Jesus and his followers steeped in piety and favored by God would add to their status. Such were the essential qualities of a "manly" leader in the imperial context. Beginning the narrative with an incense offering, portraying Jesus and his family as pious observers of cultic purity regulations, setting Jesus in the temple "daily," having his followers model this behavior—all of this adds to the picture of Jesus as fulfilling the masculine ideal. This man, as Peter argues before the high priest, God raised to his right hand as leader/founder and savior (ὁ θεὸς ἀρχηγὸν καὶ σωτῆρα ὕψωσεν τῇ δεξιᾷ αὐτοῦ, Acts 5:31, see also 3:15).[33]

Excursus: The Hellenistic Temple in Jerusalem

It may seem problematic to set aside the "Jewishness" of the temple to argue for Luke's more general interest in showing Jesus and his apostles as models of piety who again meet or surpass the standards of the imperial masculine ideal. After all, the author of Luke-Acts is fully aware of the notion of a Jewish/Gentile divide as he depicts the Jews of Asia accusing Paul of defiling the temple by allowing Gentiles to enter (Acts 21:28). On the other hand, he also shows Paul moving easily between Gentile and Jewish cultic associations, being friends with the "Asiarchs," high-ranking provincial/religious officials (19:31), and also a pious adherent to the Jerusalem cult practice (21:26). In this sense, Luke's depiction of Paul may also give us a more realistic sense of the inherent links between Jewish and Gentile cultures.

In spite of the structural divide between Jew and Gentile that was built into the temple, and in spite of the ideological interest in the "purity" of the temple, the temple shared a great deal with its Hellenistic environs. It may be precisely the similarities with other Greco-Roman temples that produced the anxiety over cultic purity in the Jerusalem temple. In this sense, the scholarly focus on the temple as strictly and distinctively Jewish may be more of a problem than the interpretation I am suggesting here. Because there is such a persistent strand of scholarship that isolates Judaism from its larger cultural context, it may be useful to recall just how Greek the Jewish temple was by the first century C.E.

As is well known, during the Second Temple period, the temple and Jerusalem in general became gradually more Hellenized. Lee Levine cites the wide-ranging evidence for this, beginning especially with the Hasmoneans. By way of example: the declarations and posted documentation of Simon as leader and high priest closely follow Hellenistic practices of establishing rulers (1 Maccabees 14:27–49). Likewise, the coins minted by the Hasmoneans to establish political legitimacy blended ancient Hebrew script with symbols borrowed from the Hellenistic world. Later, under Alexander Jannaeus, the coins would include Greek inscriptions as well. Beginning with John Hyrcanus I, the Hasmoneans adopted Greek names in addition to their Hebrew ones. Burial monuments likewise appropriated Hellenistic forms.[34]

In Herodian Jerusalem, the boundaries between Judaism, Hellenism, and "Romanness" become even more blurred. Herod's ambitious building program, designed to win the favor of his Roman superiors, stands as the premier example of Romanization in the east, a process that included the spread of things Greek.[35] Most significant for our purposes is Herod's architectural expansion of the temple. The project itself—the funding of the magnificent renovation of a public structure—fits the pattern of Roman euergetism.[36] Such benefaction no doubt had the intended effect, helping to gain support for Herod from the local Jewish elite. Meanwhile, the style of the renovated structure was a nod in the direction of the emperor. The enclosed porticoes of the new structure were modeled after the Egyptian Hellenistic temples dedicated to Julius Caesar.[37] The size of the Temple mount was doubled, creating the largest *temenos* (sacred space) known in the ancient world. Though sacred space, it resembled the open civic esplanades of Roman cities.[38]

The Hellenized aspect of the Jerusalem temple can also be seen in the coins collected for the annual half-shekel temple tax required of all Jews. Surprisingly, the only acceptable coins for the temple tax were Tyrian coins that bore the image of Heracles-Melkart, patron deity of Tyre on one side and an eagle on the prow of a ship on the other. Presumably, these coins, which were widely disseminated throughout the Middle East, were specified because of their high grade of silver. What is even more fascinating is the possibility that these coins were actually minted at the Temple itself following their discontinuance at Tyre.[39] According to Ya'akov Meshorer, this would explain, among other things, the otherwise complete absence of silver coins issued by

Herod during his reign, despite the fact that neighboring countries of lesser status were themselves minting silver coins. If Meshorer is right, in order to meet the requirement for Tyrian coins, the Jerusalem temple authorities were minting coins for the temple tax with images of a god that was typically associated with the Phoenicians.[40]

There are also intangible similarities between the Jerusalem temple cult and the other cults of the empire, which are perhaps the most significant. In both cases, it was the literate elite men of the culture who were closely involved with the maintenance of the temple cults. With pagan temples, the members of the priesthood were derived from and controlled by the upper classes of the society. These were affluent men who could sponsor the monuments, festivals, and sacrifices associated with the Roman cults. In the majority of cases, the magistrate and the priesthood were one and the same.[41] While this was true during the Republic, under the Principate the links between the priesthood and the imperial office became even stronger. Not only did Augustus become a member of every single priestly college, but appointments to the priesthood became closely linked with patronage of the emperor.[42]

So, too, the Jerusalem priesthood, while not engaged in the euergetism of the Roman priesthood, was certainly made up of elite members, especially the literate elite. Because part of the priests' duties was to copy and preserve scrolls, it was necessary for them to be educated as scribes. As noted earlier, Meir Bar-Ilan points out that "in the days of the Second Temple, scribes came almost exclusively from rich and distinguished families, most of whom were priests or levites."[43] This was because only affluent families could afford to give up the potential income from these sons so that they could acquire the education needed for a scribal career. In the Jewish context, the roles of magistrate and priest were even more closely connected. The temple priests, especially the high priests, were understood to be the ruling authority for the community. Finally, under the colonizing forces of Rome, it was members of the local ruling elite, such as the Jerusalem temple authorities, who were handpicked to mediate between Roman rule and the local people.

The Passover Meal and Masculinity in Luke-Acts

Aside from the temple, there is another cultic setting in the Gospel, namely the Passover meal. Even here we can see the link between cultic ritual and the portrayal of Jesus as one with masculine ruling authority. Like all the New Testament authors, Luke has to contend with the reality of Jesus' suffering and crucifixion at the hands of imperial authority. As was seen in the Gospel of

Mark, this reality creates a fundamental ambiguity at the heart of any attempt to stress the manliness of Jesus. In contrast, Luke works to overcome this ambiguity in the narration of this last ritual meal with the disciples. Following tradition, Luke portrays the final Passover meal as both an anticipation and a prescribed memorial of Jesus' suffering and death. But in this Gospel, the meal also becomes the setting for a critique of Gentile rulers and an anticipated coronation. Jesus instructs his disciples to model themselves after him by becoming leaders who serve, rather than "benefactors" who lord it over their subjects (Luke 22:25–27). Here again, the idea of the good king who serves his subjects is evoked. The Lukan Jesus then makes the idea of kingship explicit, honoring the disciples' loyalty by conferring on them a kingdom, just as his Father has conferred on him. He also promises them places on thrones judging the twelve tribes of Israel (Luke 22:28–30). In placing this coronation scene in the context of the cultic meal setting, Luke links the cultic remembrance of Jesus' death with a ritual in which the ruling authority of Jesus and his followers is emphasized once more.[44]

Conclusion

As we have seen, the Gospels of Mark and Matthew work with the ideology of imperial masculinity in ambiguous and at times resistant ways. In Paul's letters, we find him operating comfortably in the arena of Greco-Roman masculinity, responding to threats against his own manliness and hard at work attacking the masculine status of his opponents. We also find the subtle indications that belief in Jesus offers the kind of manly self-control so prized in the hierarchal Roman world. With Luke-Acts, we see this promise come to fruition. Indeed, only this two-volume work provides a narrative illustration of the link between belief in Jesus and the attainment of manly status. Thus, not only do we find multiple allusions that link Jesus with the emperor; not only do we find Jesus associating with various Roman officials; we also see Jesus' followers achieving their own ideal manly status in the Roman Empire. Luke accomplishes this by featuring his heroes in connection with the many cultural spheres in which ideal masculinity held symbolic power. Whether through evocations of the educational system and the training in masculinity it provided, associations with the imperial governmental structure and the power and status it represented, or connections to temple and cult practice that linked imperial masculinity to the gods, Jesus and his followers emerge from this two-volume work as models of Greco-Roman masculinity.

8

"He Must Increase"

The Divine Masculinity of the Johannine Jesus

This is he of whom I said, "After me comes a man who ranks ahead of me because he was before me."

—John 1:30

Since the Council of Chalcedon in 451 C.E., Jesus has been confessed as "perfect in Godhead and ... perfect in manhood, truly God and truly man."[1] The Gospel of John played a central role in the development of this confession with its unabashed display of the divinity of Jesus. And while the council intended the confession to point to the full *humanity* of Jesus, the English translation "perfect in manhood" captures well the relationship between ancient gender ideology and divinity. That is to say, the desire to show the true divinity of Jesus, a desire that shapes the "high" Christology of this Gospel, results in a particularly masculine Christology. The Gospel presents an image of Jesus as one who ranks above all others and models the traits that defined ideal masculinity in the first-century Greco-Roman world.

The concern for status is readily apparent in the quotation from John the Baptist that opens this chapter. The quotation provides an example of how the relationship between status and masculinity pervades the Gospel of John. It occurs early in the presentation of John. In this Gospel, he is never actually "the Baptist" but rather the witness to Jesus. What is striking is that John witnesses to Jesus through hierarchal patterns and gendered imagery that amount to self-emasculation. John's first testimony identifies the respective rank of both of them. Jesus "ranks ahead" of John because he was before him (1:15, 30). John also places himself in a position of humility and submission—he is not worthy to untie Jesus' sandal, a task typically reserved for women and slaves (1:27). Later John will tell his disciples, "He must increase, but I must decrease" (3:30). John must move down the hierarchy, becoming less masculine compared to Jesus. As a result, Jesus' status is elevated. He emerges as the more masculine leader.

This is just one example of the way the Gospel accents the superior masculine status of Jesus vis-à-vis other characters. As we will see, elsewhere in the text the superior status of Jesus is repeatedly put on display, whether it is in relation to his disciples, his opponents, or past Jewish heroes. This chapter will bring to light the various ways that the Johannine Jesus demonstrates ideal manliness with respect to these other characters through his self-revelation as the Son of God the Father. It will also explore the ways that the gender identity of Jesus is complicated, as was the case with the Gospel of Matthew, by the association of Jesus with Wisdom.

What Makes the Johannine Jesus a Man?

To begin, in John's Gospel the masculinity of Jesus is conveyed in the most straightforward way through his relationship to God. That is to say, the relationship of Jesus the Son to God the Father is introduced in the Prologue and continues as a central theme throughout the narrative. No other Gospel is so permeated with referents to the Father/Son relationship of Jesus with God. It uses "Father" as a referent to God some 118 times, compared to four times in Mark, forty-four in Matthew, and twenty in Luke. Similarly, the Fourth Gospel uses "the Son" as a reference to Jesus nineteen times, compared to one instance in Mark and its parallel in Matthew (Mark 13:32//Matthew 24:36).[2] A Q saying found in Matthew 11:27 and Luke 10:22 also refers to Jesus as "the Son" in language much like that in the Fourth Gospel, so that scholars often refer to the saying as a "Johannine logion." These frequent occurrences of father-and-son language (not to mention masculine leader titles such as King of Israel, Messiah, or rabbi) provide a continual reminder of the masculinity of both God and Jesus.

Contemporary interpretations of the Gospel sometimes treat this language as metaphorical. For them, the relationship between Jesus and God is *like* that of father and son. Feminist scholars often stress the intimacy of the relationship, rather than the literal and gendered implications of the language.

However, drawing on parallels between the Johannine Prologue and Aristotle's account of human reproduction (*epigenesis*), Adele Reinhartz raises the possibility that the Gospel's father/son terminology should be understood more literally.[3] The opening words of the Gospel, ἐν ἀρχῇ echo Aristotle's notion of the "first principle" of generation. The term accompanies the λόγος, which refers to both the rational purpose for the thing created and the source of movement that sets the creative process in motion. Thus, the role of the Logos in the Fourth Gospel may recall "the role of the motive cause in Aristotelian embryology, that is, the principal mover in the process of generation."[4] By using such language of generation and embryology, the Prologue, in its own way, may be closer to a birth narrative than has been recognized.

Added to this are the various uses of γίνομαι in the Gospel that link with Aristotelian thought, especially its occurrence in the phrase ὁ λόγος σάρξ ἐγένετο (1:14). While this phrase is often rendered "the Word became flesh," Reinhartz suggests that it would better be translated as "the Word was born flesh" so as not to miss the generative sense of the verb. Pointing also to the term μονογενής (only begotten), Reinhartz argues that, seen against the background of Aristotle's *epigenesis*, the Prologue to the Gospel of John communicates that "Jesus' uniqueness rests in the fact that he is the only one in the human or indeed divine realms who has come forth from, or been generated directly by, the divine seed."[5] Since in Aristotle's view ideal generation results in the perfectly formed male, understanding the Prologue through this lens would accentuate the maleness of both God and Jesus.[6] In other words, from an Aristotelian perspective, Jesus and God are not simply metaphorically related as father and son. Instead, their relationship is the result of ideal masculine generation.

The Passion(s) and Self-Mastery of the Johannine Jesus

That such ideal masculinity becomes flesh in the Johannine Jesus is paradoxically manifested in his lack of interest in the flesh. He distances himself from the flesh in his discussion with Nicodemus—"what is born from the flesh is flesh, but what is born from the spirit is spirit" (3:6)—and later pronounces that "the spirit gives life, the flesh is useless" (6:63). On the other hand, Jesus' own unique flesh is vitally important for the believer. To partake in the Logos that has become corporeal through a divine seed enables a transcendence of corporeality and thus a participation in the realm of divine masculinity. In other words, the Johannine Jesus gives his flesh on behalf of the life of the world, and believers will be given "eternal life" (6:51).

Meanwhile, during the earthly ministry of Jesus, he confirms his lack of interest in the flesh in more earthly ways. That is to say, he displays his ideal masculinity, as one would expect, through a complete control of the passions. For example, while none of the Gospels suggest that Jesus had the slightest interest in sexuality, the Gospel of John seems to emphasize that fact. Two scenes in the Gospel of John seem particularly designed to evoke expectations in the reader with respect to male/female intimacy, but in both instances the expectations remain unfulfilled.

The first such scene occurs between Jesus and the Samaritan women (4:1–42). As is commonly recognized, this story appears to follow the pattern of a biblical betrothal scene. In such scenes, a man and a woman typically meet at a well, talk, draw water, feast with the woman's family, and become engaged. Isaac, Jacob, and Moses all meet their future wives in such a fashion (Genesis 24:10–61, 29:1–20; Exodus 2:15–21). Thus, the scene in John 4—Jesus meeting a woman at a well—naturally raises the expectation of an emerging relationship between this man and woman.[7] Lyle Eslinger has argued that with its talk of drinking and deep wells, the first half of the scene is replete with sexual innuendo, encouraging the reader to expect a union between Jesus and the woman.[8] Yet, even while Jesus skirts close to the matter of the woman's sexuality, raising the issue of the woman's marital history (4:16–18), he speaks in the end only of spiritual matters. Far from any yielding to temptations of the flesh, Jesus appears completely removed from the realm of sexuality.

Similarly evocative allusions occur in John 20:1–2, 11–18 where Mary Magdalene's actions parallel the longing of the woman searching for her lover in Song of Songs.[9] Just as the woman in Song of Songs searches in the dark three times for her lover (Song 3:1–3), so three times Mary's visit to the tomb in the dark leads to her triple lament that she does not know where Jesus has been laid (John 20:2, 13, 15). The woman in the Song of Songs questions the "watchman" regarding her lover's whereabouts, using a Hebrew word that can also mean gardener. Likewise, Mary questions a man whom she takes to be a "gardener." Finally, once she finally finds her lover, the woman holds him and will not let him go (Song 3:4). But at this point, Jesus seems nothing like the male lover from the poem as he warns Mary not to touch him (John 20:17). In short, even when the narrative suggests passionate associations between Jesus and a woman by evoking so erotic a text as the Song of Songs, apparently Jesus is so far beyond such desires that they need not be addressed. There is no need to tell the reader of Jesus' self-control, as with Augustus or Philo's Moses—the Johannine Jesus makes such control evident.

When it comes to control over anger, the Johannine Jesus does not do so well. Indeed, there are several places in the Gospel that indicate a Jesus who loses his temper. Early in the narrative, Jesus is overcome with protective jealousy for his "Father's house" (2:13–17). Taking even more extreme measures than in the synoptic version of this tradition, the Johannine Jesus wields a whip of cords on unsuspecting cows and sheep. He overturns furniture in a violent display of his anger, no doubt making a mess of coins and tables. Plutarch would likely flinch at this undignified display and loss of control. Still, as we have seen, Plutarch's view of the relationship between anger and masculinity was not the only view in the ancient world. Plutarch, after all, was responding to others who thought that such displays demonstrated the bold, active, righteous character of a man. Given the way later Christians such as Basil and Lactantius defended the anger of God as a temporal anger against evil and sin, it is likely that Jesus' demonstration of anger in the temple would be viewed in a similar way. Indeed, one could well imagine support for Jesus' angry displays as a sure sign of his masculinity. Here is Jesus—bold, active, hater of evil, exhibiting the appropriately righteous anger of a virtuous man.

The Johannine Jesus also gets angry or at least emotional at the death of his friend Lazarus (11:33–38), but this is not the undignified loss of control that worried the philosophers. Both Jesus' anger and his tears at the death of Lazarus seem more intended as a show of compassion than a loss of self-control.[10] Indeed, this is how the narrative onlookers understand it, as we see in their response: "See how he loved him!" (11:36). Moreover, when the Johannine Jesus faces his own impending death, he shows nothing of the uncertainty depicted in the synoptic traditions (Mark 14:32–42 and parallels). Instead, he observes almost matter-of-factly that his "soul is troubled" (John 12:27). Rather than expressing anguish, the Johannine Jesus faces death with the strength and courage of a superhero. Indeed, in this equivalent to the synoptic Gethsemane scene, the Johannine Jesus nearly scoffs at the weakness of the synoptic Jesus. "And what should I say—'Father, save me from this hour?' No, it is for this reason that I have come to this hour" (12:27). Instead of praying for deliverance, this Jesus states, "Father, glorify your name" (12:28).

This is not the only place where Jesus speaks confidently of his death. Elsewhere he makes clear that he lays down his life on his own accord; no one takes his life from him (10:17–18). Later, he argues that there is no greater love than giving one's life for friends (15:13). Thus, the Johannine Jesus accentuates even more strongly than the other Gospel narratives that his death will be a noble, voluntary death for the benefit of others. Significantly, when he speaks of his own death, the Johannine Jesus never engages in predictions of his suffering and crucifixion. In fact, the verb for suffer (πάσχω) does not occur in the Gospel. In this sense, there is no "passion" narrative in the Fourth Gospel.

Or, perhaps better, the Fourth Gospel presents an "anti-passion" narrative. For this reason, when Jesus refers to his crucifixion, he uses language with far more positive connotations; rather than being crucified by the Roman authorities, he will "be lifted up" (ὑψωθῆαι)(3:14, 8:28, 12:32). Thus Jesus' death in the Fourth Gospel is not one of suffering and martyrdom, but the means by which he will "draw all people to himself" (12:32). In other words, the Johannine Jesus does not interpret his death as a ransom, as in the Markan tradition, but instead speaks of it as a death given for friends, a death that will unite all people.

The Johannine Jesus' strong self-assurance shades into control over others in the arrest scene (18:1–12). There he approaches the large cohort bent on arresting him, asking whom they seek. At their response, "Jesus of Nazareth," Jesus appears to overpower the soldiers and police with words alone. At his revelatory ἐγώ εἰμι, they retreat and fall to the ground (18:6). Here is another place where the status of Jesus is boldly displayed. The scene is clearly intended to show Jesus' divine status, which is unwittingly recognized by his opponents. Once this point is made, the scene continues with Jesus allowing the arrest to proceed and scolding Peter for his attempt at armed resistance (18:10–11). Jesus has controlled his own arrest from beginning to end. In doing so, he shows himself to be the ruler rather than the ruled.

This is true as the narrative moves through the trial and crucifixion scenes in this "anti-passion" narrative. As many have noted, the Johannine Jesus moves through his trial before Pilate as through he were the judge. He challenges and questions the assumptions of Pilate, especially Pilate's claim to have power over Jesus (18:34, 37; 19:11). In the closing scene, there is an ambiguous moment when Pilate brings Jesus out to the crowd and either sits on the judge's bench himself or seats Jesus there.[11] The latter possibility would seem out of the question in terms of the logic of the narrative, were it not for the fact that Jesus has been presented as judge throughout the narrative. Moreover, the arrest scene has already demonstrated that the author does not shy away from straining credulity to make a point about the masculinity of the Johannine Jesus.

As for the crucifixion scene itself, only in John's Gospel does Jesus orchestrate his final moments with a symbolic exchange with his mother and disciple. His measured attention to these two characters is a long way from the Markan Jesus' cry of anguish and abandonment. Even Jesus' statement "I am thirsty" is made not from a place of weakness but "in order to fulfill the scripture." Once this has occurred, Jesus pronounces, "It is finished." In the end, Jesus is the one who, bowing his head, "gives up his spirit" (19:26–30). In this way, Jesus has control of his life and of his death. No one takes it from him (John 10:18).

The Gospel of John also features resurrection accounts that present an alternative image to the echoes of Roman apotheosis in the synoptic Gospels. The traditions of apotheosis that are evidenced in the writings of Paul, Matthew, and Luke follow typical patterns of Roman apotheosis where a hero is rewarded for his extraordinary, virtuous, and manly conduct by assuming his place among the gods. So, too, did Augustus, Apollonius, and even Philo's Moses approach the heights of divinity and achieve some sort of immortality on account of their ideal masculinity. But the Johannine Jesus does not take his place alongside God as a result of his heroic behavior. Instead, throughout the narrative he affirms what the Prologue already stated: Jesus (the incarnate Logos) was with God from the beginning. While the language of "lifting up" (3:14, 8:28, 12:32) recalls the notions of apotheosis that were in play in the synoptic traditions, in John's Gospel Jesus is the one who has "come from above" and has descended. This means that when he asks Mary Magdalene to report that he is ascending "to my father and to your father, to my God and your God" (20:17), it is an ascent that *returns* him to his place with God. All of this highlights the truly different Christology of John's Gospel and the different way that the masculinity of Jesus is expressed here, even compared to the divine men examined in chapter 3. In the Gospel of John the divine Logos becomes incarnate, *necessarily*, as the ideal man. In other words, the desire to show the true divinity of Jesus, a desire that shapes the "high" Christology of this Gospel, results in a particularly masculine Christology.

The Missing Body of the Manly Jesus

If we compare the presentation of the Johannine Jesus, in all his ideal form, to that of Augustus, Moses, and Apollonius, another distinction emerges. The accounts of these extraordinary men would lead us to expect a description of Jesus' handsome countenance. Nevertheless, although there are plenty of references to "flesh" and "glory" in the Gospel, there is no description whatsoever of Jesus' body. Nor are there stories of men and women fawning over his beauty.[12] The text provides no clues as to the appearance of his eyebrows, eyelids, neck, complexion, hair, or other such traits to support the presentation of a manly man. Of course, this lack is not unique to the Gospel of John. Nowhere in the New Testament is there a physical description of Jesus, apart from the transfiguration scene that mentions his brilliant white clothes. Still, this *lack* of description itself may be an indicator of gender and social status. This is true of all the Gospel narratives, but it may be especially the case in the context of John's Gospel, which thematizes the notion of freedom and slavery (8:32–33; 13:16; 15:15, 20).

In his study of the male body in Roman Egypt, Dominic Montserrat notes an absence of physical description of free men in papyri of the first three centuries c.e.[13] Whereas the bodies of runaway slaves were typically described in specific detail, including height, weight, hair color, complexion, facial hair, gait, and so on, descriptions of free men were much more circumspect. Even when the papyri contain an order to arrest a free man (thereby removing his privileged status), only names and occupations are stated. While Montserrat acknowledges the practical aspect of detailed bodily descriptions of runaway slaves, he suggests there may be a subtext to their inclusion. Much of the language used to describe the slaves is couched in passivity, subjection, and infantilization. A slave could not be a "real man" in this world, and "the adjectives applied to his body serve both to set him physically apart and render him ridiculous."[14]

In contrast, the bodies of free men are rarely described in the Egyptian papyri, the two exceptions being when free men were victims of violence and when men served as witnesses to documents. In the latter case, the descriptions remain quite general compared to the detailed descriptions of slaves. In the first case, the emphasis is on the nature of the wounds that "rendered [the man] passive and vulnerable."[15] In light of this material evidence, the lack of description of Jesus' appearance, and especially the lack of emphasis on his wounds, is suggestive. If descriptions of a wounded body potentially meant a glimpse at a vulnerable or feminized Jesus, the Gospel provides the reader little opportunity for such a glimpse. Thus, Jesus' status as a free man is reinforced by the reticence of the Passion narrative. Notably, where the narrative does attend to wounds, Jesus' *unbroken* legs are contrasted to the broken legs of the thieves beside him (19:32–33). The wound that the already dead body of Jesus receives, a pierced side, pointedly does not indicate vulnerability but rather the saving power of Jesus even after his death (19:34–35). The blood and water that flow from Jesus recall similar imagery from earlier in the Gospel, symbolizing the life-giving power of Jesus (e.g., 4:13, 6:54).[16]

The Power and Authority of the Johannine Jesus

Woven through the narrative presentation of the Johannine Jesus is a discourse on power. From the very beginning of the Gospel, in a proleptic view of the benefits that come to Jesus' believers, Jesus is depicted as the dispenser of power. To those who believed in his name, "he gave power to become children of God" (1:12). The rest of the Gospel represents Jesus as one with the power to bestow such a gift. Unlike the synoptics, "power" in this Gospel is never expressed in terms of δύναμις (ability or demonstration of power). Instead, it is always ἐξουσία (authority), indicating absolute, ruling, authoritative power— the kind of power reserved for men who have proved themselves as men.

Along this line, the Johannine Jesus claims an astounding range of authority in the Gospel, from that of executing judgment (5:27) to power over his own life and death (10:18), to power over the lives and deaths of others (5:21, 6:40, 11:1–44). Indeed, only in this Gospel does Jesus claim the power to raise himself from death.[17] If this were not impressive enough, added assurance of the totality of Jesus' power comes in the midst of the Farewell Discourse. There the Johannine Jesus assures his disciples that "the ruler of this world" has no power over him (14:30). In prayer, Jesus claims that the Father has given the Son "power over all flesh" (17:2, my translation). Later, as we have seen, when Pilate threatens Jesus with his authority over him, Jesus points out that Pilate has no authority over him on his own accord (19:11).

Considering the Gospel through the multiple oppositions of masculinity also provides a different perspective on the rhetoric of slavery and freedom. The Johannine Jesus promises his followers the knowledge of truth and the attainment of freedom (8:31–32). As a free man in a ruling status, Jesus has the ability to make slaves free (8:34–36). This is, in fact, what happens to his disciples. Those who do Jesus' bidding are no longer slaves but are the beloved (φίλοι) of God (15:15). The implication is that Jesus' followers can expect a rise in status. Not only are they no longer slaves; the language of friendship evokes the philosophical rhetoric of intimacy between free men. In this way, the salvific benefits offered by the Johannine Jesus offer his followers a chance to become more manly, that is, to enjoy the benefits that a truly free man would enjoy. We might compare this to Philo's claim that the law desires for the soul to be trained in manliness. In the Fourth Gospel, relationship with Jesus offers the same sort of benefit. To be sure, even with this new status as "beloved," there is still an assumption that the disciples remain slaves with respect to their master Jesus (15:20, cf. 13:16). Nevertheless, they achieve manliness thanks to their association with a person of still higher social status.[18]

To summarize so far, the Fourth Gospel presents Jesus as a quintessential man. He reveals no weakening to the passions that might undercut his manly deportment. Rather, he proves himself masculine through disciplined self-control throughout his ministry and in the face of suffering and death. He is a free man who offers the possibility of freedom to others. At the same time, he insists on his fundamental authority and has followers who readily submit themselves to him.

Still, while recognizing the manliness of Jesus, this discussion has not yet attended to the ways that this Gospel, like the Gospel of Matthew, evokes the figure of Sophia. As mentioned in the introduction, consideration of masculine Christology in the Fourth Gospel demands attention to claims by some scholars that the Johannine Jesus, as Wisdom incarnate, evokes a feminine dimension of the divine. With this in mind, we turn now to a discussion of the implications of this Wisdom imagery for the gender construction of Jesus in the Gospel of John.

Wisdom and the Relative Gender of the Johannine Jesus

As was the case with the Matthean Jesus, it is clear that the portrayal of the Johannine Jesus is influenced by Jewish Wisdom traditions.[19] As one who saw this connection early on, Raymond Brown argued that John sees in Jesus the "supreme example of divine Wisdom active in history, and indeed divine Wisdom itself."[20] When this comment was made in the mid-sixties, the gender implications of the association between Wisdom and Jesus were a nonissue. The only attention Brown gives to gender identity is in a comment that Sophia is personified as a woman because of the feminine gender of חכמ, the Hebrew word for wisdom.[21]

Others, however, have attached a great deal of importance to the feminine aspect of Wisdom and its implications for Johannine Christology. For example, Engelsman argues the Fourth Gospel's presentation of Jesus produces "the most feminine of the Gospels."[22] Feminist theologian Elizabeth Johnson relies heavily on wisdom imagery from the Fourth Gospel and elsewhere in the New Testament to find an alternative vision to the male God.[23] Going a step further, Martin Scott sees the Gospel as intentionally attending to the divine feminine. He argues:

> The point of John's Wisdom Christology is precisely that Jesus So-
> phia is not mere man, but rather the incarnation of both the male and
> the female expressions of the divine, albeit within the limitations
> of human flesh.

In Scott's reading, one needs to imagine a gender-blending in the Johannine Jesus: "Jesus is a *man* who exhibits all the characteristic traits of the *woman* Sophia."[24]

While also celebrating "divine Woman Wisdom," Elisabeth Schüssler Fiorenza makes quite a different case for the use of Wisdom traditions in the

Fourth Gospel. In her view, any feminine aspect of God in the Gospel has been marginalized and silenced by the male rhetoric of the Gospel. The Johannine Jesus has displaced Sophia.[25] As she puts it:

> By introducing the "father-son" language in the very beginning and using it throughout the Gospel, the whole book reinscribes the metaphorical grammatical masculinity of the expressions "logos" and "son" as congruent with the biological masculine sex of the historic person of Jesus of Nazareth. The Fourth Gospel thereby not only dissolves the tension between the grammatical feminine gender of Sophia and the "naturalized" gender of Jesus but also marginalizes and "silences" the traditions of G*d as represented by Divine Woman Wisdom.[26]

A similar point was made even earlier by Wayne Meeks, who noted that "in the Fourth Gospel there is no trace of the usual feminine Sophia; she has become entirely the masculine Logos, the Son of Man."[27] Judith McKinlay, although taking a different approach, arrives at essentially the same place. She points out that the Gospel draws on multiple images to portray Jesus, so that the feminine Wisdom stands as one among many other masculine images. In her view, "Certainly the Wisdom parallels allow the feminine dimension to remain as part of the expression of the divine, but with that divinity expressed through a male Jesus, the feminine has now receded even further than before."[28] Michael Willett goes further, reading the Gospel's portrayal of Jesus as Wisdom as an affirmation of *maleness*, at least within the Johannine community. Although women in the community might have been attracted to leadership roles, ultimately, "Wisdom becoming flesh in the male Jesus, to whom a male disciple bore witness, would have reinforced the primary leadership positions in the community held by males."[29]

Such wide-ranging interpretations reflect the difficulty of the question. What are we to understand about the gender construction of the Johannine Jesus? On the one hand, he is presented in full masculine glory; on the other hand, he speaks the language of Sophia. In the case of Matthew's Gospel, I argued that because the pursuit of Wisdom made possible the attainment of masculinity, arguing for the introduction of a feminine dimension in the Matthean Jesus was probably misguided. In the case of John's Gospel, it will be helpful to explore more fully the ways that Wisdom is gendered in literature that is roughly contemporary to the Gospel.[30] Doing this reveals that the adoption of Wisdom imagery does not necessarily lead to either displacement or revelation of the feminine dimension of the divine. Instead, the literature reveals a fluidity of gender connotations around the figure of Wisdom. In other words, Wisdom is not consistently personified as feminine (though there are certainly instances of this) but can also be viewed in gender-neutral and masculine ways as well. Or, as Judith Lieu argues, just because Wisdom is personified as woman in some instances, that does not mean that every reference to Wisdom has gender implications.[31] Keeping this in mind and seeing the gender fluidity at play in the literary presentations of Wisdom will lead to new insights regarding the gender identity of the Johannine Jesus.

In examining the various personifications of Wisdom, it is best to begin with texts in which Sophia appears at her most erotically feminine. Ben Sira presents a Wisdom figure designed to arouse desire and pursuit from her followers. For example, Webster provocatively notes the progression of the seeker in Sirach 14:22–27 as he "penetrates [Sophia's] locative, visual, auditory space to climax in the midst of her."[32] The image then shifts to Sophia as mother and young bride, feeding her follower with bread and giving him water to drink (Sirach 15:2–3). The theme of sustenance is repeated later in the book as Sophia urges those who desire to come and eat their fill of her fruits. "For the memory of me is sweeter than honey, and the possession of me sweeter than the honey comb" (Sirach 24:20).

One can easily find similar themes associated with the Johannine Jesus. He is also sought and pursued (John 1:37; 6:2, 24); he also offers sustenance to his followers (4:14, 6:51–58). But the evocation of these Wisdom themes is designed to indicate that Johannine Jesus surpasses this Wisdom figure. Whereas those who eat of Sophia will hunger and thirst for more (Sirach 24:21), those who eat and drink of Jesus will be eternally satisfied (John 4:14, 6:58). In fact, in each of the cases in which Jesus is designated as the true version of something—*true* bread, *true* light, and *true* vine (John 1:9, 6:32, 15:1)—one hears Sophia traditions in the background (bread, Sirach 15:3; light, Wisdom 7:26, 29; vine, Sirach 24:17). This seems to imply that the Sophia traditions as expressed apart from Jesus are false, perhaps because they are linked to Torah and/or Moses, and not to Jesus.[33] Indeed, Jesus does surpass Moses in the Gospel, as one who provides something greater than the manna from Moses (see John 6:31–34, 58). Given Philo's first-century depiction of Moses as a paradigm of masculinity, it is tempting to understand Jesus in the Gospel of John as surpassing even that ideal. In any case, it seems clear that the masculine figure of Jesus as *true* bread, light, and vine does imply superiority and does effect a displacement of the feminine personification of Wisdom, especially with respect to the sustaining functions of Wisdom.[34]

However, it is also apparent that Wisdom is not personified as a woman in every Second Temple wisdom text. For instance, the Wisdom of Solomon contains mixed gender imagery. To be sure, Sophia is here also sought after and desired as a bride (Wisdom 6:12–14, 8:2). On the other hand, masculine imagery is also used in these personifications. Wisdom penetrates "all spirits" and "pervades and penetrates all things" (Wisdom 7:23–24). She "passes into holy souls" (Wisdom 7:27).[35] Such active penetration connotes a masculine act in this ancient world. Even more significantly, Wisdom teaches self-control, prudence, justice, and courage—just those traits that make a man a man (Wisdom 8:7).

In addition, the Wisdom of Solomon features Wisdom imagery that seems to have no gender connotations. Wisdom is spoken of as a spirit (Wisdom 1:6–7, 9:17), a fashioner of all things (Wisdom 7:22), and a breath of the power of God (Wisdom 7:25). Throughout these texts, Wisdom is still referred to with feminine pronouns, but there is no emphasis on erotic connotations such as is found in Sirach. This diversity of language suggests that the presence of Wisdom imagery did not in all cases suggest a feminine image.

Perhaps most informative, however, is yet another example from Philo. As discussed in chapter 3, Philo's discussion of Wisdom provides a marvelous example of how fluid and functional gender categories could be in the ancient world. Philo has no qualms in arguing that Sophia is, in principle, masculine, because she has the generative power of masculinity. Still, Philo needs to explain why she has a feminine name. In this context, it is worth repeating his explanation:

> All the virtues have women's titles, but powers and activities of per-
> fect men. For that which comes after God, even if it were chiefest of
> all other things, occupies a second place, and therefore was termed
> feminine to express its contrast with the Maker of the Universe, who
> is masculine, and its affinity to everything else. (*Fug.* 51–52)

This gender fluidity extends to discussions of Wisdom in relation to humanity. Wisdom can be feminine or masculine, impregnator or impregnated, depending on her partner in procreation.

Such gender fluidity provides another way of understanding the gender construction of the Johannine Jesus. The Fourth Gospel can be seen as a narrative expression of ideas that Philo relates philosophically. With respect to the people who populate the Gospel, Jesus is certainly an exemplar of masculinity. Yet, when it comes to his relationship with the God the Father, he assumes a less masculine status. He is obedient, submissive, and can do nothing on his own (John 5:19, 30; 6:38; 7:16; 12:49; 15:10). In other words, when compared to God, Jesus takes a less masculine position in much the same way that John the Baptist did in relation to Jesus. Similarly, if Philo understands Wisdom as masculine relative to human beings (men) and feminine in relation to God, so too can Jesus be seen as relatively masculine and feminine. For Philo, the feminine aspect of Wisdom is only that (s)he is second to God. The same could be said of the Johannine Jesus.

Thus, Jesus fulfills the expectations of masculinity in every way, even when submitting to the yet higher power of God, the father. As Logos, Jesus is masculinity at its active, generative, and spiritual best, at least in terms of the gender ideology of the ancient world. When compared to the ultimate male, God, the Johannine Jesus assumes a second, less masculine position in the gender hierarchy. In the end, Jesus is such a supreme example of masculinity that he takes on divine status.

Conclusion: Relating to the Johannine Jesus

Examining the Gospel of John through the lens of hegemonic masculinity in the ancient Mediterranean world has enabled a more nuanced analysis of gender and Christology in the Fourth Gospel. Much of the evidence suggests that Jesus is presented in this Gospel as the manliest of men. This presentation would be fully commensurate with his characterization as divine Word made flesh. Like Philo's Moses, whose ideal masculinity approaches the heights of divinity, so the deified Jesus is incarnate as the ideal man. Like Augustus, this Johannine Jesus is "savior of the world" (4:42).

To be sure, this masculine Christology is complicated by the links between Jesus and Sophia in the Gospel. In our contemporary setting, one might fruitfully read such links as indicators of a feminine dimension to the divine. But in the context of the first century, a feminine aspect in the presentation of Jesus would speak more to his position vis-à-vis God than to a positive expression of feminine qualities. In other words, highlighting Jesus' "feminine" side through the presence of Wisdom motifs would be to emphasize the ways in which he is second to the ultimate male, God.

The same principle applies to the Gospel's depiction of female characters in general. Many have looked to the Gospel's positive portrayal of women as a resource for feminist reflections on leadership in the church.[36] Characters such as the Samaritan women, Martha, and Mary Magdalene have been read as exemplars of faithful discipleship and leaders in the Johannine community. This analysis, however, suggests that in the end, the positive depiction of these characters takes shape only in the broader framework of the Gospel's masculine Christology. Yes, there are strong female characters in the narrative. Nevertheless, their consistently positive portrayal may be because as women they are already in the properly submissive position with respect to the dominant ultramale characters in the Gospel, Jesus and God. The words of John the Baptist that opened this chapter point to the importance of proper position with respect to Jesus, especially from a character that potentially represented competition with Jesus. As we saw, John lowers himself, using feminizing images to express his status vis-à-vis Jesus. The downplaying of Petrine authority that has long been recognized in the Gospel may be for similar reasons. The status of Peter was clearly growing in some strands of early church tradition, represented in the New Testament by the Gospel of Matthew (16:17–19). Meanwhile, the Johannine tradition seems to neutralize Peter's status, so that the overall impression of Peter left by the narrative is less than favorable.[37] But the female characters pose no threat to the divine/human gender hierarchy. They are very clearly "women" with respect to Jesus and God in a way that is not so readily apparent with the male characters. Ironically, then, the prominence and positive depiction of women in the Gospel functions to preserve and accentuate masculine images of Jesus and God.[38]

In sum, the Gospel assimilates many of the typical values ascribed to hegemonic masculinity in the Greco-Roman culture, especially the equation of superior masculinity with divinity. It also assimilates the fluid gender gradient that was a defining characteristic of ancient gender ideology. For this reason, the masculinity of Jesus is repeatedly defined in relation to other characters. Ranging from John the Baptist, who expressly ranks below Jesus, to his relationship with the men and women of the Gospel, to his position vis-à-vis God, Jesus can appear more or less masculine. The use of the divine wisdom motif reinforces this gender fluidity. Like personified Wisdom, the personified Logos ranks higher on the gender gradient than all of creation. As Logos, he was with God from the beginning and all things come into being through him. But with respect to God, like Wisdom, he is less masculine. Indeed, he can do nothing on his own (John 5:30).

9

Ruling the Nations with a Rod of Iron

Masculinity and Violence in the Book of Revelation

And from his mouth comes a sharp sword, so that he may strike down the nations, and rule them with an iron rod.
—Revelation 19:15 (my translation)

Although the title of this book is *Behold the Man*, in the Book of Revelation, Jesus as a human male is nowhere to be found. The book challenges the imagination when it comes to imagining Jesus, the man. That is to say, the postresurrection Jesus who is encountered in this text is a long way from the Jesus of the Gospels. Rather than the teaching, preaching, healing, suffering, dying, resurrecting Jesus, in Revelation one encounters Jesus as an angel, a lamb, and a warrior with flaming eyes on a white horse.

These images of Jesus are woven throughout the text—the angelic Son of Man is introduced in Revelation 1:13–16 and reappears at 14:14. The lamb, by far the most prominent image, first appears in 5:6 and is then featured throughout the rest of the book. The mounted warrior leads his army though the war scene in chapter 19 (Revelation 19:11–21). But if these figures are not easily recognizable as human, they are nevertheless gendered figures. And, as the reader might expect at this point in the book, their gender identity is tension-filled and complex.

The tension lies between the imitation of ideal imperial masculinity and the mirroring of Roman imperial violence. The first type of imitation produces a masculine identity for God and Christ that is commensurate with ideal ruling authority—both are worthy of honor and worship, according to Roman standards. The second type produces figures of rage and vengeance and general lack of control that was indicative of unmanly conduct. Thus, on the one hand, the gendered identity of Revelation's Christological figures is informed by the same sort of imperial imitation seen in the Gospels. On the other hand, something quite different is also on display.

The difference lies, in part, in the fact that Revelation draws more heavily on military imagery than any other New Testament text. That is to say that Revelation is unique in presenting its soteriological figures as those who are successful in battle. In so doing, the author of Revelation engages an obvious and central aspect of Roman imperial masculinity, the waging of war. Augustus, after all, began his *Res Gestae* with the acknowledgment that he "often waged war, civil and foreign, on the earth and sea, in the whole wide world" (3). The *Aeneid*, Virgil's foundational Roman epic, is a song of "arms and the man." So when the Book of Revelation employs images of warfare, it engages a very basic element of imperial masculinity.[1]

At the same time, however, soteriological figures in Revelation deviate from standards of Roman hegemonic masculinity precisely in the ways they engage their enemies of war. Consider that in the same sentence in which Augustus writes of his frequent warfare, he reminds his audience of how he preferred to preserve rather than destroy foreign nations, and how he spared anyone who sought pardon (*Res ges. divi Aug.* 3). This is hardly the case in Revelation. Instead, as I will argue, along with engaging the Roman rhetoric of warfare and victory, the Book of Revelation reveals a far more monstrous masculinity—an ideology driven more by vengeance than by an interest in cultural standards. Or from a different perspective, one might argue that the Christ figure in Revelation is in certain respects far more unmanly than manly. In what follows, this gender tension will be explored in each of three main Christological figures.

The Angelic Son of Man

Perhaps because Revelation is all about seeing, the Christological images in this book are more fully described than others in the New Testament. Detailed description occurs already in the opening chapter, with Revelation's most anthropomorphic of Christological images, the Son of Man. This figure has a head and hair white like wool, blazing eyes, a long robe with golden sash across the chest, feet like glowing bronze, and a voice like rushing waters (Revelation 1:12–15). Needless to say, such traits are not found in the physiognomic handbooks that assisted ancient specialists in identifying gender. Were a physiognomist to look closely at the Son of Man for the telltale shape of his eyebrows or nature of his gaze, he would risk blindness—his face is like the sun shining at full force (1:16). But he might be able to see that the Son of Man also bears a weapon, a two-edged sword that issues from his mouth.

Even if the physiognomic handbooks are of no help, Revelation is not the only ancient text in which one finds a figure with a white head and flaming eyes, girded in gold, with glowing metallic limbs. Daniel, too, sees a vision of a figure with similar features—face like lightning, flaming eyes, burnished bronze limbs (Daniel 10:4–6). Also, the "Ancient One" in Daniel has hair like pure wool (7:9–10), and Ezekiel speaks of the approaching glory of God sounding like "mighty waters" (Ezekiel 43:2). Similar descriptions accompany the appearance of the Son of Man in 1 Enoch 46:1. The head of this figure, too, is white as wool. All of these echoes point to the supernatural aspect of the Son of Man in Revelation, in particular to his depiction as an angel.[2] In fact, he is a terrifying angel judging by the reaction of John, who, upon seeing the angel, falls at his feet as though dead (Revelation 1:17). As with other appearances of angels and divine beings in the New Testament, this Son of Man urges John not to be afraid. But because he says this with a two-edged sword issuing from his mouth, perhaps there is good reason to be afraid.

As the narrative continues, the Son of Man is depicted as one with imperial authority issuing instructions to various locals (2:1–3:22). As David Aune argues, the so-called seven letters at the beginning of Revelation actually resemble imperial edicts more than any standard epistolary form. Like ancient imperial edicts, the proclamations of the Son of Man open with a formal introduction of the issuing authority, then move to a direct address to the addressees. Like the imperial edict, the main body of these statements expresses decisions and sanctions, with a final clause intended to reinforce obedience.[3] Also relevant is the repetition of the τάδε λέγει formula at the beginning of each of the proclamations that introduces the direct speech (literally, "these he says"). This same (and perhaps standard) formula was found on a Persian inscription in Asia Minor that recorded an edict from Darius I to a local official.[4] So, for example, the message to Thyatira begins with the announcement: "These are the words [τάδε λέγει] of the Son of God, who has eyes like flaming fire and feet like shining metal" (2:18, my translation). The announced speaker then addresses the church in the first person, "I know your works..." and proceeds to list their merits and shortcomings. The message concludes with a promise of authority for those who obey and punishment for those who do not (2:26–28). This is the form for all seven messages from the Son of Man to the communities in Asia Minor. Thus, as Aune observes,

"In his role as the eternal sovereign and king of kings, Jesus is presented as issuing solemn and authoritative edicts befitting his status."[5] In fact, this is Aune's thesis for the imperial imagery of Revelation in general, namely, that the author strategically employs it to polarize "God/Jesus and the Roman emperor, who is but a pale and diabolical imitation of God."[6]

This would be a clever strategy, if it were the case—imitating imperial authority to show how imperial authority is a poor imitation of God. But a more obvious cultural interaction, and one suggested by several other readers of Revelation, is that the author simply mirrors the emperor in his depictions of God/Jesus.[7] Such an approach would be in keeping with a strategy that we have seen throughout the New Testament, namely, to use the widespread cultural image of imperial authority to represent the ruling authority of the Christian savior and god. In Revelation, however, there is more than imitation of magisterial authority at work.[8] As already mentioned, there is another type of imitation present that is hinted at in the "imperial edicts" of the Son of Man. This is the mimicry of imperial violence.

The indication of this mimicry is seen already in the Son of Man who claims that he is throwing the so-called Jezebel on a bed and will strike her children dead (2:22). This is the promised consequence for those in Thyatira who are following alternative teachings, such as eating meat from animals sacrificed in Roman temples. The reference to throwing the woman Jezebel "on a bed" is often interpreted as causing her illness, because κλίνη can refer to a pallet for a sick person. Not surprisingly, commentators are hesitant to see violence in the image, let alone sexual violence. But given the double reference to the woman's sexual deviance—prostitution and adultery (πορνεία, μοιχεία)—for her to be thrown on a bed unavoidably (however disturbingly) evokes images of sexual humiliation, if not assault.[9] After all, in this passage the Son of God announces, "I will give to each of you as your actions deserve" (2:23, my translation).

Thus, we see early hints that the author of Revelation has no qualms in presenting a violent side of his images of Christ.[10] Such violence only builds as the visions continue. For example, Son of Man reappears in chapter 14, this time seated on a cloud with a golden crown. He has traded his two-edged sword, not for a plowshare, but for a sharp sickle. The figure is joined by another sickle-bearing angel (ἄλλος ἄγγελος).[11] The sickles, it soon becomes clear, are for judgment. Because dispensing justice was a central function of the emperor, and here the Son of Man is crowned and seated, imperial imitation is again at work. The harvesting imagery barely conceals the bloodbath that this judgment involves. Indeed, as both angels sweep their sharp tools across an earth that is ripe for harvest (14:16–19), the scene soon turns horrific.

The shorn grapevines of the second sickle are thrown into the great winepress of the wrath of God. But it is blood, not grape juice, that flows from the press (14:20). And not just a little blood. As if to point ahead to another Christological figure, the blood that flows from the wine press is as "high as a horse's bridle" spread for a distance of almost two hundred miles.[12]

The violence in this imagery—the punishment of Jezebel, the killing of her children, the excessive bloodshed resulting from God's anger—raise a question about the masculinity of both God and his son. On the one hand, the author clearly understands such divine violence to be the result of righteous judgment and punishment. On this point, Robert Mounce's gendered observations about God's anger are telling. Noting how the nouns for "wrath" and "anger" are found thirteen times in Revelation 6–19, he concludes, "Any view of God that eliminates judgment and his hatred of sin in the interest of an emasculated doctrine of sentimental affection finds no support in the strong and virile realism of the Apocalypse."[13] Indeed, both John and Mounce would likely agree (contra Plutarch) that in some cases anger is a sign of masculinity.[14]

On the other hand, everything that the Roman imperial rhetoric has taught us so far is that such excessively punitive conduct is unbefitting the manly ideal of self-restraint and moderation, even in times of war. Recall the critique of Augustus, in the midst of challenges to his masculinity, that he was excessively cruel. To be sure, the emperors hardly lived up to this ideal themselves, in spite of the rhetoric. But it is notable that those who most blatantly fell short of the ideal, at least in the eyes of their critics, were also those whose masculine status was suspect. Thus, in depicting an angry and vengeful God, the author is walking a perilous line between manly and unmanly depiction. As we will see, the violent imagery is not limited to God and the Son of Man. Other Christological images participate in divine violence as well.

The Warrior Rider

The close link between the Son of Man and the warrior rider is seen in the overlap of images of the wine press and the bloodstained robes of the warrior. For, later in the text, the one found treading in the wine press of the fury of the wrath of God is the rider on the white horse (19:11–16). Notably, the missing two-edged sword turns up with him as well. Thus, although this warrior rider is not named the Son of Man but rather the Word of God, the connection between these Christological figures is clear. Once again, a detailed description of the figure is included—he wears many crowns and is clothed with a robe dipped in blood (19:12–13). Such a description conveys both sides of the tension that runs through the gendered Christology of Revelation. The crowns highlight the imperial aspects of the figure. They symbolize divine honor and glory, as well as victory and royalty.[15] The bloodstained robe tells another story, or at least another dimension of the story.

It is not the story of Christ's self-sacrifice, although more than one interpreter has wanted very much to make it so. Mitchell Reddish, for example, argues that the blood on the robe must be Jesus' own, because the description takes place before the battle scene. For this reason, "the bloodstained garment is a reminder of the cross."[16] Along the same line, Reddish quotes with approval the observation of Hanson and Preston that "in the Apocalypse, Christ conquers not by shedding the blood of his enemies, but by shedding his own blood *for his enemies*."[17]

But although the theme of Christ's vicarious death is present in Revelation (though nowhere does it state that this death was for his enemies!), here it is all too clear that the reason for the warrior's bloodied robe is the fact that it has been dipped (βεβαμμένον from βάπτω) in the blood of people killed by God.[18] In fact, as many have recognized, the scene in Revelation echoes Isaiah 63:2–3, where it is God who wears the bloodied robes.[19] In this case, the poet asks God directly about his stained garments: "Why are your robes red and your garments like theirs who tread the winepress?"

God answers,

> I have trodden the winepress alone and from the peoples no one
> was with me; I trod them in my anger and trampled them in my
> wrath; their juice spattered on my garments and stained all my
> robes. (Isaiah 63:3)

Notably, in Revelation, it is not God alone, but his earthly accomplice who tramples God's enemies in anger. His two-edged sword is used to strike down the nations, so that they can be ruled with a rod of iron (19:15). Imperial authority is recalled once more in the midst of this violent imagery, as the rider is described, or rather inscribed, with the name "King of Kings and Lord of Lords" (19:16).

Finally, the appearance of the rider ushers in the "great supper of God," with a main course of carrion. Yet another angel calls for the birds to feast on the flesh of kings, captains, the mighty, horses and riders, indeed the flesh of all, free and slave, small and great (19:17–18). The scene recalls the prophetic image from Ezekiel 39:17–20, in which God commands the Son of Man to invite the birds and wild animals to a great sacrificial feast of the enemies of God who are slaughtered in battle. So also, in the battle scene of Revelation, the enemy "beast" and false prophet are captured and the armies of the kings of the earth are all killed by the sword of the rider.

The battle scene of chapter 19 suggests that in Revelation, the ideal ruler—the Christ of leniency and clemency—has been replaced by a Christ figure who rules nations with an iron rod and slaughters entire armies with a sword. To be sure, the audience is told that the rider is called "faithful and true" and that he judges and wages war justly (19:11). In this way, Revelation presents a display of divine violence founded on a basis of manly virtues. Indeed, the statement in 19:11 seems intended to relieve the tension between the rhetoric of ideal masculine deportment and the image of wrathful, unremitting vengeance on the part of God and his son.

But if the tension is allowed to remain—that is, if the contemporary reader does not excuse the violence of God as a "just violence" (as the first-century audience of Revelation certainly did)—a more interesting aspect of the gender dynamics of Revelation becomes apparent. In fact, by revealing this tension, Revelation may offer the most accurate depiction of imperial masculinity that we have seen thus far in the New Testament. For all the pretensions to an imperial masculine ideal—justice, peace, and the Roman way—the fact remained that Rome, like all empires, was built on the unseemly foundation of blood. Revelation captures that reality all too clearly, but it does so in the construction of its own masculine rulers and alternative imperial city. This is a point to which we will return. First, however, there is the matter of the most prominent Christological image, that of the lamb.

The Lamb

The lamb is first introduced to the audience by way of the distraught seer who is weeping bitterly because no one is worthy to break the seal on the heavenly scroll. The seer is reassured by one of the elders that the Lion of the tribe of Judah, the root of David, has conquered and is thus worthy to open the scroll (5:4–5). (Unlike the Son of Man, the lion *is* featured in the physiognomic handbooks as the most masculine of the animal world.[20]) Of course, what appears is not a lion at all, but a lamb standing as if it had been slaughtered.

At this point, a common interpretive refrain involves the experience of shock on the part of the reader. Loren Johns's description of this reading experience provides a good illustration. "But wait!" he writes. "What John sees is a *lamb*, standing slaughtered, with seven horns and seven eyes. This is a powerful and mind-wrenching switch of images for which the reader is unprepared."[21] Many scholars then go on to suggest that the image of the lamb offers a resistant Christology. For Johns, it represents nonviolent resistance to evil.[22] Similarly, for Brian Blount, the lamb symbolizes weakness and vulnerability, even while it stands as an active figure of nonviolent resistance.[23] As Chris Frilingos remarks, such readings "alight on the lamb as a symbolic rejection of societal values: in a world that idealizes domination, the broken Lamb portends a reversal of the status quo."[24] His own reading, one of the few that attend to the gendered identity of the lamb, understands its slaughtered state as an indication of effeminacy. This, too, would suggest rejection of societal values, though this is not the direction taken by Frilingos. While such readings of "the broken lamb" are powerful and empowering for communities sorely in need of a change in status quo, the nonviolent interpretation of the lamb raises questions.[25]

In fact, before moving more deeply into examination of the lamb, we should pause to take account of the interpretive dilemma that Revelation creates for its readers as a whole. For it is especially this lion turned lamb that epitomizes the dilemma. On the one hand, the book is filled with violent imagery such as that outlined above. On the other hand, as we have seen, some readers of Revelation see its main message to be one of nonviolence. David Barr, for instance, while recognizing the violent imagery, insists on Revelation's ultimate subversion of violence. For Barr, it is "absolutely fundamental to the Apocalypse that the violence through which Jesus is said to conquer evil is the violence done to him."[26] Blount, too, perceives the dilemma as he imagines a response to his argument for the nonviolent resistance of Revelation. " 'Nonviolent?' some critics mutter. What about all the blood-letting that takes place throughout the book?"[27]

A key verse for the nonviolent reading of Revelation is the call for endurance rather than violence in 13:10. "If you are to be taken captive, into captivity you go; if you kill with the sword, with the sword you must be killed. Here is a call for the endurance and faith of the saints." Further arguments for the subversion of violence include the fact that the sword of the Son of Man issues from his mouth. For this reason, it represents "oppositional witness not violent combat."[28] Finally, proponents of this reading often note that for all the imagery of war in the book, actual battles are never depicted. Or, as Barr states, "We have all the paraphernalia of Holy War, but no war."[29]

I admit to ambivalence about this approach to Revelation, perhaps in the same way that Revelation is ambivalent about violence. Admittedly, there is no call for violence on the part of the "saints." Followers of Jesus are not encouraged to take up arms against Rome, but to endure. Rather, the violence of Revelation is portrayed as divine violence against God's enemies. It is also true that because the victory has already been won in the visions of Revelation, the audience is not privy to the actual battle scene. But there are still bodies strewn about the field, and blood flows from the deaths of nearly all the inhabitants of the earth. There is no war, but there is war's deadly aftermath on display. And while I understand how this nonviolent reading, coupled with a hope in God's utter annihilation of the evil enemy, may be critically important for certain communities, it does not dispense with the bloodied bodies. Moreover, for an interpretation such as this, which focuses on the relationship of Revelation's images with the construction of masculinity, it is important to take account of such images alongside Roman imperial masculinity.

So, I return to the lamb. First, this particular lamb was not likely intended as a symbol of weakness. This is not a typical lamb, after all, but one with seven horns and seven eyes. In other apocalyptic literature, the presence of horns is invariably a sign of strength and power. The horns on the beasts of Daniel wage war (Daniel 7:21), symbolize kings who grow in power (Daniel 7:24–25), or represent military strength (Daniel 8:5–7). In 1 Enoch, the Maccabeans are portrayed as lambs who grew horns, that is, became stronger (90:9). This same text links the power symbolized by the horn with vision or insight. When "one great horn sprouted on one of the sheep," he brought vision to the others, opening their eyes (1 Enoch 90:10). In other words, he brought them wisdom. So, too, a lamb with seven horns and seven eyes should be understood as a figure symbolizing strength and wisdom.[30]

Another unusual aspect of this lamb is the fact that it is "standing" as if slaughtered. Being slaughtered and standing do not typically go together, unless this slaughtered state is a thing of the past, which it decidedly is in Revelation. Like the angelic Son of Man or the warrior rider, the image of the standing-as-if-slaughtered lamb is one of the resurrected Jesus. It is true that the scene offers an interpretation of the "slaughtering" that did occur. The praise sung to the lamb celebrates his worthiness gained through his slaughter and the resulting ransom (by his blood) of people from every tribe, language, people, and nation. By now, such language should be easily recognized as indicating a noble death. This heavenly acclamation highlights the manly death of Jesus by way of the slaughter of the lamb. That it is an honorable death is confirmed by other aspects of the acclamation. Because of his death, the lamb is not only worthy to open the scroll, but also to receive power, wealth, wisdom, might, honor, glory, and blessing (Revelation 5:12). Such an acclamation would be familiar to anyone in the Roman world who had heard the praise at a public procession, honoring a man of high status. A later appearance of the lamb robed in white and sharing God's throne further accents his status and divine authority (7:9–17; also 22:3).

Finally, a further indication of the masculine status of the lamb is the heavenly worship that surrounds his appearance. As Aune has shown, the vision of the throne room of Revelation 4–5 has much in common with popular images of Roman court ceremonials.[31] The twenty-four elders prostrating and casting their golden crowns before God and the lamb with hymns and acclamations fit similar descriptions of senators before the imperial throne. The main difference between the Roman court ceremony and the heavenly display in Revelation is precisely the fact that it is heavenly. As Aune notes, the throne room in Revelation is the Roman court in heightened form. It is the rulers of the entire cosmos who are in view. Taken together, the appearance of the lamb, its vicarious death, and the divine honors that result all suggest this is quite a manly lamb after all, in spite of the reference to being slaughtered.

And in any case, after this initial introduction, the image of the slaughtered lamb recedes into the background. In its place come visions of the wrathful lamb from whom every slave and free man hides (6:15–17), the above-mentioned robed lamb on the throne (7:9–17; also 22:3), the lamb standing on Mt. Zion accompanied by 144,000 male virgins (14:1–5), the conquering lamb, who is also named "Lord of Lords and King of Kings" (17:14), and finally the lamb as bridegroom (19:7–9, 21:9). Among these multiple references, only once is the "slaughtered lamb" mentioned again, at 13:8 when the audience learns of the book of life of the lamb that was slaughtered. So while the audience *knows* it is through Jesus' death that he conquers, what they *witness* in Revelation are the vengeful results, or at least the fantasy about the results of his conquering.

That is to say that once again, these images of the lamb, like the figures of the Son of Man and the warrior, represent multiple sides of imperial masculinity and arguably the unseemly loss of ideal masculine deportment. Whereas it was God's anger that produced the bloodbath of chapter 19, in chapter 6 it is the wrath of the lamb as well as God that evokes terror. As Revelation 6:16 depicts, it seems that the full range of human existence—kings, generals, those of high status, the rich, the slaves, the free—would rather be crushed to death by rocks than face the lamb and "the one seated on the throne." Such a reaction is more in keeping with those under the thumb of tyrannical rule than that of an ideal ruler. It is certainly not a response one would expect if the lamb symbolizes nonviolence.

Given this disturbing hint of tyranny in the image of the lamb, it may be useful to recall once again the tyrant of 4 Maccabees, Antiochus Epiphanes.[32] As discussed earlier, 4 Maccabees is very much about masculinity. Janice Capel Anderson and Stephen Moore have shown how the brothers and even the mother are displayed as models of masculine courage and self-control. In contrast, the text insinuates the unmanliness of the tyrant, Antiochus. As each of the seven brothers maintains his reason and self-control in the face of torture, Antiochus becomes increasingly agitated and out of control, losing a grip on his own masculine deportment.[33]

Particularly interesting for our purposes is the appeal that Antiochus makes before the torture begins:

> Just as I am able to punish those who disobey my orders, so I can be a
> benefactor to those who obey me. Trust me, then, and you will
> have positions of authority in my government if you will renounce
> the ancestral tradition of your national life.... But if by disobedi-
> ence you rouse my anger, you will compel me to destroy each and
> every one of you with dreadful punishments through tortures.
> (4 Maccabees 8:6–7, 9)

Like the imperial edicts cited earlier, Antiochus promises rewards and punishments depending on his subjects' response to his demands. To make his point more strongly, as his speech concludes Antiochus orders the instruments of torture to be brought before the brothers (and so before the readers as well). The torture implements are listed in detail, as are the gruesome results. Brothers, mother, and audience are all privy to repeated viewings of blood-smeared torture implements, severed ligaments, crushed bones, dripping gore, and so on.

Martyrdom and torture are also themes in the Book of Revelation, but in Revelation, the graphic and gory description does not involve the suffering of the martyred, nor for that matter the suffering of the lamb. Instead, it is the torture of the enemy that is described in detail. Those who "worship the beast," the narrator informs us, will be tortured by fire and sulfur. This future threat shifts to the present as we hear that "the smoke of their torture goes up forever and ever" (14:10–11).

But the most disturbing aspect of the comparison of 4 Maccabees and Revelation concerns the role of the torturer. If in 4 Maccabees Antiochus is the tyrant who presides over the torture of his opposition, in Revelation it is the lamb. The enemies are tortured "in the presence of the lamb and the holy angels" (14:10). God is implicated, as well. His enemies receive a double dose of his ire—they drink the "wine of his rage poured undiluted into the cup of his anger" (14:10, my translation). Such phrasing recalls the debate regarding the manliness of such angry displays. Surely the author understands this wrathful display as righteous anger. But it is remarkable how closely the conduct of God and his son recalls that of the tyrant Antiochus IV.

Like Antiochus, the saving figures of Revelation will be benefactors to those who obey, giving them an authoritative role in the kingdom. Those who obey will also have their rods of iron, as we will see. But also like Antiochus, God and the lamb will punish and torture those who refuse to obey. Notably, there is even some overlap between what obedience requires. Antiochus tortures the brothers who refuse to abandon the cultic obligations of their communal life in exchange for a governmental office. So also, God and the lamb torture those who participate in the cultic obligations of communal life under Rome—"worship of the beast" or the imperial cult. Which raises the question: Are God and the lamb also "tyrants" whose conduct suggests they have lost key traits of hegemonic masculinity such as self-restraint, reason, and clemency? Of course, the author and the audience for whom the work is intended would not entertain such a question. But the contemporary reader might do well to at least dwell on its implications.

Here we should take another cue from Moore and look one last time at Antiochus, this time as he is confronted by his final victim. Before his death, this youngest brother predicts the demise of Antiochus. Because of his cruelty, "justice has laid frequent and eternal fire and tortures that will never unleash [him]" (4 Maccabees 12:12, my translation). Thus, in terms of the meting out of divine justice, as Moore observes, 4 Maccabees and Revelation are "of a piece."[34] Notably, the son punctuates Antiochus's unmanly conduct, stating, "As a man [ἄνθρωπος], were you not ashamed, you beast, to cut out the tongues of those who have similar feelings and are made of the same stuff as you, and to hurt and torture them like this?" (4 Maccabees 12:13, my translation). In other words, Antiochus is more beast than (hu)man in his conduct.

What does this imply for the gender identity of the lamb? For one thing, it seems the conclusions of Frilingos need to be reversed. Remarking on Revelation 14, he suggests that the lamb's presence during the eternal torture of the enemy "transforms the creature from passive victim to active 'victimizer,' a gendered mutation . . . from effeminacy to masculinity."[35] To be sure, the Christology of the early Christians frequently demanded this type of mutation. But in Revelation, this shift has already occurred before the opening vision of the book. Jesus' death, while important to the book, is an event in the past and is clearly understood as a vicarious, noble sacrifice. Instead, what is unveiled in this Apocalypse is not only the honorable nature of Jesus' death, but also the results of this "conquering," including the tyrannical conduct of the victors as they mete out "justice" against their opposition. But this means that, at least on the basis of chapter 14, the lamb moves not from effeminacy to masculinity, but rather in the reverse direction. If his "conquering" death made him a manly lamb, his vindictive rage moves him down the gender hierarchy, closer to the uncontrolled emotions of the "unman." In other words, while the author introduces the lamb through imitation of the divine honors awarded the imperial ruler, by chapter 14, this imitation has shifted (however unwittingly) to the violence of the imperial beast.

"To the one who conquers, I will give . . . "

Finally, conquering is not reserved for the Christological figures in the Book of Revelation. From the beginning of the work, the Son of Man offers multiple rewards to anyone who conquers. That this conquering also means death for believers is implicit throughout the text, but it is seen most clearly at 12:10–11. Here a heavenly voice announces the coming of the salvation, power, and kingdom of "our God." The voice goes on to proclaim that "our brothers" have conquered Satan, the accuser, through the blood of the lamb, but also with their own blood: "They did not love their life even when faced with death" (12:11, my translation). In other words, they died willingly, like Jesus did.

But although conquering involves death, it is the promise of life and ruling authority that is used to encourage the followers of Christ. Those who conquer are offered permission to eat from the tree of life (2:7), the promise of no second death (2:11), and the inscription of their names in the book of life (3:5). In other words, those who are willing to die for the cause are all promised eternal life in contrast to the destruction that awaits those who oppose God and Christ, and who worship the beast. But it is especially the promise of authority, kingship, and priesthood that highlights the masculine status gained by those who endure. Those in Thyatira are promised authority over the nations, to rule them (like the Son of Man) with an iron rod (2:26–27). The Laodiceans are promised a place with the Son of Man on his throne, just as through his own conquering death he earned a place on his father's throne (3:21). In short, if the Christians in these communities are able to endure and conquer, dying a noble, manly death, they will be rewarded with immortality and participation in divine ruling authority. This sounds very much like achieving an ideal masculinity in the context of the Greco-Roman world.

Other benefits of enduring and conquering are revealed in the course of the book. Because those who endure are saved from the wrath of God and the lamb, they are able to witness the utter destruction of their enemies. If their conquering means death for them, it is only temporary death. On the other hand, as we have seen, their conquering means the eternal torture and death of their opponents. Indeed, chapter 14 is not the only place where horrific images of the enemy's demise are found in Revelation. The torrents of blood flowing from the winepress of God's wrath have already been mentioned.

And there is also the fate of the whore of Babylon, whose flesh is devoured and burned with fire (17:16).[36] The whore, of course, is Rome—a vicious parody of the austere goddess Roma who graced temples throughout the empire.[37] Envisioning this, it seems, is also part of the reward for those who conquer.

Finally, there are two more explicitly gendered images of those who are redeemed, both associated with the lamb, and seemingly at odds with one another. There are the 144,000 male virgins who stand with the lamb on Mt. Zion (14:1–5) and the pure bride prepared for marriage to the lamb (19:7). The male virgins have been interpreted in multiple ways, with many commentators quick to argue that they should not be taken literally.[38] But such a claim does not take us very far, for what in this book should be taken literally? On the other hand, here and elsewhere, the author frequently uses particularly gendered symbolic language to make a point. In this case, the point involves sexual purity—"those who have not defiled themselves with women." As Adela Yarbro Collins and others have pointed out, such continence was relevant in two arenas: in the temple and on the battlefield.[39] Notably, the scene that opens chapter 14 evokes both settings. The 144,000 are standing on Mt. Zion, the location of the Jerusalem temple. The male virgins are referred to with the sacrificial language "first fruits" and "without defect." In other words, they are perfect male specimens offered as sacrifice to God and to the lamb. This same language also recalls the status that is promised to those who conquer: they are to be priests to God (1:6). At the same time, the vision of 144,000 men standing en masse with the lamb suggests an army ready for battle, or "properly pure warriors for God."[40] Thus, in multiple ways, these 144,000 who have been redeemed from the earth are presented as not just male, but thoroughly masculine and aligned with the lamb as their leader.

Another image of the lamb, however, takes us from war camp to wedding feast for the lamb and his bride that follows on the destruction of the whore/ Rome (19:7–9). In complete contrast to the corrupt and demolished Rome, the new city of Jerusalem is free from defect and beautifully adorned for her husband, the lamb. If the new Jerusalem is also symbolic of the redeemed people of God, then the ideal celibate men of Mt. Zion have undergone a gender transformation; they are now wives to the lamb.[41] Still, this is not the first time that the masculine becomes feminine in relation to God, or to Jesus. As we have seen throughout the book, gender identities are fluid and relative in the ancient world.

Resisting or Representing Imperial Masculinity in Revelation?

An increasingly common way of understanding the Book of Revelation is to view it as resistance literature, and for obvious reasons. The most transparent element of this book is its animosity towards Rome, expressed in a violent fantasy of utter annihilation of the city and all who have an interest in its well-being. Collins has suggested that such a fantasy likely served a cathartic function for those who perceived Rome as their enemy.[42] More recently, with the introduction of postcolonial theory, analysis of the nature of resistance in Revelation has become ever more nuanced. Scholars have explored the ways that Revelation becomes entangled in the making of empire even as it actively resists it. For instance, Robert Royalty juxtaposes the sharp critique of imperial wealth that runs through Revelation with the image of the jewel-encrusted new Jerusalem that ultimately descends from heaven to replace Rome. As he puts it, "Opposition to the dominant culture in the Apocalypse is not an attempt to redeem that culture but rather an attempt to replace it with a Christianized version of the same thing. . . . The text creates a new culture of power that mimics the dominant ideology; only the names and labels are changed."[43] Similarly, Stephen Moore argues that "to construct God or Christ, together with their putatively salvific activities, from the raw materials of imperial ideology is not to shatter the cycle of empire but merely to transfer it to a transcendental plane, thereby reinscribing and reifying it."[44]

The use of this raw material to which Moore refers is found in the imitation of imperial edicts in the proclamation to the churches, or in the scenes of heavenly worship modeled after imperial court ceremony. But the raw material for other aspects of Revelation is not found in Roman ideology, at least not Roman masculine ideology. Of the range of expressions of masculine ideology discussed in chapters 2 and 3, none of them involved a blatant celebration of violence, destruction, or cruelty. On the contrary, Caesar Augustus, while thoroughly successful on the battlefield, emphasizes his clemency and moderation toward those he conquered. As we saw early on, rulers who had reputations for cruelty and excessive violence were often charged with effeminacy as well. Such character defects went hand in hand from the perspective of the ancient elite. It is for this reason that Augustus's enemies accused him of both. This is not to say that Augustus and the emperors who followed were not cruel or violent. It is only to say that such behavior was not promoted as particularly masculine—in fact, quite the opposite was true.

So when Revelation portrays a wrathful God who wreaks eternal vengeance on his enemies, it is not drawing on Roman masculine ideology. On the other hand, it may well be mimicking forms of Roman imperial practice. Indeed, more than just mimicking, it seems to magnify such practices. Here Moore's comments about the God in Revelation are certainly right:

> What Revelation seems to be saying is this: If you gouge out the eyes of one of God's witnesses, or even refuse to heed them God will gouge out both of your eyes in return. And not only that but he will puncture your eardrums as well, and tear out your tongue, and sever your spine and plunge you into a timeless torment. Or what amounts to much the same thing, he will have you tortured for all eternity in the presence of his Son and his angels (14:9–11).[45]

Or, to put it a different way, part of the unveiling of Revelation is to pull back the curtain of imperial ideology and reveal the reality of imperial practice. In this way, Revelation exposes the gap between Roman masculine ideology and imperial practice. The only problem is that in doing so, the man or men standing behind the curtain are not the Roman rulers, but God and his son— the avenging angel, the warrior rider, and the horned lamb. In other words, the Book of Revelation mirrors the worst of the violence of Rome in its own saving figures. It is not only the civilized masculinity of Roman imperial rhetoric that is on display, but also a more beastly "unmanliness." In resisting Rome, the author knew enough to imitate and surpass the images of imperial rule with his own visions of God and the lamb's heavenly rule. In this way, the saving figures of Revelation appear as ideal masculine figures worthy of honor. But also present in this resistance to Rome is a call for vengeance. "How long will it be before you judge and avenge our blood on the inhabitants of the earth?" the martyred souls ask God (Revelation 6:10). The immediate response is that they must wait until the full number of martyrs is complete, but the rest of Revelation provides a different answer to the question, displaying divine vengeance in all its fury through the imitation and surpassing of imperial violence. The message is that just as the establishment of *Pax Romana* involved warfare and bloodshed, so massive amounts of blood will be spilt on the way to constructing the peaceful city of Jerusalem. For the author, it appears not to matter that the masculine honor of God and Christ is impugned in the process. What matters most is the concluding vision of the new Jerusalem, the city from which God and those who have "conquered" will rule the nations with a rod of iron.

10

Conclusion

The Multiple Masculinities of Jesus

One of the most persistent questions in the study of the development of Christianity is: how did it happen? How did a tiny Jewish splinter group evolve into the religion of the Roman Empire, so that by the late fourth century, the Jesus who was crucified by the Romans could be transformed into the imperial Jesus that guided Constantine? Although this book has not been an attempt to answer that complex question, a gender-critical analysis such as this one provides more insight into this transformation.

Several studies focusing on late antiquity have already suggested solutions that move in this direction. Michele Salzman, for example, shows how Christian bishops drew in the upper classes through appeals to traditional Roman values such as *nobilitas* and *honos*.[1] Matthew Kuefler's proposal draws on a more explicitly gendered reading of this period. As discussed in the introduction, some have suggested that the emergence of the Principate precipitated a crisis of masculine identity.[2] According to Kuefler, the church offered a new venue in which the increasingly marginalized Roman aristocracy could exercise manly power. Summarizing the crisis conditions of late antiquity, Kuefler explains:

> The threat to masculinity in late antiquity posed by the growing distance between expectation and reality—between the military ideal of manliness and the actual collapse of the empire, between the centrality of political office to

aristocratic identity and the political impotence of the aristocracy, between the ideal of patriarchal marital and familial authority and the declining *patria potestas*—all could be reconciled through the creation of a kind of counterculture that interpreted disjunction as paradox and was invigorated by its dissection from traditional standards rather than frustrated by it. The use of paradox allowed Christian men to claim real manliness in apparent unmanliness.[3]

In other words, during a time of gender crisis, with paradox as their main tool, the Latin fathers convinced the elite class that what was formerly considered unmanly behavior was actually more masculine than the behavior of their non-Christian peers. Especially relevant for this study is Kuefler's understanding of the role of the New Testament in this project. He notes how these Christian writers used biblical models of paradox and inversion, such as Jacob and Paul, to support their point. Additionally, he argues, "The whole of the life of Jesus as remembered in the Gospels, culminating in his ignominious death, also demonstrated how the measure of this world is not God's measure."[4]

Kuefler's study is one of the few that considers the role that ideologies of masculinity played in early Christianity, and his insights into the ambiguous figure of the eunuch are particularly useful. Still, one might conclude from his work that Jesus, "as remembered in the Gospels," was completely immune to the "measure of this world." But having examined a range of New Testament presentations of Jesus in light of ancient masculine ideology, we can see that this is clearly not the case. Often, it was very much the measure of the world that helped determine the shape of Christological expressions. From the Philippians hymn that depicts the extraordinary conduct of Jesus resulting in divine honors to Revelation's armed warrior rider who vanquishes the enemy, the evidence for worldly measures of ideal masculinity are clearly in view.

Such cases suggest that there is more than paradox and inversion at work in New Testament constructions of Jesus. In fact, it is difficult to find a true case of gender inversion, where the feminine is elevated over the masculine, with respect to any New Testament image of Jesus. Instead of simple inversion, a far more complex intersection between New Testament Christology and ancient ideologies of masculinity has emerged from this study. New Testament authors drew on a variety of discourses on ancient masculinity that produced multifaceted Christological constructions. In some cases, these Christological expressions were fully commensurate with broader cultural demands of ideal masculinity. In other cases, New Testament authors made use of more marginalized discourses on masculinity that nevertheless highlighted the masculine status of Jesus and his followers. In still other cases, the presentations of

Jesus expose the contradictions, ambiguity, and ambivalence that were also inherent in Greco-Roman hegemonic masculine ideology. What follows is a brief recapitulation of the different discourses on masculinity used by New Testament authors in their varied portrayals of Jesus as a true man of honor and status.

The Noble and Manly Death of Jesus

Perhaps the earliest and most prominent strategy for construction of a manly Jesus was a reliance on the Greco-Roman noble death traditions. This is not surprising, because it was Jesus' death that most called his masculine honor into question. From a Christological perspective, the vicarious death traditions highlight the saving benefits of Jesus. His death was a salvific death on behalf of others. From a gender-critical perspective, such traditions move the death of Jesus from the cultural arena of humiliating emasculation to that of manly self-sacrifice. Tapping into this Greco-Roman tradition was an important means of revirilizing the otherwise shameful death of Jesus.

Although the earliest application of the dying formula likely predates Paul, he was nevertheless an "early adopter" of the phrase. He used it often to emphasize the vicarious nature of Jesus' suffering and death, shoring up the masculine image of Jesus as well as his own. The Gospel of Mark also made use of this tradition in narrative form. The Markan Jesus himself could teach the audience, by way of instructions to the disciples, that his death was a "ransom for many." Other New Testament writings continue the practice. Meanwhile, references to the crucifixion are already elided in Paul's letter to the Romans, and even more so in later texts like the Pastoral Epistles.

Masculinity through Imperial Imitation

The hegemonic masculinity that is evident in the Greco-Roman period was a masculinity largely defined by the elite men of the empire, beginning especially with Caesar Augustus. As the first emperor, Augustus built on long-standing Greco-Roman traditions of the ideal ruler to build an image of himself as the ideal man. Notably, Augustus had the resources to display this image across the empire. Such displays were further promoted by local elite men hoping to increase their own status vis-à-vis recognition of the ideal manliness of Augustus and other imperial rulers. The writers of the New Testament could hardly hope to compete against this imperial machine in presenting their own manly depiction of Jesus. Still, their convictions about the power and authority of Jesus led to a body of literature that resisted the emperor while promoting its own version of an imperial rule. In every New Testament text examined here, the authors found ways to associate Jesus with some aspect of imperial masculinity. Scholars have long noted this influence in the titles used for Jesus. To call Jesus "savior of the world," "King of kings," or "Lord of lords," and to depict him as one whom his subjects honor and worship, is to evoke the figure of the emperor.

But imperial imitation occurs in more subtle ways than the use of titles, particularly with respect to gender ideology. In some instances, this imitation takes the form of presenting Jesus as the ideal ruler. To present Jesus, as Paul did for example, as one who serves his subjects, judges rightly, and exhibits leniency and clemency is to present him as the ideal manly ruler. The definition for such an ideal ruler comes straight from the Greco-Roman tradition and its cult of virtues. Note that there is no inversion of this ideology, nor is there a paradoxical application to the figure of Jesus. Instead, there is a ready assimilation of the "good king" in the figure of Jesus.

Closely integrated to the idea of the good king, and central to Greco-Roman masculine ideology, are the achievement and display of virtues. In addition to those virtues listed above, various places in the Gospels illustrate a Jesus who is authoritative, wise, dutiful, and (of crucial importance) self-controlled. These virtues are often expressed in the synoptic Gospels through Jesus' role as teacher and healer. Such a display of virtues not only reinforces the ideal manliness of Jesus; it also puts him in the rank of the elite men of the empire. Particularly his extraordinary sense of duty (*pietas*) as seen in the Gospel of Luke and his bravery and self-control in the face of death as exhibited in John are rewarded with heavenly exaltation and a place next to God.

Indeed, as we have seen, the tradition of Jesus' resurrection has strong links to the Roman apotheosis traditions. The Philippians hymn suggests an early link to these traditions, and Matthew and Luke both make use of it in their Gospels. Taken together, traditions of noble death and apotheosis go a long way toward restoring the failed masculinity of Jesus implied by the crucifixion. Moreover, as with the divine men examined in chapter 3, the resurrection/apotheosis traditions associated with Jesus reinforce and eventually strengthen the cultural link between masculinity and divinity.

New Testament scholars have long debated whether various New Testament authors understood Jesus to be divine during his life or only after his death. Such a question is difficult to answer historically because once a figure is divinized, there is a natural tendency to read this status back into their life. This is explicit in the birth stories of Augustus and Apollonius, and apparent also in the way Moses is regarded by others in Philo's *Life*. Moreover, from the perspective of ancient gender ideology, to present someone as an ideal—or "perfect," to use the author of Matthew's expression—implies an ideal masculinity that is commensurate with divine status. To recall Gradel's argument, this does not necessarily mean an ontological divinity (though with respect to Jesus, this will become, of course, a crucial part of later Christian doctrine) as much as a relative divinity.[5] As an ideal masculine figure, Jesus is of higher status than all others, save his heavenly father, and therefore necessarily divine.

The Hypermasculinity of the Ascetic Jesus

In some cases, the depictions of Jesus made use of alternative expressions of masculinity that were in circulation in the broader culture. For example, the sayings of Jesus that suggest an ascetic detachment from the household or family structures do not put him in the mainstream of masculine deportment, but they emphasize his masculinity nonetheless. His instructions to his disciples to embrace a life of simplicity sound much like a Cynic philosopher in search of virtue. The radical image of the voluntary eunuch evoked in Matthew's Gospel is a celibate figure who is "for the Kingdom of God." This alternative means to masculinity is also seen in Paul, who urges a celibate lifestyle for those who can achieve it.

The depiction of certain ascetic aspects of Jesus is one place where imperial masculinity is not guiding the Christological interpretation of Jesus. But, as I have argued throughout, this does not mean that masculinity is no longer in view. Rather, it suggests that while the imperial image was important, perhaps even central, to the virilization of Jesus, it was not used exclusively. The New Testament authors were not opposed to adopting different, sometimes marginalized cultural discourses in their interpretations of Jesus. In the same way that they could use multiple traditions from the Torah and prophets to articulate their understanding of Jesus, so too they were open to multiple ways of presenting his manly conduct. Some of these ways involved direct imitation of the emperor, while others involved the use of discourses from philosophical circles.

Mimicking a Militant Masculinity

Finally, there is the Christology of Revelation. As we have seen, the book is a complex mix of thinly veiled attacks on Roman domination and imitation of imperial military power with all the accompanying pomp and circumstance, along with disturbing representations of "unmanly" political tyranny at its worst. The militant masculinity on display in this work is unique in the New Testament. Elsewhere in the New Testament, the masculine ideology that informs the gendered identity of Jesus is the civilized masculinity of the literate elite. But in Revelation, the manliness of war is on display. Only this book evokes armed warriors stained with blood and battlefields strewn with corpses. Along with this masculinity come a raging vengeance upon and torture of the enemy that are all too familiar in military settings.

The mix of masculinities reflecting both imperial court majesty and the gruesome battlefield points to the ambiguous way in which this author related to cultural expressions of Greco-Roman masculine ideology. To present Jesus as an honorable figure deserving of worship and fidelity meant linking him with standard hegemonic expressions of imperial masculine deportment. God sitting majestically on his throne, issuing judgment of the wicked and the righteous, is, in effect, the image of the emperor writ large—now ruling on a cosmic level rather than just the earthly sphere. At the same time, the apocalyptic genre of the Book of Revelation exposes the experience of "unmanly" tyranny and violent force that was the underside of civilized imperial masculinity. In Revelation, this exposure occurs primarily not through the depiction of Roman violence against its subjects but rather in Rome's defeat before the armies of the Son of Man. At this point, the image of the ideal ruler filled with clemency and benevolence is left behind in favor of ruling authorities (God and the lamb) who take no prisoners and torture the enemy eternally. To be sure, the book includes poignant and powerful images of God dwelling in the midst of mortals wiping every tear from their eyes (Revelation 21:3–4). But meanwhile, the devil, beast, and false prophet are tormented day and night, forever and ever (Revelation 20:10).

Resisting Rome while Embracing Its Masculine Ideal

As we have seen, the disturbing Christological figures in Revelation are born out of political resistance to Rome. And, as we have seen, the assimilation of other aspects of hegemonic masculinity can be understood as strategies of resistance as well. Those places that clearly depict Jesus as surpassing the emperor in power and ruling authority are no doubt intended as challenges to claims of imperial rule. So, too, the places that emphasize Jesus as an ideal ruler may be understood as texts of resistance. In both cases, the ideology of ideal masculine rule is embraced by the author and displayed in the figure of Jesus. Here there is no inversion of masculine ideology, even while there may be resistance to Roman rule.

On this point, the work of James C. Scott has proven particularly helpful.[6] He suggests that subordinate groups or colonized subjects rarely have the privilege of giving voice to the total collapse of a dominant ideology. While Scott does not apply his work to ancient texts such as the New Testament, his insights into cultural resistance are suggestive regarding the form that ideological critique of early Christian writers might take:

> For the great bulk of political life, including most violent conflict, the stakes are less than the conquest of a new world. The conflict will accordingly take a dialogic form in which the language of the dialogue will invariably borrow heavily from the terms of the dominant ideology prevailing in the public transcript.... We may consider the dominant discourse as a plastic idiom or dialect that is capable of carrying an enormous variety of meanings, including those that are subversive of their use as intended by the dominant. The appeal to would-be hegemonic values sacrifices very little in the way of flexibility given how malleable the terms are and has the added advantage of appearing to disavow the most threatening goals. For anything less than completely revolutionary ends the terrain of dominant discourse is the only plausible arena of struggle.[7]

This study has shown the degree to which New Testament authors borrowed heavily from the terms of the dominant discourse on masculinity. And, as we have seen, Greco-Roman masculinity was intricately bound to the broader imperial project. Central to this project was the notion of Rome as a humane civilization brought about through the will of the gods by means of a divinely sanctioned emperor. The idea is found in the well-known verse in Virgil's *Aeneid*: "Remember Rome, these are your skills: to rule over peoples, to impose morality, to spare your subjects and to conquer the proud" (6.851–853). A similar sentiment is expressed in Pliny's *Natural History*, where Italy is eulogized as

> a land which is at once the nursling and the mother of all other lands, chosen by the providence of the gods to make heaven itself more glorious, to unite scattered empires, to make manners gentle, to draw together in converse by community of language the jarring and uncouth tongues of so many nations, to give [hu]mankind civilisation, [*humanitatem homini*], and in a word to become throughout the world the single fatherland of all the races. (3.39)

Thus, as Greg Woolf argues, by the late first century B.C.E., *humanitas* has been formulated as a thoroughly Roman idea, embodying concepts of culture and conduct that Romans regarded as the hallmarks of the aristocracy. In his words, "*Humanitas*...distinguished an elite as cultivated, enlightened, humane and so fitted to rule and lead by example, but it also encapsulated a set of ideals to which all men might aspire."[8] Moreover, as the earlier discussion of Augustus illustrated, the Roman emperor, as the ideal man, was supposed to represent the *humanitas* of the empire. Likewise, the provincial authorities were supposed to represent the emperor, ruling their subjects with virtue, moderation, and self-control.

What the New Testament authors have done, in a variety of ways, is to embrace this masculine ideal and represent it in the figure of Jesus. And at times that very same figure is used to resist Roman political domination. In this sense, Scott's sense of the malleability of the dominant discourse and its use in acts of resistance is certainly right. But, in the case of New Testament depictions of Jesus, it is not so clear that the dominant masculine ideology is resisted. Rather, expressions of hegemonic masculinity in the New Testament figure of Jesus often coexist with implicit and explicit critiques of Roman rule. It is this coexistence, more than the paradox and inversion noted earlier, that contributes to the eventual success of Christianity in the empire.

To put it another way, most cases of resistance to Roman political power in the New Testament can be located in the imitation of imperial masculinity in the figure of Jesus. In this way, Leif Vaage is on target with his claim that it is precisely the way that the New Testament writings resist Roman rule that led to Christianity's eventual success. He notes that by adopting Roman imperial discourse, or, "talking the talk" of Rome, the New Testament writers also imported the imperial impulses that led to Christianity's success.[9] But, I would add that when it comes to gender ideology, "talking the talk" of Rome was not always a strategy of resistance. From a gender-critical perspective, constructing Jesus as an ideal man was necessitated by the demands of masculine ideology. This deeply embedded ideology was not resisted, but was positively embraced both as a means of promoting the status and authority of Jesus *and* as a tool for resisting the dominant political structure. So the Jesus who was crucified by the Roman authorities, the Jesus whose masculinity was stripped bare by the nature of his demise, was already in the New Testament being clothed in Roman masculine garb. From there, the move to the front of Constantine's army was not a difficult one to make. In the end, one could argue that the price that was paid for "using the master's tools," to recall Needham's work,[10] was becoming a tool of the master. Insofar as this was a strategy of resistance, it was perhaps too dangerous to adopt. Dollimore's warning is particularly apt on this point: "Often the subordinate incorporates, in the act of appropriation, more than it knows of the ruling order, and often to its cost."[11] Of course,

Dollimore's statement is only a warning if one believes, as I do, that imperial impulses are not a good thing for the Christian tradition to embrace.

New Testament Christology and Gender Ideology

The story that Kuefler tells of the success of Christianity in late antiquity is a story of threatened masculinity and the church's response. But this same story might well be moved to the first century and the earliest stages of the Christian community. The New Testament depictions of Jesus suggest that in many cases not just a threatened masculinity but the seemingly failed masculine deportment of Jesus resulted in a reaffirmation and elevation of his masculine status. The story of the crucified and resurrected Jesus was also the story of a failed and restored (and improved) masculinity.

This is the gendered story, born out of the emasculating death of Jesus, that is at the center of the Christian Gospel. I would argue that this, too, contributed to the long-term success of Christianity. Such a story is particularly effective for producing an ever-more-entrenched gender ideology that associates masculinity especially with divinity, but also with the virtues—self-control, courage, moderation, and so on. By drawing on the range of discourses on masculinity that were culturally accessible, the New Testament writers made their own powerful contributions to hegemonic masculine ideology in the figure of Jesus—fully man and fully god.

But the figure of Jesus in the New Testament does something more than this. Even in the midst of the highly successful revirilization of Jesus, there are moments of contradictions and ambivalence regarding the masculine ideal. The Gospel of Mark, for example, even while it promotes the idea of a manly death, still lays bare the reality of the crucifixion. From a gender-critical perspective, its stark portrayal of Jesus' death is an unmasking (all too briefly) of the ultimate demands of the ideology of masculinity. The Markan Jesus' anguished cry from the cross is the sound of the cultural expendability of men who are expected to die on demand. The Book of Revelation, too, shows the contradictions of an imperial masculinity that speaks of peace while it wages war.

Finally, the varied discourses used to construct a manly Jesus point to the constructed nature of all such gendered discourses. Theoretically, such an observation is neither profound nor new. But seeing such gender construction at work in the New Testament gives concrete examples of how and why it occurs. Moreover, while I have found an abundance of evidence that shows an interest in the manly construction of Jesus, in the end it is not "manly" but "construction" that I want to emphasize. If many of the expressions of New Testament Christology were driven (not surprisingly) by the cultural demands of ancient gender ideology, it is time to loosen the grip of some of these ancient constructions and allow room for Christological constructions more fitting for the demands of our contemporary setting. As noted in the introduction, many feminist scholars have already begun this work. My hope is that this analysis of the multiple, complex intersections between ancient gender ideology and first-century Christologies can be an additional resource in this project. It is well past the time when we might naively find "Jesus the feminist" in the New Testament. However, we can be critically attuned to the way gender ideologies were always deeply embedded in the religious language and symbols of the ancient world, even in New Testament images of Jesus. Such critical sensitivity can only benefit our attempts to navigate a new course through the ideological complexities and contradictions of our own time.

Notes

CHAPTER I

1. Robert Warren Conant, *The Virility of Christ: A New View* (Chicago: The author, 1915), 12–13.

2. Ibid., 14–15.

3. Bruce Barton, *The Man Nobody Knows: A Discovery of Jesus* (Indianapolis: Bobbs-Merrill, 1925), "How it Came to Be Written."

4. Quoted in David Morgan, *Visual Piety: A History and Theory of Popular Religious Images* (Berkeley: University of California Press, 1998), 119. See also Erika Doss, "Making a 'Virile, Manly Christ': The Cultural Origins and Meanings of Warner Sallman's Religious Imagery," in *Icons of American Protestantism: The Art of Warner Sallman*, ed. David Morgan (New Haven: Yale University Press, 1996), 80. For additional discussion of the manly Jesus of both Barton and Sallman, see Stephen D. Moore, *God's Beauty Parlor: And Other Queer Spaces in and around the Bible* (Stanford, Calif.: Stanford University Press, 2001), 105–17.

5. Rosemary Radford Ruether, *Sexism and God-Talk: Toward a Feminist Theology* (London: SCM, 1983), 116.

6. See, for example, Alicia Craig Faxon, *Women and Jesus* (Philadelphia: United Church Press, 1973); Joan Chamberlain Engelsman, *The Feminine Dimension of the Divine* (Philadelphia: Westminster Press, 1979); Joseph A. Grassi and Carolyn Grassi, *Mary Magdalene and the Women in Jesus' Life* (Kansas City, Mo.: Sheed & Ward, 1986); Elisabeth Moltmann-Wendel, *The Women around Jesus* (New York: Crossroad, 1992); and Carla Ricci, *Mary Magdalene and Many Others: Women Who Followed Jesus* (Minneapolis: Fortress Press, 1994).

7. Ruether, *Sexism and God-Talk*, 137.

8. See, for example, Anne E. Carr, *Transforming Grace: Christian Tradition and Women's Experience* (San Francisco: Harper & Row, 1990); Elizabeth A. Johnson, *She Who Is: The Mystery of God in Feminist Theological Discourse* (New York: Crossroad, 1992); Maryanne Stevens, *Reconstructing the Christ Symbol: Essays in Feminist Christology* (New York: Paulist Press, 1993); Elisabeth Schüssler Fiorenza, *Jesus: Miriam's Child, Sophia's Prophet: Critical Issues in Feminist Christology* (New York: Continuum, 1994); Ellen K. Wondra, *Humanity Has Been a Holy Thing: Toward a Contemporary Feminist Christology* (Lanham, Md.: University Press of America, 1994); Julie M. Hopkins, *Towards a Feminist Christology: Jesus of Nazareth, European Women, and the Christological Crisis* (Grand Rapids, Mich.: William B. Eerdmans, 1995); Julie M. Hopkins and Elisabeth Dieckmann, *Feministiche Christologie: Wie Frauen Heute Von Jesus Reden Können* (Mainz, Germany: Matthais-Grünewald Verlag, 1996); and Lisa Isherwood, *Introducing Feminist Christologies* (London: Sheffield Academic Press, 2001).

9. For a discussion of various feminist approaches to wisdom imagery and Christology, see Schüssler Fiorenza, *Jesus: Miriam's Child, Sophia's Prophet*, 155–62.

10. Johnson, *She Who Is*, 154.

11. Ibid., 165.

12. Caroline Walker Bynum, *Jesus as Mother: Studies in the Spirituality of the High Middle Ages* (Berkeley: University of California Press, 1982). See also Isobel Combes, "Nursing Mother, Ancient Shepherd, Athletic Coach: Some Images of Christ in the Early Church," in *Images of Christ: Ancient and Modern*, ed. Stanley E. Porter, Michael A. Hayes, and David Tombs (Sheffield, England: Sheffield Academic Press, 1997), 113–25.

13. Anne McGuire, "Women, Gender, and Gnosis in Gnostic Texts and Traditions," in *Women and Christian Origins*, ed. Ross Kraemer and Mary Rose D'Angelo (New York: Oxford University Press, 1999), 257–99; Michael A. Williams, "Uses of Gender Imagery in Ancient Gnostic Texts," in *Gender and Religion: On the Complexity of Symbols*, ed. Caroline Walker Bynum, Stevan Harrell, and Paula Richman (Boston: Beacon Press, 1986), 196–227; Michael A. Williams, "Variety in Gnostic Perspectives on Gender," in *Images of the Feminine in Gnosticism*, ed. Karen L. King (Philadelphia: Fortress Press, 1988), 2–22; Karen L. King, "Sophia and Christ in the Apocryphon of John," in *Images of the Feminine in Gnosticism*, ed. Karen L. King (Philadelphia: Fortress Press, 1988), 158–76.

14. Happily, there is now an abundance of such scholarship—too much to credit in one note. I cite here some of the foundational feminist work, along with several more recent examples: Phyllis Trible, *God and the Rhetoric of Sexuality* (Philadelphia: Fortress Press, 1978); Phyllis Trible, *Texts of Terror: Literary-Feminist Readings of Biblical Narratives* (Philadelphia: Fortress Press, 1984); Elisabeth Schüssler Fiorenza, *In Memory of Her: A Feminist Theological Reconstruction of Christian Origins* (New York: Crossroad, 1983); Elisabeth Schüssler Fiorenza, *Bread Not Stone: The Challenge of Feminist Biblical Interpretation* (Boston: Beacon Press, 1984); Adela Yarbro Collins, ed., *Feminist Perspectives on Biblical Scholarship* (Chico, Calif.: Scholars Press, 1985); Letty M. Russell, *Feminist Interpretation of the Bible* (Philadelphia: Westminster Press, 1985);

Elisabeth Schüssler Fiorenza and Shelly Matthews, eds., *Searching the Scriptures*, vol. 1, *A Feminist Introduction* (New York: Crossroad, 1993); Elisabeth Schüssler Fiorenza, Shelly Matthews, and Ann Graham Brock, eds., *Searching the Scriptures*, vol. 2, *A Feminist Commentary* (New York: Crossroad, 1994); Luise Schottroff, *Let the Oppressed Go Free: Feminist Perspectives on the New Testament* (Louisville, Ky.: Westminster John Knox Press, 1993); Harold C. Washington et al., eds., *Escaping Eden: New Feminist Perspectives on the Bible* (Sheffield: Sheffield Academic Press, 1998); Caroline Vander Stichele and Todd C. Penner, *Her Master's Tools? Feminist and Postcolonial Engagements of Historical-Critical Discourse* (Atlanta: Society of Biblical Literature, 2005); Hee An Choi and Katheryn Pfisterer Darr, eds., *Engaging the Bible: Critical Readings from Contemporary Women* (Minneapolis: Fortress Press, 2006); Linda Day and Carolyn Pressler, eds., *Engaging the Bible in a Gendered World: An Introduction to Feminist Biblical Interpretation in Honor of Katharine Doob Sakenfeld* (Louisville, Ky.: Westminster John Knox Press, 2006). In addition, during the past several years Amy-Jill Levine and Marianne Blickenstaff have edited a multivolume series titled *Feminist Companion to the New Testament and Early Christian Writings* (Sheffield, England: Sheffield Academic Press).

15. Greg Woolf, "Becoming Roman, Staying Greek: Culture, Identity and the Civilizing Process in the Roman East," *Proceedings of the Cambridge Philological Society* 40 (1994): 120.

16. Those familiar with New Historicism and Cultural Materialism will detect the influence of these approaches here. For useful introductions, see Catherine Gallagher and Stephen Greenblatt, *Practicing New Historicism* (Chicago: University of Chicago Press, 2000) and John Brannigan, *New Historicism and Cultural Materialism* (New York: St. Martin's Press, 1998). See also my discussion in Colleen M. Conway, "New Historicism and the Historical Jesus in John: Friends or Foes?" in *John, Jesus and History: Critical Appraisals of Critical Views*, ed. Paul Anderson, Felix Just, and Tom Thatcher (Atlanta: Scholars Press, 2007), 203–19.

17. For an annotated bibliography on postcolonial criticism in general and within biblical studies, see Stephen D. Moore, *Empire and Apocalypse: Postcolonialism and the New Testament* (Sheffield, England: Sheffield Phoenix Press, 2006). Seminal work includes Homi K. Bhabha, *The Location of Culture* (London: Routledge, 1994), Gayatri Chakravorty Spivak, "Can the Subaltern Speak?" in *Marxism and the Interpretation of Culture*, ed. Cary Nelson and Lawrence Grossberg (Urbana: University of Illinois Press, 1988), 271–313, and Edward W. Said, *Orientalism* (London: Routledge and Kegan Paul, 1978). Said's work is now published in a twenty-fifth anniversary edition with a new preface by the author (New York: Vintage Books, 2003).

18. See, for example, Stephen D. Moore and Fernando F. Segovia, *Postcolonial Biblical Criticism: Interdisciplinary Intersections* (London: T & T Clark International, 2005); R. S. Sugirtharajah, *The Bible and Empire: Postcolonial Considerations* (Cambridge, England: Cambridge University Press, 2005); Roland Boer and Gerald O. West, eds., *A Vanishing Mediator? The Presence/Absence of the Bible in Postcolonialism* (Atlanta: Society of Biblical Literature, 2001); Musa W. Dubu, *Postcolonial Feminist*

Interpretation of the Bible (St. Louis: Chalice Press, 2000); R. S. Sugirtharajah, *The Postcolonial Bible* (Sheffield, England: Sheffield Academic Press, 1998).

19. The term and analysis of colonial "mimicry" comes from Bhabha, *The Location of Culture*.

20. For a discussion of the emergence of masculinity studies in relation to the New Testament and a review of early work in this area, see Stephen D. Moore, "'O Man, Who Art Thou?': Masculinity Studies and New Testament Studies," in *New Testament Masculinities*, ed. Stephen D. Moore and Janice Capel Anderson (Atlanta: Society of Biblical Literature, 2003), 1–22.

21. See especially John J. Winkler, *The Constraints of Desire: The Anthropology of Sex and Gender in Ancient Greece* (New York: Routledge, 1990) and David M. Halperin, John J. Winkler, and Froma I. Zeitlin, *Before Sexuality: The Construction of Erotic Experience in the Ancient Greek World* (Princeton, N.J.: Princeton University Press, 1990). More recently, see Ralph M. Rosen and I. Sluiter, eds., *Andreia: Studies in Manliness and Courage in Classical Antiquity* (Leiden, the Netherlands: Brill, 2003) and Marilyn B. Skinner, *Sexuality in Greek and Roman Culture* (Oxford: Blackwell, 2005). For a recent classified bibliography of masculinity studies, see Stephen D. Moore and Janice Capel Anderson, eds., *New Testament Masculinities* (Atlanta: Society of Biblical Literature, 2003).

22. For examples of feminist critique of Foucault see Nancy Hartsock, "Foucault on Power: A Theory for Women?" in *Feminism/Postmodernism*, ed. Linda J. Nicholson (New York: Routledge, 1990); Lois McNay, *Foucault and Feminism: Power, Gender and Self* (Cambridge, England: Polity, 1992); and Caroline Ramazanoglu, *Up against Foucault: Explorations of Some Tensions between Foucault and Feminism* (London: Routledge, 1993). For a critique of a Foucaldian approach to classical studies, see Amy Richlin, "Foucault's *History of Sexuality*: A Useful Theory for Women?" in *Rethinking Sexuality: Foucault and Classical Antiquity*, ed. David H. J. Larmour, Paul Allen Miller, and Charles Platter (Princeton, N.J.: Princeton University Press, 1998). An overview of the debate can be found in Marilyn B. Skinner, "Zeus and Leda: The Sexuality Wars in Contemporary Classical Scholarship," *Thamyris* 3 (1996): 103–23. For further discussion, see Moore, "'O Man, Who Art Thou?': Masculinity Studies and New Testament Studies," 20–22.

23. Judith Butler, *Gender Trouble: Feminism and the Subversion of Identity* (New York: Routledge, 1990).

24. Ibid., 140. In simplest terms, this turn from identity to performance is what troubles many feminists who have worked hard to establish an identity politics, especially an identity for women in the political sphere.

25. Some of the early works include Harry Brod, ed., *The Making of Masculinities: The New Men's Studies* (Boston: Allen & Unwin, 1987); Harry Brod and Michael Kaufman, *Theorizing Masculinities* (Thousand Oaks, Calif.: Sage Publications, 1994); David D. Gilmore, *Manhood in the Making: Cultural Concepts of Masculinity* (New Haven, Conn.: Yale University Press, 1990); and Kaja Silverman, *Male Subjectivity at the Margins* (New York: Routledge, 1992).

26. Tim Carrigan, Bob Connell, and John Lee, "Toward a New Sociology of Masculinity," in *The Making of Masculinities: The New Men's Studies*, ed. Harry Brod (Boston: Allen & Unwin, 1987), 86.

27. Ibid., 92.

28. But see F. Gerald Downing, "A Bas Les Aristos: The Relevance of Higher Literature for the Understanding of the Earliest Christian Writings," *Novum Testamentum* 30 (1988): 212–30. Downing discusses the multiple ways in which social classes may have overlapped, and he focuses on the ways that cultural ideas may have been disseminated to widely varying audiences in the Greco-Roman world.

29. Sally Robinson, "Pedagogy of the Opaque: Teaching Masculinity Studies," in *Masculinity Studies and Feminist Theory: New Directions*, ed. Judith Kegan Gardiner (New York: Columbia University Press, 2002), 151.

30. Bryce Traister, "Academic Viagra: The Rise of American Masculinity Studies," *American Quarterly* 52 (2000): 274–304. There are exceptions, as in the studies of black masculinity that emerges not as a reaction to crisis but as "the gradual and often rebellious appropriation of prohibited masculine positionality." See Traister for a bibliography of these studies.

31. Michel Foucault, *The History of Sexuality*, vol. 3, *The Care of the Self* (New York: Vintage Books, 1988), 95.

32. See Carlin A. Barton, *The Sorrows of the Ancient Romans: The Gladiator and the Monster* (Princeton, N.J.: Princeton University Press, 1993); Brent D. Shaw, "Body/Power/Identity: Passions of the Martyrs," *Journal of Early Christianity Studies* 4 (1996): 269–312; and Mathew Kuefler, *The Manly Eunuch: Masculinity, Gender Ambiguity, and Christian Ideology in Late Antiquity* (Chicago: University of Chicago Press, 2001).

33. Examples of such contemporary studies include Sally Robinson, *Marked Men: White Masculinity in Crisis* (New York: Columbia University Press, 2000); Anthony W. Clare, *On Men: Masculinity in Crisis* (London: Chatto & Windus, 2000); Brian Taylor, *Responding to Men in Crisis: Masculinities, Distress and the Postmodern Political Landscape* (London: Routledge, 2006); and Tim Edwards, *Cultures of Masculinity* (London: Routledge, 2006).

34. Edwards argues that there is little evidence "to endorse an overall masculinity in crisis thesis other than to say that masculinity is perhaps partially constituted *as* crisis" (*Cultures of Masculinity*, 24).

35. Traister, "Academic Viagra: The Rise of American Masculinity Studies," 296.

36. Dale B. Martin, "Contradictions of Masculinity: Ascetic Inseminators and Menstruating Men in Greco-Roman Culture," in *Generation and Degeneration: Tropes of Reproduction in Literature and History from Antiquity through Early Modern Europe*, ed. Valeria Finucci and Kevin Brownlee (Durham, N.C.: Duke University Press, 2001), 106. Similarly, Catherine Gallagher remarks that one of the early interests of new historicists was to show that "under certain historical circumstances, the display of ideological contradictions is completely consonant with the maintenance of oppressive social relations." Gallagher, "Marxism and the New Historicism," in *The New Historicism*, ed. H. Aram Veeser (New York: Routledge, 1989), 44.

37. Moore is addressing the Markan narrative in particular, but his remarks are appropriate for the passion tradition in general. Moore, " 'O Man, Who Art Thou?': Masculinity Studies and New Testament Studies," 11.

38. Oscar Cullmann, *The Christology of the New Testament*, trans. Shirley C. Guthrie and Charles A. M. Hall, rev. ed. (Philadelphia: Westminster Press, 1959). See also Reginald Horace Fuller, *The Foundations of New Testament Christology* (New York: Scribner, 1965) and Ferdinand Hahn, *The Titles of Jesus in Christology: Their History in Early Christianity* (New York: World Publishing Co., 1969).

39. Marinus de Jonge, *Christology in Context: The Earliest Christian Response to Jesus* (Philadelphia: Westminster Press, 1988).

40. Frank J. Matera, *New Testament Christology* (Louisville, Ky.: Westminster John Knox Press, 1999), 3.

41. For examples, see C. Kavin Rowe, *Early Narrative Christology: The Lord in the Gospel of Luke* (Berlin: Walter de Gruyter, 2006); Richard A. Burridge, "From Titles to Stories: A Narrative Approach to the Dynamic Christologies of the New Testament," in *Person of Christ*, ed. Stephen R. Holmes and Rae Murray (London: T & T Clark, 2005), 37–60; Terrence L. Donaldson, "The Vindicated Son: A Narrative Approach to Matthean Christology," in *Contours of Christology in the New Testament*, ed. Richard N. Longenecker (Grand Rapids, Mich.: Eerdmans, 2005), 100–121; Elizabeth Struthers Malbon, "The Christology of Mark's Gospel: Narrative Christology and the Markan Jesus," in *Who Do You Say That I Am? Essays on Christology*, ed. Mark Allan Powell and David R. Bauer (Louisville, Ky.: Westminster John Knox Press, 1999), 33–48; Mark Coleridge, *The Birth of the Lukan Narrative: Narrative as Christology in Luke 1-2* (Sheffield, England: JSOT Press, 1993); M. Eugene Boring, "Narrative Christology in the Apocalypse," *Catholic Biblical Quarterly* 54 (1992): 702–23.

42. For discussion of the shift from origin to reception and its implications for the study of New Testament Christology, see Dieter Zeller, "New Testament Christology in Its Hellenistic Reception," *New Testament Studies* 47 (2001): 312–33.

CHAPTER 2

1. Diogenes reports that the same saying was attributed to Socrates. Plutarch reports that Plato was grateful to be a man rather than a beast, a Greek rather than a barbarian, and born in the time of Socrates (*Marius* 46.I).

2. The term comes from Jonathan Walters, "Invading the Roman Body: Manliness and Impenetrability in Roman Thought," in *Roman Sexualities*, ed. Judith P. Hallett and Marilyn B. Skinner (Princeton, N.J.: Princeton University Press, 1997), 29–43.

3. On similarities and differences in sexual practices between Greeks and Romans, see Craig A. Williams, *Roman Homosexuality: Ideologies of Masculinity in Classical Antiquity* (New York: Oxford University Press, 1999), 62–95. Such differences have little effect on the basic ideology that I will outline in this chapter.

4. Jane Gardner, "Sexing a Roman: Imperfect Men in Roman Law," in *When Men Were Men: Masculinity, Power, and Identity in Classical Antiquity*, ed. Lin Foxhall and J. B. Salmon (London: Routledge, 1998), 136–52.

5. Carlin A. Barton, *Roman Honor: The Fire in the Bones* (Berkeley: University of California Press, 2001), 38.

6. Thomas W. Laqueur, *Making Sex: Body and Gender from the Greeks to Freud* (Cambridge, Mass.: Harvard University Press, 1990).

7. Ibid., 26.

8. For a discussion of the gender implications of the Hebrew sacrificial system as reflected in Leviticus and other biblical texts, see Nicole Ruane, *Sacrifice, Purity and Gender in Priestly Law* (Cambridge University Press, forthcoming).

9. John J. Winkler, "Laying Down the Law: The Oversight of Men's Behavior in Classical Athens," in *Before Sexuality: The Construction of Erotic Experience in the Ancient Greek World*, ed. John J. Winkler, David M. Halperin, and Froma I. Zeitlin (Princeton, N.J.: Princeton University Press, 1990), 182.

10. Maud W. Gleason, *Making Men: Sophists and Self-Presentation in Ancient Rome* (Princeton, N.J.: Princeton University Press, 1995), xxii.

11. Quoted in Elizabeth Cornelia Evans, *Physiognomics in the Ancient World*, vol. 59, Transactions of the American Philosophical Society (Philadelphia: American Philosophical Society, 1969).

12. Ibid., 7 8.

13. Ibid., 8–9.

14. Maud W. Gleason, "The Semiotics of Gender: Physiognomy and Self-Fashioning in the Second Century C.E.," in *Before Sexuality: The Construction of Erotic Experience in the Ancient Greek World*, ed. John J. Winkler, David M. Halperin, and Froma I. Zeitlin (Princeton, N.J.: Princeton University Press, 1990) 399–402. Tamsyn Barton, *Power and Knowledge: Astrology, Physiognomics, and Medicine under the Roman Empire* (Ann Arbor: University of Michigan Press, 1994).

15. Barton, *Power and Knowledge*, 117. Note that both *kinaidos* (or *cinaedus*) and *androgyne* were derogatory references to one perceived as less than a man. See chapter 3, "From Octavian to Augustus," for a more detailed discussion of *cinaedus*.

16. Gleason, "The Semiotics of Gender," 412–13. This is Gleason's composite translation of Adamantios, 2.52, 1.415–16; Polemo, 61, 1.276F; and Anon. Lat. 98, 2.123–24F. See Gleason, "The Semiotics of Gender," 352.

17. The same story is told of Cleanthes by Diogenes, 7.173.

18. Gardner, "Sexing a Roman," 140–41.

19. Ibid., 145–46.

20. Theodor Mommsen, Paul Krueger, and Alan Watson, eds., *The Digest of Justinian* (Philadelphia: University of Pennsylvania Press, 1985).

21. Gardner, "Sexing a Roman," 146.

22. Walters, "Invading the Roman Body," 30.

23. For another lively discussion of men versus unmen in the ancient world, see Stephen D. Moore, *God's Beauty Parlor: And Other Queer Spaces in and around the Bible* (Stanford, Calif.: Stanford University Press, 2001), 135–46.

24. On the contradiction between the demands for generativity and self-control in the masculine role, see Dale B. Martin, "Contradictions of Masculinity: Ascetic Inseminators and Menstruating Men in Greco-Roman Culture," in *Generation and*

Degeneration: Tropes of Reproduction in Literature and History from Antiquity through Early Modern Europe, ed. Valeria Finucci and Kevin Brownlee (Durham, N.C.: Duke University Press, 2001), 81–108,

25. Amy Richlin, *The Garden of Priapus: Sexuality and Aggression in Roman Humor*, rev. ed. (New York: Oxford University Press, 1992), 66–67.

26. Percival Turnbull, "The Phallus in the Art of Roman Britain," *Bulletin of the Institute of Archeology* 15 (1978): 199–206.

27. Williams, *Roman Homosexuality*, 127.

28. Mathew Kuefler, *The Manly Eunuch: Masculinity, Gender Ambiguity, and Christian Ideology in Late Antiquity* (Chicago: University of Chicago Press, 2001), 19.

29. J. Rufus Fears, "The Cult of Virtues and Roman Imperial Theology," *Aufstieg und Niedergang der römischen Welt* II.17.2 (1981): 850.

30. Ibid.

31. See discussion in Kuefler, *The Manly Eunuch*, 19.

32. On the similarities between the "subject" of Stoic philosophy and first-century B.C.E./C.E. romance novels, see Judith Perkins, *The Suffering Self: Pain and Narrative Representation in the Early Christian Era* (London: Routledge, 1995), 77–103.

33. Catharine Edwards, *The Politics of Immorality in Ancient Rome* (Cambridge, England: Cambridge University Press, 1993), 63–97.

34. Kuefler, *The Manly Eunuch*, 26–29.

35. Edwards, *The Politics of Immorality in Ancient Rome*, 85.

36. Later Jerome will reflect the same attitude regarding sex in marriage and quote a lost text of Seneca in support of his position: "Any love for another's wife is scandalous; so is too much love for one's own wife. A prudent man should love his wife with discretion, and so control his desire and not be led into copulation. Nothing is more impure than to love one's wife as if she were a mistress. . . . Men should appear before their wives not as lovers but as husbands" (Adversus Jovinianum 1.49).

37. See, for example, Suetonius *Jul* 4.4; Seneca *Ep.* 52.12; Juvenal 9.133; Ammianus 17.11.

38. While a detailed discussion of "homosexuality" would take us too far afield, scholars such as Veyne and Williams have convincingly argued that whom one had sex with was much less important than how one had sex. Except for the case of sex with free men or married women in Rome, one could acceptably have sex with men, usually boys, or women. See Philippe Ariès and André Béjin, *Western Sexuality: Practice and Precept in Past and Present Times* (Oxford: Blackwell, 1985) and Williams, *Roman Homosexuality*.

39. Williams, *Roman Homosexuality*, 142–53.

40. Richlin, *The Garden of Priapus*, 91–92.

41. Edwards, *The Politics of Immorality in Ancient Rome*, 84.

42. Marcus Aurelius, *Meditations*, trans. Maxwell Staniforth (Baltimore: Penguin Books, 1964).

43. On the "passion therapists" that arose in the second century to advise men on how best to control their anger, see David Brakke, "The Passions and the Social

Construction of Masculinity," paper presentation, Hellenistic Moral Philosophy Section, SBL Annual Meeting (Orlando, November 21–24, 1998).

44. Plutarch's provides a compromise. Olympian gods never got angry; only the lesser divine forces such as furies and daimones (*Cohib. ira* 9). See William V. Harris, *Restraining Rage: The Ideology of Anger Control in Classical Antiquity* (Cambridge, Mass.: Harvard University Press, 2001), 120.

45. KD 1. Hermannus Usener, ed., *Epicurea*. Studia Philologica 3 ("L'Erma" di Bretschneider: Rome, 1963), 71.

46. Harris, *Restraining Rage*, 394–95.

47. Brakke, "The Passions and the Social Construction of Masculinity," 26.

48. For further discussion of the dilemma that the anti-anger sentiment created for early Christians, see Harris, *Restraining Rage*.

49. Basil, *Ascetical Works*, trans. Monica Wagner, vol. 9, The Fathers of the Church (Washington: Catholic University of America Press, 1950).

50. See Barton, *Roman Honor*, 39.

51. Williams, *Roman Homosexuality*, 142.

52. Ibid., 141.

53. W. Martin Bloomer, "Schooling in Persona: Imagination and Subordination in Roman Education," *Classical Antiquity* 16 (1997): 60.

54. Morgan points out that the Greek educational system relied on traditional literature more heavily than the Roman system did. Roman education also involved gnomic maxims, but the Romans were also interested in looking to the examples of great men of the past for instruction. So Quintilian claims, "Strong as the Greeks are in precepts, the Romans are as strong in examples, which is better" (12.2.30). Teresa Morgan, *Literate Education in the Hellenistic and Roman Worlds* (Cambridge, England: Cambridge University Press, 1998), 144–45.

55. Ibid., 135–36.

56. Ibid.

57. Amy Richlin, "Gender and Rhetoric: Producing Manhood in the Schools," in *Roman Eloquence: Rhetoric in Society and Literature*, ed. William J. Dominik (London: Routledge, 1997).

58. Joy Connolly, "Mastering Corruption: Constructions of Identity in Roman Oratory," in *Women and Slaves in Greco-Roman Culture: Differential Equations*, ed. Sandra R. Joshel and Sheila Murnaghan (London: Routledge, 2001), 135.

59. Catherine Atherton, "Children, Animal, Slaves and Grammar," in *Pedagogy and Power: Rhetorics of Classical Learning*, ed. Yun Lee Too and Niall Livingstone (Cambridge, England: Cambridge University Press, 1998), 226.

60. Maud W. Gleason, "Truth Contests and Talking Corpses," in *Constructions of the Classical Body*, ed. James I. Porter (Ann Arbor: University of Michigan Press, 1999), 301.

61. Laur, II 49. Cited in Raffaella Cribiore, *Gymnastics of the Mind: Greek Education in Hellenistic and Roman Egypt* (Princeton, N.J.: Princeton University Press, 2001), 220.

62. Ibid., 220.

CHAPTER 3

1. Angela Hobbs, *Plato and the Hero: Courage, Manliness, and the Impersonal Good* (Cambridge, England: Cambridge University Press, 2000), 14–15.

2. Portions of the following section appear in Colleen Conway, "Philo of Alexandria and Divine Relativity," *Journal for the Study of Judaism* 34 (2003): 471–91.

3. Mary Beard, John A. North, and S. R. F. Price, *Religions of Rome: Volume 1: A History* (Cambridge, England: Cambridge University Press, 1998), 141.

4. Paul Zanker, *The Power of Images in the Age of Augustus* (Ann Arbor: University of Michigan Press, 1990), 188–92, esp. 92.

5. Larry W. Hurtado, *One God, One Lord: Early Christian Devotion and Ancient Jewish Monotheism,* 2nd ed. (Edinburgh: T&T Clarke, 1998).

6. Martha Himmelfarb, *Ascent to Heaven in Jewish and Christian Apocalypses* (New York: Oxford University Press, 1993).

7. Ittai Gradel, *Emperor Worship and Roman Religion* (Oxford: Oxford University Press, 2004).

8. Ibid., 69.

9. Ibid., 26.

10. Ibid., 101.

11. Studies that were helpful to the following discussion include Fergus Millar and Erich Segal, *Caesar Augustus: Seven Aspects* (Oxford: Clarendon Press, 1984); Kurt A. Raaflaub, Mark Toher, and G. W. Bowersock, eds., *Between Republic and Empire: Interpretations of Augustus and His Principate* (Berkeley: University of California Press, 1990); Anton Powell, ed., *Roman Poetry and Propaganda in the Age of Augustus* (London: Bristol Classical Press, 1992); Ronald Mellor, *Augustus and the Creation of the Roman Empire: A Brief History with Documents* (New York: Palgrave Macmillan, 2006); and Karl Galinsky, *The Cambridge Companion to the Age of Augustus* (Cambridge, England: Cambridge University Press, 2005).

12. See especially Zanker, *The Power of Images in the Age of Augustus.* Zanker has been highly influential, but not without critics. See for example, John Elsner, "Cult and Sculpture: Sacrifice in the Ara Pacis Augustae," *Journal of Roman Studies* 81 (1991), 50–61. Also Jas Elsner, *Art and the Roman Viewer: The Transformation of Art from the Pagan World to Christianity* (Cambridge, England: Cambridge University Press, 1995), esp. 164–67, and J. Pollini, "Man or God: Divine Assimilation and Imitation in the Late Republic and Early Principate," in *Between Republic and Empire: Interpretations of Augustus and His Principate,* ed. Kurt A. Raaflaub, Mark Toher, and G. W. Bowersock (Berkeley: University of California Press, 1990), 334–57.

13. Judith P. Hallett, "Perusinae Glandes and the Changing Image of Augustus," *American Journal of Ancient History* 2 (1977): 151–71.

14. As Hallett notes, the gendered attacks against Fulvia continued even many years after her death, as indicated in Velleius Paterculus's comment, *nihil muliebre praeter corpus gerens,* "she had nothing womanly about her save for her body" (2.74). See also Plutarch's accusations against her lack of interest in womanly pursuits (*Antony* 10.3). Ibid.: 157 and 67, nt. 38.

15. See nos. 3, 4, and 5 in ibid.: 152–53.

16. For an overview on the use of sexual slander in the ancient world, see Jennifer Wright Knust, *Abandoned to Lust: Sexual Slander and Ancient Christianity* (New York: Columbia University Press, 2006).

17. Craig A. Williams, *Roman Homosexuality: Ideologies of Masculinity in Classical Antiquity* (New York: Oxford University Press, 1999), 98–99.

18. Ibid., 172–77, esp. 177.

19. Such gendered attacks were common across the ancient world, especially in the form of sexual slander. See Knust, *Abandoned to Lust*, 15–50.

20. Zvi Yavetz, "The *Res Gestae* and Augustus' Public Image," in *Caesar Augustus: Seven Aspects*, ed. Fergus Millar and Erich Segal (Oxford: Clarendon Press, 1984) 3.

21. Jane Bellemore, ed., *Nicolaus of Damascus Life of Augustus* (Bristol, England: Bristol Classical Press, 1984). According to Bellemore, Velleius Paterculus, Suetonius, and Dio Cassius all seemed to rely on the autobiography and to be independent of each other. The latter two cite the autobiography directly (*Suet. Aug.* 2.3, 27.4 and 62.2; Dio 44.35.3). Vellius, the earlier work, shares some of the material that Suetonius claims to be quoting from Augustus. Nicolaus, the earliest source of all, writes as a contemporary of Augustus. His Ἀγωγή τοῦ Βίου Καίσαρος was written around 25–23 B.C.E. Augustus stopped work on his autobiography in 25 B.C.E.

22. Nicolaus was a Greek, the son of an affluent father who provided him with a Hellenistic education. He is reported to have tutored the children of Antony and Cleopatra in Rome. Later (ca. 20 B.C.E) he left the imperial household and served as a close advisor to Herod of Judaea. See ibid., xv–xvii.

23. In categorizing ancient biographies, Charles Talbert considers Nicolaus's work as the type that seeks to correct a mistaken impression of a man. Charles H. Talbert, "Biographies of Philosophers and Rulers as Instruments of Religious Propaganda in Mediterranean Antiquity," *Aufstieg und Niedergang der römischen Welt* II.16.2 (1978): 1619–51. The evidence suggests that in large part what Nicolaus wants to refute is an unmanly image of the young Octavian.

24. I have relied primarily on Bellemore's text and translation. All paragraph markings refer to her text.

25. On the medical logic that probably lies behind this statement, see Dale B. Martin, "Contradictions of Masculinity: Ascetic Inseminators and Menstruating Men in Greco-Roman Culture," in *Generation and Degeneration: Tropes of Reproduction in Literature and History from Antiquity through Early Modern Europe*, ed. Valeria Finucci and Kevin Brownlee (Durham, N.C.: Duke University Press, 2001), 83–84. Expenditure of semen was regarded as a potential loss of strength; and, according to Aristotle, sexual intercourse lowered the voice (*Hist. an.* 581a21). One would think the latter would be desirable for masculine deportment, but it may reflect a fear of becoming *too* low and thus impairing one's public-speaking ability.

26. Yavetz, "The *Res Gestae* and Augustus' Public Image," 3.

27. Hallett adds to the picture the various reports of Octavian's adulterous affairs (e.g., Suetonius, *Augustus*, 71.1), suggesting that during the decade between Perusia

and Actium, Octavian may not have objected to a reputation as womanizer, given the alternative being suggested by his enemies. Hallett, "Perusinae Glandes and the Changing Image of Augustus," 160.

28. Elsewhere Dio reports that Antony dressed like an Egyptian and posed for pictures with Cleopatra. He represented Osiris or Dionysus, while she posed as Selene of Isis (50.5.2–3).

29. On the dates of construction, see Zanker, *The Power of Images in the Age of Augustus*, 73. Zanker notes that as early as 28 b.c.e., the adjacent park is already open to the public.

30. Konrad Kraft, "Der Sinn Des Mausoleum Des Augustus," *Historia* 16 (1967). See also Yavetz, "The *Res Gestae* and Augustus' Public Image," 6–7, and Zanker, *The Power of Images in the Age of Augustus*, 72–77.

31. This gender construction also took place quite literally through the building program of Augustus. The art and architecture of Rome are more than can be ana-lyzed here. Two provocative studies that do are Barbara Kellum, "The Phallus as Signifier: The Forum of Augustus and Rituals of Masculinity," in *Sexuality in Ancient Art: Near East, Egypt, Greece, and Italy*, ed. Natalie Kampen (Cambridge, England: Cambridge University Press, 1996), 170–83, and Indra Kagis McEwen, *Vitruvius: Writing the Body of Architecture* (Cambridge, Mass.: MIT Press, 2003).

32. Zanker, *The Power of Images in the Age of Augustus*, 35.

33. Edwin S. Ramage, *The Nature and Purpose of Augustus' "Res Gestae"* (Weis-baden, Germany: Franz Steiner Verlag, 1987), 102.

34. Suetonius reports that Augustus left with the Vestal Virgins three rolls to be read in the Senate after his death, one of which contained a list of his accomplish-ments. Along with posting this list at the entrance to the Mausoleum, it was to be copied and posted in many other temples of Augustus throughout the empire (*Aug.* 101). Three copies have been discovered in Asia Minor alone, the most complete of which was found in the temple of Rome and Augustus in Ancyra. See the introduction by Frederick W. Shipley, trans., *Velleius Paterculus. Res Gestae Divi Augusti*, Loeb Classical Library 152 (Cambridge, Mass.: Harvard University Press, 1979), 333.

35. G. W. Bowersock, "The Pontificate of Augustus," in *Between Republic and Empire: Interpretations of Augustus and His Principate*, ed. Kurt A. Raaflaub, Mark Toher, and G. W. Bowersock (Berkeley: University of California Press, 1990), 393.

36. Yavetz, "The *Res Gestae* and Augustus' Public Image," 14.

37. Michael Grant, *From Imperium to Auctoritas: A Historical Study of Aes Coinage in the Roman Empire, 49 B.C.–A.D. 14* (Cambridge, England: Cambridge University Press, 1946), 443.

38. Ramage, *The Nature and Purpose of Augustus' "Res Gestae,"* 42–43.

39. For a concise review of the debate through the twentieth century, see ibid., 136–39.

40. Yavetz, "The *Res Gestae* and Augustus' Public Image," 12.

41. Ibid.

42. Brian Bosworth, "Augustus, the *Res Gestae* and Hellenistic Theories of Apotheosis," *Journal of Roman Studies* 89 (1999): 13.

43. Ernst H. Kantorowicz's concept of the king's two bodies evident in medieval political theology is relevant here. One of these bodies is a "body natural" that is subject to passions and death; the other is the "body politic," which is not subject to passions or death because the body of the king never dies. Ernst Hartwig Kantorowicz, *The King's Two Bodies: A Study in Mediaeval Political Theology* (Princeton, N.J.: Princeton University Press, 1957), 13. For scholars who have considered his ideas in relation to the Roman emperor, see Florence Dupont, "The Emperor-God's Other Body," in *Fragments for a History of the Human Body: Part Three*, ed. Michael Feher (New York: Zone, 1989), 397–419, and McEwen, *Vitruvius: Writing the Body of Architecture*, 227.

44. McEwen, *Vitruvius: Writing the Body of Architecture*, 251.

45. John Pollini, "The Augustus from Prima Porta and the Transformation of the Polykleitan Heroic Ideal: The Rhetoric of Art," in *Polykleitos, the Doryphoros, and Tradition*, ed. Warren G. Moon (Madison, Wis.: University of Wisconsin Press, 1995), 268.

46. The following discussion is modified from Conway, "Philo of Alexandria and Divine Relativity."

47. For a detailed discussion of Philo's use of θήλεια νόσος see Holger Szesnat, " 'Pretty Boys' in Philo's De Vita Contemplativa," *Studia Philonica Annual* 10 (1998): 87–107.

48. Maud W. Gleason, "The Semiotics of Gender: Physiognomy and Self-Fashioning in the Second Century C.E.," in *Before Sexuality: The Construction of Erotic Experience in the Ancient Greek World*, ed. John J. Winkler, David M. Halperin, and Froma I. Zeitlin (Princeton, N.J.: Princeton University Press, 1990), 389–415.

49. Such a change was conceivable from the ancient perspective. The elder Pliny asserts that "the transformation of females into males is not an idle story" and goes on to cite several examples, including an eyewitness account of a woman changing into a man on the day of her marriage (*Nat.* 7.4.36–38).

50. While it is clear that Philo sees both the potential to progress in manliness (piety) and the danger of slipping into femininity (degradation), he conceives of this only for the man. In her study of Philo's perception of women, Dorothy Sly has convincingly demonstrated that Philo "simply did not raise the question" of women's spiritual growth. Dorothy Sly, *Philo's Perception of Women* (Atlanta: Scholars Press, 1990), 223.

51. For further discussion of divine impregnation in Philo, see Richard Arthur Baer, *Philo's Use of the Categories Male and Female* (Leiden, the Netherlands: Brill, 1970), 55–64.

52. Jean Laporte, "Philo in the Tradition of Biblical Wisdom Literature," in *Aspects of Wisdom in Judaism and Early Christianity*, ed. Robert Louis Wilken (Notre Dame, Ind.: University of Notre Dame Press, 1975), 118–19.

53. Baer, *Philo's Use of the Categories Male and Female*, 57–58, nt. 6.

54. For a comparison of the Platonic model of the philosopher-king and Philo's description of Moses, see Carl R. Holladay, *Theios Aner in Hellenistic-Judaism: A Critique of the Use of This Category in New Testament Christology* (Missoula, Mont.: Scholars Press, 1977), 103–98; Wayne Meeks, "Moses as God and King," in *Religions in Antiquity: Essays in Memory of Erwin Ramsdell Goodenough*, ed. Jacob Neusner, 354–71 (Leiden, the

Netherlands: Brill, 1968); and E. Ramsdell Goodenough, *By Light, Light: The Mystic Gospel of Hellenistic Judaism* (New Haven, Conn.: Yale University Press, 1935).

55. Daniel H. Garrison, *Sexual Culture in Ancient Greece* (Norman: University of Oklahoma Press, 2000), 119.

56. On the scholarly debate about whether Philo means what he says when he calls Moses a god, see Conway, "Philo of Alexandria and Divine Relativity."

57. Wendy J. Cotter, "Greco-Roman Apotheosis Traditions and the Resurrection Appearances in Matthew," in *The Gospel of Matthew in Current Study: Studies in Memory of William G. Thompson S.J*, ed. David E. Aune (Grand Rapids, Mich.: Eerdmans, 2001), 147–48. Cotter's discussion of Ovid's *Metamorphoses* points to the deified Julius seeing into the future and predicting both the rise of Augustus as ruler of the world and his apotheosis.

58. Ibid., 148.

59. Baer, *Philo's Use of the Categories Male and Female*, 19.

60. This Baer also recognizes. "Philo frequently associates maleness with the realm of the asexual, insofar as it is shown that becoming male is roughly equivalent to becoming a virgin." Ibid., 66.

61. Sharon Lea Mattila, "Wisdom, Sense Perception, Nature and Philo's Gender Gradient," *Harvard Theological Review* 89 (1996): 106.

62. Annewies van den Hoek, "Endowed with Reason or Glued to the Senses: Philo's Thoughts on Adam and Eve," in *The Creation of Man and Woman*, ed. G. P. Luttikhuizen (Leiden, the Netherlands: Brill, 2000).

63. Erkki Koskenniemi, "Apollonius of Tyana: A Typical Theios Anhr?" *Journal of Biblical Literature* 117 (1998): 455–67. See also Erkki Koskenniemi, *Apollonios Von Tyana in Der Neutestamentlichen Exegese* (Tübingen, Germany: Mohr, 1994).

64. Philostratus claims that Julia Domna, wife of Septimius Severus, commissioned the transcription of the notebooks of Damis, a purported disciple of Apollonius and source for his biography. For discussions of the myth or reality of Damis, see especially E. L. Bowie, "Apollonius of Tyana: Tradition and Reality," *Aufstieg und Niedergang der romischen Welt* II.16.2 (1978), 1652–99. See also Graham Anderson, *Philostratus: Biography and Belles Lettres in the Third Century A.D.* (London: Croom Helm, 1986) and Maria Dzielska, *Apollonius of Tyana in Legend and History* (Rome: "L'Erma" di Bretschneider, 1986).

65. However, by the third century, a revival of neo-Pythagorean circles (as represented, for example, by Philostratus) and Middle and Neoplatonic circles (as represented, for example, by Porphyry) may have made critique of animal and blood sacrifice less of an issue for the expression of Roman *pietas*.

66. See also *Vit. Apoll.* 8.6, where Philostratus encourages readers to listen to him and to the speech of Apollonius before Domitian in a manly way. While I closely consulted the Loeb Classical Library translation by Christopher Jones, the translated material that follows is my own, because the gendered connotations of the language are not always evident in the Jones translation.

67. In what follows, any reference to Apollonius means Philostratus's Apollonius, a phrase too cumbersome to repeat throughout the discussion.

68. Also notable is Apollonius's discussion of eunuchs during his visit to the Babylonian court, which serves as an opportunity to define σωφροσύνη. After asking his disciple, Damis, whether eunuchs are free of desire, Apollonius argues otherwise. The point is that σωφροσύνη cannot be compelled or induced by drastic measures. It must come from one's own restraint and mastery of the passions (*Vit. Apoll.* 1.34.1). Apollonius is soon proven correct when a eunuch is found in the bed of one of the king's wives (*Vit. Apoll.* 1.37).

69. This is one of the few places Apollonius has something negative to say about Greeks.

70. This letter is also preserved as Letter 42a. See Robert J. Penella, *The Letters of Apollonius of Tyana: A Critical Text with Prolegomena, Translation and Commentary* (Leiden, the Netherlands: Brill, 1979).

71. Jones's translation.

CHAPTER 4

1. For the most influential work, see Krister Stendahl, "The Apostle Paul and the Introspective Conscience of the West," *Harvard Theological Review* 56 (1963): 199–215. Reprinted in Krister Stendahl, *Paul among Jews and Gentiles and Other Essays* (Philadelphia: Fortress Press, 1976), 78–96. Also E. P. Sanders, *Paul and Palestinian Judaism: A Comparison of Patterns of Religion* (Philadelphia: Fortress Press, 1977). More recently, see Mark D. Nanos, *The Mystery of Romans: The Jewish Context of Paul's Letter* (Minneapolis: Fortress Press, 1996) and Mark D. Nanos, *The Irony of Galatians: Paul's Letter in First-Century Context* (Minneapolis: Fortress Press, 2002).

2. Raymond Pickett, *The Cross in Corinth: The Social Significance of the Death of Jesus* (Sheffield, England: Sheffield Academic Press, 1997); David G. Horrell, *The Social Ethos of the Corinthian Correspondence: Interests and Ideology from 1 Corinthians to 1 Clement*, Studies of the New Testament and Its World (Edinburgh: T & T Clark, 1996); and Stephen M. Pogoloff, *Logos and Sophia: The Rhetorical Situation of 1 Corinthians* (Atlanta: Scholars Press, 1992).

3. A strong appeal for a political interpretation of Paul came first from Neil Elliott, *Liberating Paul: The Justice of God and the Politics of the Apostle* (Maryknoll, N.Y.: Orbis Books, 1994). See also Richard A. Horsley, ed., *Paul and Empire: Religion and Power in Roman Imperial Society* (Harrisburg, Pa.: Trinity Press International, 1997); Richard A. Horsley, ed., *Paul and Politics: Ekklesia, Israel, Imperium, Interpretation*, (Harrisburg, Pa.: Trinity Press International, 2000); and Richard A. Horsley, ed., *Paul and the Roman Imperial Order* (Harrisburg, Pa.: Trinity Press International, 2004). Also Richard A. Horsley, ed., *Hidden Transcripts and the Arts of Resistance: Applying the Work of James C. Scott to Jesus and Paul* (Atlanta: Society of Biblical Literature, 2004).

4. Jennifer Wright Knust, *Abandoned to Lust: Sexual Slander and Ancient Christianity* (New York: Columbia University Press, 2006), 85.

5. Stanley K. Stowers, *A Rereading of Romans: Justice, Jews, and Gentiles* (New Haven, Conn.: Yale University Press, 1994).

6. As recognized by Johan Christiaan Beker, *Paul the Apostle: The Triumph of God in Life and Thought* (Philadelphia: Fortress Press, 1980), 198–99, and Charles B. Cousar, *A Theology of the Cross: The Death of Jesus in the Pauline Letters* (Minneapolis: Fortress Press, 1990), 21. Also Leif E. Vaage, "Why Christianity Succeeded (in) the Roman Empire," in *Religious Rivalries in the Early Roman Empire and the Rise of Christianity*, ed. Leif E. Vaage (Waterloo, Ont.: Wilfrid Laurier University Press, 2006), 274.

7. The "undisputed" epistles are letters whose genuine Pauline authorship is not a point of scholarly debate. They include Romans, 1 and 2 Corinthians, Galatians, Philippians, 1 Thessalonians, and Philemon.

8. Henk S. Versnel, "Making Sense of Jesus' Death: The Pagan Contribution," in *Deutungen Des Todes Jesu Im Neuen Testament*, ed. Jörg Frey and Jens Schröter (Tübingen, Germany: Mohr Siebeck, 2005), 230–31.

9. For a complete list of the occurrences of the dying formula in the New Testament, see Henk J. de Jonge, "The Original Setting of the χριστός ἀπέθανεν ὑπερ Formula," in *The Thessalonian Correspondence*, ed. Raymond Collins (Louvain, Belgium: Leuven University Press, 1990), 235. De Jonge notes that in Paul's undisputed letters the formula occurs eight times (1 Thessalonians 5:10; 1 Corinthians 15:3; 2 Corinthians 14, 15; Romans 5:6, 8, 14:15), with variations or allusions to the formula in another seven or eight instances (Romans 14:9; 1 Corinthians 1:13, 5:7 8:11; 2 Corinthians 5:21; Galatians 2:21, 3:13).

10. One line of scholarship has attempted to identify the sitz-im-leben for the use of this formula. For a brief review, see ibid. De Jonge argues for a setting in Christian paraenesis, as opposed to a Eucharistic setting, or Christian catechesis.

11. For a recent argument to this effect, see J. D. G. Dunn, "Paul's Understanding of the Death of Jesus," in *Sacrifice and Redemption*, ed. S. W. Sykes (Cambridge: Cambridge University Press, 1990), 35–56. Dunn argues that the reference in Romans 3:25 to *hilasterion* can only have a sacrificial meaning (41). Similarly, the phrase "in or through his blood" (Romans 3:25, 5:9) cannot otherwise be understood (43). But Dunn, even in 1990, is swimming against a growing stream of scholarship that is decidedly opposed to situating the early Christian use of the dying formula in an Israelite/Jewish or Old Testament setting.

12. See, most recently, Versnel, "Making Sense of Jesus' Death."Also Jeffrey B. Gibson, "Paul's 'Dying Formula': Prolegomena to an Understanding of Its Import and Significance," in *Celebrating Romans: Template for Pauline Theology*, ed. Sheila E. McGinn (Grand Rapids, Mich.: Eerdmans, 2004), 20–41, and David Seeley, *The Noble Death: Graeco-Roman Martyrology and Paul's Concept of Salvation*, Journal for the Study of the New Testament Supplement 28 (Sheffield, England: JSOT Press, 1990). Addressing the shift from a Jewish/Old Testament context for interpreting the death of Jesus to a Hellenistic one, Versnel marks two studies in the 1970s that "launched a radical and comprehensive critique, leveled . . . at the very concept of the OT as source of the notion of vicarious death" (216). He has in mind Klaus Wengst, *Christologische Formeln Und Lieder Des Urchristentums*, Studien Zum Neuen Testament 7 (Gütersloh, Germany: Gütersloher Verlagshaus Gerd Mohn, 1972), and Sam K. Williams, *Jesus'*

Death as Saving Event: The Background and Origin of a Concept (Missoula, Mont.: Scholars Press for *Harvard Theological Review*, 1975).

13. Williams, *Jesus' Death as Saving Event*, 153–61.

14. For an interesting analysis of this phenomenon through the lens of the Laudatio Turiae funerary inscription, see Emily A. Hemelrijk, "Masculinity and Femininity in the Laudatio Turiae," *Classical Quarterly* 54 (2004): 185–97. See also her early study *Matrona Docta: Educated Women in the Roman Élite from Cornelia to Julia Domna* (London: Routledge, 1999).

15. Janice Capel Anderson and Stephen D. Moore, "Taking It Like a Man: Masculinity in 4 Maccabees," *Journal of Biblical Literature* 117 (1998): 267.

16. Ibid., 265–72.

17. For more on the idea of the "manly" Christian woman, see Kerstin Aspegren, *The Male Woman: A Feminine Ideal in the Early Church*, ed. René Kieffer (Uppsala, Sweden: Uppsala University, 1990).

18. Or to put it another way, Jesus is "a woman forever in the process of becoming a man." The quote is a result of Stephen Moore's "queering" of Paul's letter to the Romans. While Moore refers to the submissiveness of Jesus to God combined with the self-mastery demonstrated in his death as represented in Romans, his remark could apply more generally to Paul's attention to Christ crucified, along with his repeated references to the vicarious manly death of Jesus.

19. "As much as anything else, 4 Maccabees is about what it means to be a true man." Anderson and Moore, "Taking It Like a Man," 253.

20. Versnel is here building a case for the influence of the contemporaneous Greco-Roman setting on the early Christian use of the notion of vicarious death, demonstrating that by the first century c.e., the idea of a vicarious death that was beneficial to others was not just a literary *topos*, but also a *topos* in real life. He cites several instances of first century c.e. funerary inscriptions that praise particular women, who, like Alcestis, die "instead of" their husbands. He also notes the popular theme of dying for a loved one that can be found in Greek novels and in historical anecdotes. His discussion is quite useful, although rather than seeing such cultural phenomena as *influencing* the early Christians, it is more accurate to see the Jewish and Christian ideas as examples of more Hellenistic material with an interest in vicarious death. Versnel, "Making Sense of Jesus' Death," 283–84.

21. Cora E. Lutz, *Musonius Rufus, "The Roman Socrates"* (New Haven, Conn.: Yale University Press, 1947).

22. Carlin A. Barton, *Roman Honor: The Fire in the Bones* (Berkeley: University of California Press, 2001), 277.

23. Jerry L. Sumney, " 'I Fill Up What Is Lacking in the Afflictions of Christ': Paul's Vicarious Suffering in Colossians," *Catholic Biblical Quarterly* 68 (2006): 671.

24. Though cross terminology is not exclusive to these letters. Demetrius Williams argues that the language of the cross is found only in polemical contexts in Paul. See Demetrius K. Williams, *Enemies of the Cross of Christ: The Terminology of the Cross and Conflict in Philippians* (London: Sheffield Academic Press, 2002).

25. For a similar argument, see Jennifer Larson, "Paul's Masculinity," *Journal of Biblical Literature* 123 (2004): 85–97.

26. This is the point that Jennifer Glancy emphasizes, especially the way Paul presents the scars on his body as representing a body that was "whippable," rather than a more honorably battle-scarred body. Jennifer A. Glancy, "Boasting of Beatings (2 Corinthians 11:23–25)," *Journal of Biblical Literature* 123 (2004): 99–135.

27. Catharine Edwards, "The Suffering Body: Philosophy and Pain in Seneca's Letters," in *Constructions of the Classical Body*, ed. James I. Porter (Ann Arbor: University of Michigan Press, 1999), 262.

28. Ibid.

29. Brent D. Shaw, "Body/Power/Identity: Passions of the Martyrs," *Journal of Early Christianity Studies* 4 (1996): 280. See also Tessa Rajak, "Dying for the Law: The Martyr's Portrait in the Jewish-Greek Literature," in *Portraits: Biographical Representation in the Greek and Latin Literature of the Roman Empire*, ed. M. J. Edwards and Simon Swain (Oxford: Clarendon Press, 1997), 39–67. Stephen D. Moore discusses both in relation to Revelation in *God's Beauty Parlor: And Other Queer Spaces in and around the Bible* (Stanford, Calif.: Stanford University Press, 2001), 192–95.

30. Shaw, "Body/Power/Identity," 278.

31. Lutz, *Musonius Rufus*, 59.

32. Helen Cullyer, "Socratic Echoes in Stoic 'Manly Courage,'" in *Andreia: Studies in Manliness and Courage in Classical Antiquity*, ed. Ralph Mark Rosen and I. Sluiter (Leiden, the Netherlands: Brill, 2003), 225. Cullyer argues further that the Stoics understood their version of *andreia* to be active; it was an exercise of virtue that was beneficial to the community (226–27).

33. As Shaw also notes, suggesting that this ideology of endurance (in particular as it came to the author of 4 Maccabees) was an appropriation of the "subtle naturalistic legitimation of Stoicism" ("Body/Power/Identity," 276–77). For another iteration of an emphasis on endurance, this time in Greek imperial orators, see Joy Connolly, "Like the Labors of Heracles: *Andreia* and *Paideia* in Greek Culture under Rome," in *Andreia: Studies in Manliness and Courage in Classical Antiquity*, ed. Ralph Mark Rosen and I. Sluiter (Leiden, the Netherlands: Brill, 2003), 287–317.

34. Cullyer, "Socratic Echoes in Stoic 'Manly Courage.'"

35. Stowers, *A Rereading of Romans*.

36. Ibid., 42.

37. Moore, *God's Beauty Parlor: And Other Queer Spaces in and around the Bible*, 163, his emphasis. For an alternative reading of Romans, gender, and imperial power, see Diana M. Swancutt, "'The Disease of Effemination': The Charge of Effeminacy and the Verdict of God (Romans 1:18–2:16)," in *New Testament Masculinities*, ed. Stephen D. Moore and Janice Capel Anderson (Leiden, the Netherlands: Brill, 2004), 193–233. Swancutt argues that in this section of Romans, Paul denounces a hypothetical stoicized Roman ruler, and in effect, the imperial ideological construct of *Romanitas*.

38. Brigitte Kahl, " 'No Longer Male': Masculinity Struggles behind Galatians 3:28?" *Journal for the Study of the New Testament* 79 (2000): 40. While Kahl's observations are quite helpful, my conclusions about the gender dynamics in this letter differ from hers.

39. Knust, *Abandoned to Lust*, 86.

40. Dale B. Martin, *Sex and the Single Savior: Gender and Sexuality in Biblical Interpretation* (Louisville, Ky.: Westminster John Knox Press, 2006), 78.

41. Stendahl's work is focused in particular on women's ordination. Krister Stendahl, *The Bible and the Role of Women: A Case Study in Hermeneutics* (Philadelphia: Fortress Press, 1966). Schüssler Fiorenza's highly influential work focused more broadly on the idea of an early Christian egalitarian community. Schüssler Fiorenza, *In Memory of Her: A Feminist Theological Reconstruction of Christian Origins* (New York: Crossroad, 1983).

42. Wayne A. Meeks, "The Image of the Androgyne: Some Uses of a Symbol in Early Christianity," *History of Religion* 13 (1974): 165–208.

43. Martin, *Sex and the Single Savior*, 84.

44. For a bibliography, see Ralph P. Martin, *Philippians* (Grand Rapids, Mich.: Eerdmans, 1980), 109–16.

45. Donald Dale Walker, *Paul's Offer of Leniency (2 Cor 10:1): Populist Ideology and Rhetoric in a Pauline Letter Fragment* (Tübingen, Germany: Mohr Siebeck, 2002).

46. Ibid., 153. Charlotte Roueche, "Acclamations in the Later Roman Empire: New Evidence from Aphrodisias," *Journal of Roman Studies* 74 (1984): 181–99.

47. Cicero goes on to cite the assassination of the "tyrant" Julius Caesar as an illustration of the "deadly effects of popular hatred" (*Off.* 2.23).

48. Walker, *Paul's Offer of Leniency*, 38–90. For an extended discussion of πραΰς in the context of Hellenistic kingship, see Deirdre Joy Good, *Jesus the Meek King* (Harrisburg, Pa.: Trinity Press International, 1999).

49. I will not rehearse arguments about the authenticity of these letters, though I assume pseudonymity for all of them. For the most recent discussion of Colossians, the most disputed among the deutero-Pauline traditions, see R. McL. Wilson, *A Critical and Exegetical Commentary on Colossians and Philemon* (London: T & T Clark International, 2005). Also Mark Christopher Kiley, *Colossians as Pseudepigraphy* (Sheffield, England: JSOT Press, 1986).

50. George H. van Kooten, *Cosmic Christology in Paul and the Pauline School: Colossians and Ephesians in the Context of Graeco-Roman Cosmology, with a New Synopsis of the Greek Texts*, Wissenschaftliche Untersuchungen Zum Neuen Testament 2. Reihe, 171 (Tübingen, Germany: Mohr Siebeck, 2003), 17–53.

51. With respect to fire, it is tempting to recall Galen's theory of the male anatomy formed precisely because of the right amount of heat (*On the Usefulness of Parts of the Body*, 2.630).

52. van Kooten, *Cosmic Christology in Paul and the Pauline School*, 24. See Cicero, *Nat. d.*, esp. 2.34.

53. Sumney, " 'I Fill Up What Is Lacking in the Afflictions of Christ,' " 676. The ideal of something "lacking" in the afflictions of Christ has long puzzled interpreters.

See Sumney for a summary of scholarship and further bibliography. He argues that what is lacking is an immediate and accessible example of the suffering demanded by obedience to the Gospel. This can not found in the exalted Christ, but can be found in the Paul of Colossians.

54. For discussion of the gendered aspects of the expanded household code in Ephesians, especially the marital imagery, see David M. Carr and Colleen M. Conway, "The Divine-Human Marriage Matrix and Constructions of Gender and 'Bodies' in the Christian Bible," in *Sacred Marriages: The Divine-Human Sexual Metaphor from Sumer to Early Christianity*, ed. Martti Nissinen and Risto Uro (Winona Lake, Ind.: Eisenbrauns, 2008).

55. Mary Rose D'Angelo, "The ANHP Question in Luke-Acts: Imperial Masculinity and the Deployment of Women in the Early Second Century," in *A Feminist Companion to Luke*, ed. Amy-Jill Levine and Marianne Blickenstaff (London: Sheffield Academic Press, 2002), 44–69; Jennifer A. Glancy, "Protocols of Masculinity in the Pastoral Epistles," in *New Testament Masculinities*, ed. Stephen D. Moore and Janice Capel Anderson (Atlanta: Society of Biblical Literature, 2003), 235–64.

56. Glancy, "Protocols of Masculinity in the Pastoral Epistles."

57. Ibid., 261.

58. Ibid., 260.

59. In his typically provocative style, Moore comments on the submissiveness of Jesus (as reflected in Romans) as follows: "Yet Jesus is not allowed to become mired in femininity, to sink into a softness, a flabbiness, from which he might not be able to extricate himself, in which he might lose his own hardness, his own manliness. For his spectacular act of submission is simultaneously a demonstration of self-mastery." Moore's observation points to the multiple ways that Paul's portrayal of Jesus links with the ideologies of masculinity in the first century.

CHAPTER 5

1. See Tat-siong Benny Liew, "Re-Mark-Able Masculinities: Jesus, the Son of Man, and the (Sad) Sum of Manhood?" in *New Testament Masculinities*, ed. Stephen D. Moore and Janice Capel Anderson (Atlanta: Society of Biblical Literature, 2003), 93–135, and Eric Thurman, "Looking for a Few Good Men: Mark and Masculinity," in *New Testament Masculinities*, ed. Stephen D. Moore and Janice Capel Anderson (Atlanta: Society of Biblical Literature, 2003), 137–61.

2. While there is some manuscript evidence to the contrary, I favor a reading that includes υἱοῦ θεοῦ in Mark 1:1, given the recurrence of the theme in 1:11, 9:7, and 15:39. Even if the phrase was a scribal addition, it is surely not an appellation that the author would dispute.

3. Here and elsewhere, I will not rehearse the history of religions background for the various titles that are applied to Jesus, because that has been done many times before. My interest is not in the potential origin of the titles, but in their application and reception, particularly with respect to their gendered aspects.

4. In fact, nowhere in the New Testament is there a description of Jesus' appearance. This is not the case with other men in the scripture tradition. Although there is a similar reticence regarding physical descriptions in the Hebrew scriptures, when it comes to kingly men, even the biblical authors make exceptions. Thus, Saul is described as a handsome, tall man with ruddy complexion and beautiful eyes (1 Samuel 9:2, 10:23, and 16:12). David, also, is said to be ruddy and handsome (17:12). But the Gospel writers refrain from physical descriptions of Jesus and almost every other character. See chapter 8, "The Missing Body of the Manly Jesus," p. 149, for further discussion of this phenomenon.

5. M. Eugene Boring, *Mark: A Commentary* (Louisville, Ky.: Westminster John Knox Press, 2006), 45.

6. Even when it does not refer to demons, ἐκβαλλω still indicates force against someone in the Gospel, with one possible exception at 1:43. There Jesus sends out the man he healed of a skin disease to be inspected by the priest. But even in this case, Jesus is portrayed rather harshly as he "sternly warns" the newly healed man (ἐμβριμησάμενος) not to speak to anyone about the healing. For other occurrences, see 5:40; 9:47; 11:15; 12:8.

7. Boring, *Mark: A Commentary*, 47. See also Ernest Best, *The Temptation and the Passion: The Markan Soteriology*, 2nd ed. (Cambridge, England: Cambridge University Press, 1990).

8. Donahue and Harrington note that in the Old Testament, wild beasts are associated with evil powers. John R. Donahue and Daniel J. Harrington, *The Gospel of Mark* (Collegeville, Minn.: Liturgical Press, 2005), 66. See, for example, Psalm 22:11–21, Ezekiel 34:5, 8, 25.

9. On the question of autonomy of the Markan Jesus, see Tat-siong Benny Liew, *Politics of Parousia: Reading Mark Inter(Con)Textually* (Leiden, the Netherlands: Brill, 1999), 126–29. Pointing to the seemingly "coerced or haphazard" travels of Jesus, Liew argues, "Jesus' movements seem more like those of a drifter or vagabond, who wanders about not because of a self-determined and pre-arranged traveling plan, but because of necessity, which may be understood in divine, human and/or fortuitous terms. Long before Jesus is physically arrested (14:46), he has already been subjected to a less conspicuous but equally confining form of arrest that governs and inhibits his comings and goings" (128–29).

10. Liew, "Re-Mark-Able Masculinities," 105.

11. An alternative interpretation of the miracle tradition in Mark was famously argued by Theodore Weeden in *Mark: Traditions in Conflict* (Philadelphia: Fortress Press, 1971). Weeden argued that the use of the miracle tradition in the first half of the Gospel was in service of a "corrective Christology" that was made apparent in the second half. According to Weeden, Mark explicitly refutes the theos aner figure—the miracle-working divine man—in favor of the suffering messiah. Although the notion of a corrective Christology is now largely dismissed by Markan scholars, the structure of the Gospel is still discussed in terms of a theological shift from the first half to the second half. Thus, Boring sees in the first half a theology of glory and in the

second a theology of the cross. The latter does not critique the former but relativizes it. Alternatively, Tolbert suggests the lack of miracles in the second half of the Gospel is due to a lack of faith on the part of the characters in this section of the narrative. Mary Ann Tolbert, *Sowing the Gospel: Mark's World in Literary-Historical Perspective* (Minneapolis: Fortress Press, 1989), 183.

12. G. W. Bowersock, "The Mechanics of Subversion in the Roman Provinces," in *Opposition Et Résistances À L'empire D'auguste À Trajan: Neuf Exposés Suivis De Discusssions*, ed. Kurt A. Raaflaub and Adalberto Giovannini (Vandœuvres-Genève, Switzerland: Fondation Hardt, 1987).

13. See especially Richard A. Horsley, *Hearing the Whole Story: The Politics of Plot in Mark's Gospel* (Louisville, Ky.: Westminster John Knox Press, 2001), 112–15.

14. On the retainer class, see Gerhard E. Lenski, *Power and Privilege: A Theory of Social Stratification* (New York: McGraw-Hill, 1966).

15. Catherine Hezser, *Jewish Literacy in Roman Palestine* (Tübingen, Germany: Mohr Siebeck, 2001), 119.

16. Best argues that this saying indicates that Jesus has already conquered Satan, and did so at the temptation. Best, *The Temptation and the Passion*, 147. See also Horsley, *Hearing the Whole Story*, 147.

17. This text is key to the political reading of Mark by Ched Myers. He argues that the conflict with Satan corresponds to Jesus' conflict with scribal Judaism. Thus, the passage is "Jesus' declaration of ideological war with the scribal establishment." Ched Myers, *Binding the Strong Man: A Political Reading of Mark's Story of Jesus* (Maryknoll, N.Y.: Orbis Books, 1988), 166. See Horsley, who also interprets the conflict as political, but unlike Myers emphasizes the conflict with Roman authority rather than with scribal Judaism and its purity code. Horsley, *Hearing the Whole Story*.

18. According to Bar-Ilan, "in the days of the Second Temple, scribes came almost exclusively from rich and distinguished families, most of whom were priests or levites." This was because only affluent families could afford to give up the potential income from these sons so that they could acquire the education needed for a scribal career. Meir Bar-Ilan, "Writing in Ancient Israel and Early Judaism Part II: Scribes and Books in the Late Second Commonwealth and Rabbinic Period," in *Mikra: Text, Translation, Reading, and Interpretation of the Hebrew Bible in Ancient Judaism and Early Christianity*, ed. M. J. Mulder and Harry Sysling (Minneapolis: Fortress Press, 1990), 22.

19. Horsley sees in the story "a demystification of (the belief) in demons and demon possession. . . . It is now evident to Jesus' followers and to hearers of Mark's story that the struggle is really against the rulers, ultimately the Romans." Horsley, *Hearing the Whole Story*, 147. However, it seems doubtful that Mark's readers would need to learn this lesson through a demystified exorcism narrative. Instead, they quite likely understood the cosmic struggle and political struggle (of which they were already aware!) to be one and the same.

20. J. Duncan M. Derrett, "Contributions to the Study of the Gerasene Demoniac," *Journal for Study of the New Testament* 3 (1979): 5–8.

21. Elizabeth Struthers Malbon, "The Christology of Mark's Gospel: Narrative Christology and the Markan Jesus," in *Who Do You Say That I Am? Essays on*

Christology, ed. Mark Allan Powell and David R. Bauer (Louisville, Ky.: Westminster John Knox Press, 1999), 39–40.

22. I refer to issues in the "Messianic Secret" debate. For a review of the long history of this discussion, see James L. Blevins, *The Messianic Secret in Markan Research, 1901–1976* (Washington, D.C.: University Press of America, 1981), and Heikki Räisänen, *The "Messianic Secret" in Mark* (Edinburgh: T. & T. Clark, 1990).

23. Malbon, "The Christology of Mark's Gospel," 44.

24. The enigmatic Son of Man title has generated more discussion than any other New Testament title for Jesus. In the Gospel traditions, Jesus uses this title as a self-reference, but no other character refers to Jesus as the Son of Man. For a discussion of scholarship, see Morna Dorothy Hooker, *The Son of Man in Mark: A Study of the Background of the Term "Son of Man" and Its Use in St. Mark's Gospel* (Montreal: McGill University Press, 1967). Recent scholarship has tended to leave behind the "backgrounds" question (where did the title come from?) in favor of examining how the Gospel narratives give shape to the figure of the Son of Man. So, in the Gospel of Mark, it is apparent that Jesus uses the title to link himself as the one who must suffer to an eschatological figure who will return in glory. See Elizabeth Struthers Malbon, "Narrative Christology and the Son of Man: What the Markan Jesus Says Instead," *Biblical Interpretation* 11 (2003): 373–85; Paul Danove, "The Rhetoric of Characterization of Jesus as the Son of Man and Christ in Mark," *Biblica* 84 (2003): 16–34; and Harry L. Chronis, "To Reveal and to Conceal: A Literary-Critical Perspective on 'the Son of Man' in Mark," *New Testament Studies* 51 (2005): 459–81.

25. Though not all will be required to die—some will see the kingdom coming with power in their lifetime (9:1).

26. Johanna Dewey, "The Gospel of Mark," in *Searching the Scriptures*, vol. 2, *A Feminist Commentary*, ed. Elisabeth Schüssler Fiorenza, Shelly Matthews, and Ann Graham Brock (New York: Crossroad, 1994), 492–93.

27. For a detailed discussion of the Greco-Roman traditions related to service and rulership, see David Seeley, "Rulership and Service in Mark 10:41–45," *Novum Testamentum* 35 (1993): 234–50.

28. Gerd Theissen, "The Political Dimension of Jesus' Activities," in *The Social Setting of Jesus and the Gospels*, ed. Wolfgang Stegemann, Bruce Malina, and Gerd Theissen (Minneapolis: Fortress Press, 2002), 240–41.

29. Anuradha Dingwaney Needham, *Using the Master's Tools: Resistance and the Literature of the African and South-Asian Diasporas* (New York: St. Martin's Press, 2000), 33.

30. John J. Pilch understands the death of the Markan Jesus to be an honorable one. John J. Pilch, "Death with Honor: The Mediterranean Style Death of Jesus in Mark," *Biblical Theology Bulletin* 25 (1995): 65–70.

31. Thurman, "Looking for a Few Good Men," 150.

32. Deborah Krause, "School's in Session: The Making and Unmaking of Docile Disciple Bodies in Mark," in *Postmodern Interpretations of the Bible: A Reader*, ed. A. K. A. Adam (St. Louis: Chalice Press, 2000), 185.

33. Stephen D. Moore, " 'O Man, Who Art Thou?': Masculinity Studies and New Testament Studies," in *New Testament Masculinities*, ed. Stephen D. Moore and Janice Capel Anderson (Atlanta: Society of Biblical Literature, 2003), 11.

34. While "a voice from heaven" has addressed Jesus (1:11) and Jesus has sought a deserted place to pray (1:35), this is the first instance of direct speech to God.

35. Thurman, "Looking for a Few Good Men," 151.

36. A common explanation for Jesus' silence is by way of the suffering servant song in Isaiah 53:7. Like the servant, Jesus is seen as a lamb led to slaughter who does not open his mouth.

37. Perhaps the difference in response is due to Pilate's formulation. The title βασιλεὺς τῶν Ἰουδαίων is not found in Jewish tradition. While the Markan Jesus affirms the more traditional "King of Israel," his "You say so" suggests that only Pilate or other outsiders would use the phrase "king of the Judeans."

38. Boring, *Mark: A Commentary*, 431.

39. Best, *The Temptation and the Passion*, lxiv.

40. Robert H. Gundry, *Mark: A Commentary on His Apology for the Cross* (Grand Rapids, Mich.: Eerdmans, 1993), 970. Gundry suggests that only one shout is intended, the second occurrence in Mark 15:37 being a back reference to Mark 15:34.

41. John R. Donahue and Daniel J. Harrington, *The Gospel of Mark* (Collegeville, Minn.: Liturgical Press, 2005), 451.

CHAPTER 6

1. Whom Virgil intended with his reference to the "boy" is perhaps left deliberately unclear. Some possibilities include the anticipated child of the marriage of Augustus and Scribonia, the anticipated child of Marc Antony and Octavia (Augustus's sister), or perhaps a reference to Augustus himself. For further discussion, see Harold Mattingly, "Virgil's Fourth Eclogue," *Journal of the Warburg and Courtauld Institutes*, 10 (1947): 14–19.

2. Ulrich Luz, *Matthew 1–7: A Commentary* (Minneapolis: Augsburg, 1989), 109–10. For a focus on the sexual taint of women, see for example, Bernard Brandon Scott, "The Birth of the Reader: Matthew 1:1–4:16," in *Faith and History: Essays in Honor of Paul W. Meyer*, ed. John T. Carroll, Charles H. Cosgrove, and E. Elizabeth Johnson (Atlanta: Scholars Press, 1991), 41–42.

3. Amy-Jill Levine, *The Social and Ethnic Dimensions of Matthean Salvation History* (Lewiston, N.Y.: E. Mellen Press, 1988). Her own interpretation is that "what unites these women is their manifestation of faith which outstrips that of their partners" (81).

4. Daniel J. Harrington, *The Gospel of Matthew*, Sacra Pagina (Collegeville, Minn.: Liturgical Press, 1991), 32. Similarly, Rudolf Schnackenburg, *The Gospel of Matthew* (Grand Rapids, Mich.: Eerdmans, 2002), 17.

5. John Nolland, *The Gospel of Matthew: A Commentary on the Greek Text* (Grand Rapids, Mich./Bletchley, England: Eerdmans/Paternoster Press, 2005), 77.

6. For a survey of feminist interpretation, see Jane Schaberg, "Feminist In-tepretation of the Infancy Narrative in the Gospel of Matthew," *Journal of Feminist Studies in Religion* 13 (1997): 35–62.

7. Elaine Wainwright, "The Gospel of Matthew," in *Searching the Scriptures*, ed. Elisabeth Schüssler Fiorenza (New York: Crossroad, 1993), 642–43.

8. For discussion of Matthew's use of "Son of God" in an imperial context, see Robert L. Mowery, "Son of God in Roman Imperial Titles and Matthew," *Biblica* 83 (2002): 100–110.

9. Warren Carter, *Matthew and Empire: Initial Explorations* (Harrisburg, Pa.: Trinity Press International, 2001), 64.

10. W. D. Davies and Dale C. Allison, *A Critical and Exegetical Commentary on the Gospel According to Saint Matthew*, vol. 1 (Edinburgh: T. & T. Clark, 1988), 239.

11. Nolland notes the way Matthew's use of προσκυνέω blurs the distinction between deferential respect and worship (*The Gospel of Matthew*, 101 nt. 80).

12. The NRSV renders Matthew's "ruler" (ἄρχων) as a leader of the synagogue following Mark's term ἀρχισυναγώγων. But given Matthew's harsh depiction of Jewish authorities throughout much of the narrative, the generalizing of the term to "ruler" in this context may be intentional.

13. Schnackenburg, *The Gospel of Matthew*, 286.

14. Cf. the account of Suetonius regarding the astrologer Publius Nigidius Figulus, who "hearing what hour the child had been delivered, cried out: 'The ruler of the world is now born'" (*Aug.* 95).

15. For an extensive discussion of the political implications of Matthew's Gospel, see Carter, *Matthew and Empire*.

16. See chapter 3, "Caesar Augustus, Son of the Deified Julius."

17. Jerome H. Neyrey, "Jesus, Gender and the Gospel of Matthew," in *New Testament Masculinities*, ed. Stephen D. Moore and Janice Capel Anderson (Atlanta: Society of Biblical Literature, 2003), 60–65.

18. Janice Capel Anderson and Stephen D. Moore, "Matthew and Masculinity," in *New Testament Masculinities*, ed. Stephen D. Moore and Janice Capel Anderson (Atlanta: Society of Biblical Literature, 2003), 79.

19. Ibid., 81.

20. For an extensive study of the image, see Celia Deutsch, *Lady Wisdom, Jesus, and the Sages: Metaphor and Social Context in Matthew's Gospel* (Valley Forge, Pa.: Trinity Press International, 1996).

21. Marinus de Jonge, *Christology in Context: The Earliest Christian Response to Jesus* (Philadelphia: Westminster Press, 1988), 233 nt. 4.

22. Although this is not always the case. Sometimes Wisdom is portrayed with more "masculine" features and sometimes it is not personified at all. See chapter 8, "Wisdom and the Relative Gender of the Johannine Jesus."

23. For a similar argument with respect to the Wisdom figure in Proverbs, see Howard Eilberg-Schwartz, *God's Phallus and Other Problems for Men and Mono-theism* (Boston: Beacon Press, 1994), 131–32. He suggests that the insertion of the

nonsexual female figure in the fatherly discourse to the son "allows sons to love God's words while keeping homoerotic associations at bay."

24. Deutsch, *Lady Wisdom, Jesus, and the Sages*, III.

25. Ibid., 40.

26. Ibid., 141.

27. Deirdre Joy Good, *Jesus the Meek King* (Harrisburg, Pa.: Trinity Press International, 1999), 63. At this point, Good parts substantially from Deutsch's reading of the passage, because the latter focuses on the adjectives "lowly" and "humble in heart" as indicative of the status reversal associated with Lady Wisdom. I am more convinced by Good's reading on this point. It is not clear that the sages were interested in status reversal in their self-identification with Wisdom. Instead, their intimate association with (Divine) Lady Wisdom would elevate their status with respect to other men who did not share such intimacy.

28. Good points to *Ned.* 83a, "The Holy One, blessed be He, causes his divine presence to rest only on him who is strong, wealthy, wise and meek; and all these are deduced from Moses." Ibid., 5.

29. The question of Jesus as personified wisdom will come up again in the discussion of Johannine Christology in chapter 8. In the Gospel of John, the allusions to wisdom are even more predominant, making their implications for the gender identity of Jesus even more pressing.

30. Anderson and Moore note the absence of the terminology typically associated with masculine virtue such as ἀνδρεῖος (manliness), ἐγκράτεια (self-control), or σωφροσύνη (moderation). Anderson and Moore, "Matthew and Masculinity," 71.

31. Warnings against adultery and lust are abundant in wisdom literature. For example, "Say to wisdom, 'You are my sister,' and call insight your intimate friend, that they may keep you from the strange woman, from the adulteress with her smooth words" (Proverbs 7:4–5). Or from Ben Sira: "Let neither gluttony nor lust overcome me, and do not give me over to shameless passion" (Sirach 23:6).

32. Here and elsewhere, Jesus uses "the Gentiles" as foils for improper (unmanly) behavior. For example, in contrast to the effective public speech of Jesus, the Gentiles are presented as "babbling" and "thinking they will be heard because of their many words" (6:7). Much like the barbarians whom Apollonius wanted to instruct in the ways of civilized masculinity, in the Gospel of Matthew, the Gentiles are those who lack proper masculine deportment.

33. See the discussion in Nolland, *The Gospel of Matthew*, 267. In contrast, Marius Reiser argues that the idea of love for one's enemies only rarely occurs in a Greco-Roman context, mainly in Socrates and a few Roman Stoics (namely Musonius, Seneca, Epictetus, and Marcus Aurelius). Marius Reiser, "Love of Enemies in the Context of Antiquity," *New Testament Studies* 47 (2001): 411–27.

34. Hans Dieter Betz, *The Sermon on the Mount: A Commentary on the Sermon on the Mount, Including the Sermon on the Plain (Matthew 5:3–7:27 and Luke 6:20–49)*, Hermeneia (Minneapolis: Fortress Press, 1995), 85–87.

35. Galen, *On the Usefulness of the Parts of the Body*, trans. Margaret Tallmadge May (Ithaca, N.Y.: Cornell University Press, 1968).

36. Schnackenburg, *The Gospel of Matthew*, 290. Also Warren Carter, *Matthew and the Margins: A Sociopolitical and Religious Reading* (Maryknoll, N.Y.: Orbis Books, 2000), 535–36.

37. Wendy J. Cotter, "Greco-Roman Apotheosis Traditions and the Resurrection Appearances in Matthew," in *The Gospel of Matthew in Current Study: Studies in Memory of William G. Thompson S.J,* ed. David E. Aune (Grand Rapids, Mich.: Eerdmans, 2001), 149.

38. Ibid., 151.

39. For a detailed reading of Matthew's Gospel as a counter-narrative that resists the values of the Roman Empire, see Carter, *Matthew and the Margins.*

40. Halvor Moxnes, *Putting Jesus in His Place: A Radical Vision of Household and Kingdom* (Louisville, Ky.: Westminster John Knox Press, 2003), 72–73.

41. For detailed arguments for a Cynic influence on early Christianity, see F. Gerald Downing, *Cynics and Christian Origins* (Edinburgh: T & T Clark, 1992).

42. See the discussion in Moxnes, *Putting Jesus in His Place,* 77.

43. For discussions of the ambiguous gender status of the eunuch, see Mathew Kuefler, *The Manly Eunuch: Masculinity, Gender Ambiguity, and Christian Ideology in Late Antiquity* (Chicago: University of Chicago Press, 2001); Anderson and Moore, "Matthew and Masculinity," 87–91; and Moxnes, *Putting Jesus in His Place,* 78–80.

44. Peter R. Brown, *The Body and Society: Men, Women, and Sexual Renunciation in Early Christianity* (New York: Columbia University Press, 1988), 10.

45. Arthur J. Dewey, "The Unkindest Cut of All? Matthew 19:11–12," *Forum* 8 (1992): 118.

46. Given its radical nature, examination of this saying is also fascinating on the level of the historical Jesus. It seems quite unlikely that the saying would emerge in the early Christian tradition if it were not rooted in the historical Jesus. For discussion and bibliography of the saying in the *Sitz im Leben* of Jesus, see Stephen C. Barton, *Discipleship and Family Ties in Mark and Matthew* (Cambridge, England: Cambridge University Press, 1994), 192. For an insightful use of queer theory with respect to the eunuch saying and the historical Jesus, see Moxnes, *Putting Jesus in His Place,* 91–107.

47. Though Barton argues that from a sociological perspective the call to celibacy marginalizes Matthew's group from contemporary Judaism. Barton, *Discipleship and Family Ties in Mark and Matthew,* 201.

48. Though Kuefler entertains the possibility of a literal translation (*The Manly Eunuch,* 259).

CHAPTER 7

1. Mary Rose D'Angelo was the first to call attention to the author's use of ἀνήρ, though her count of the occurrences in Acts is different from mine. Mary Rose D'Angelo, "The ANHP Question in Luke-Acts: Imperial Masculinity and the Deployment of Women in the Early Second Century," in *A Feminist Companion to Luke,*

ed. Amy-Jill Levine and Marianne Blickenstaff (London: Sheffield Academic Press, 2002), 48–49.

2. Ibid., 54–55.

3. For an analysis of the construction of male and female characters in Acts 1–7, see Caroline Vander Stichele and Todd Penner, " 'All the World's a Stage': The Rhetoric of Gender in Acts," in *Luke and His Readers: Festschrift A. Denaux*, ed. R. Bieringer, Gilbert van Belle, and Jozef Verheyden, Bibliotheca Ephemeridum Theologicarum Lovaniensium 182 (Louvain, Belgium: Leuven University Press, 2005), 373–96.

4. Elsewhere in Luke-Acts, the title is used for the governors Felix (Acts 24:3) and Festus (Acts 26:25).

5. D'Angelo, "The ANHP Question in Luke-Acts," 68.

6. Clare K. Rothschild, *Luke-Acts and the Rhetoric of History: An Investigation of Early Christian Historiography*, Wissenschaftliche Untersuchungen Zum Neuen Testament. 2. Reihe; 175 (Tübingen, Germany: Mohr Siebeck, 2004).

7. W. Martin Bloomer, "Schooling in Persona: Imagination and Subordination in Roman Education," *Classical Antiquity* 16 (1997). For a different perspective on the socializing effect of declamation exercises, see Robert A. Kaster, "Controlling Reason: Declamation in Rhetorical Education at Rome," in *Education in Greek and Roman Antiquity*, ed. Yun Lee Too (Leiden, the Netherlands: Brill, 2001). Kaster emphasizes the often-lurid cases presented to the student, forcing him to consider what would happen if he were to lose control and act unreasonably.

8. Perhaps such practice in speaking in character would also help explain the author's altruistic attention to the poor that occurs throughout the narrative.

9. For additional discussion of the importance of declamation and of the Greco-Roman educational system in general for understanding the literary aspects of Acts, see Todd C. Penner, "Civilizing Discourse: Acts, Declamation, and the Rhetoric of the *Polis*," in *Contextualizing Acts: Lukan Narrative and Greco-Roman Discourse*, ed. Todd C. Penner and Caroline Vander Stichele (Leiden, the Netherlands: Brill, 2004), 65–104. Penner's focus on the narrative formation of a Christian *politeia* complements my argument regarding the characterization of civilized literate males among the early Christians.

10. For such honors bestowed on Pompey and Julius Caesar, see Robert K. Sherk, *Rome and the Greek East to the Death of Augustus* (Cambridge, England: Cambridge University Press, 1984), 95, 99–101.

11. Victor Ehrenberg, A. H. M. Jones, and D. L. Stockton, eds., *Documents Illustrating the Reigns of Augustus and Tiberius*, 2nd ed. (Oxford: Clarendon Press, 1976), 98b.50.

12. Ibid., 98b.35–37. For additional material relating to Roman imperial propaganda, see the summary in Gary Gilbert, "Roman Propaganda and Christian Identity in the Worldview of Luke-Acts," in *Contextualizing Acts: Lukan Narrative and Greco-Roman Discourse*, ed. Todd C. Penner and Caroline Vander Stichele (Leiden, the Netherlands: Brill, 2004), 237–42.

13. Mary Beard and John Henderson, "The Emperor's New Body: Ascension from Rome," in *Parchments of Gender: Deciphering the Bodies of Antiquity*, ed. Maria Wyke (Oxford: Oxford University Press, 1998), 197.

14. Gilbert, "Roman Propaganda and Christian Identity in the Worldview of Luke-Acts," 246–47.

15. A centurion typically came from the equestrian rank. See Peter Garnsey and Richard P. Saller, *The Roman Empire: Economy, Society, and Culture* (Berkeley: University of California Press, 1987), 23, 199.

16. David Gowler points to this as an indication of the patron/broker/client relationship between the centurion and the Jewish community. As he puts it, "The centurion serves as a broker of imperial favor" so that the "Jewish elders are both obligated and loyal to their patron; one of the primary responsibilities of clients was to praise the patron and the benefits he brings." David B. Gowler, "Texture, Culture, and Ideology in Luke 7:1–10: A Dialogic Reading," in *Fabrics of Discourse: Essays in Honor of Vernon K. Robbins*, ed. David B. Gowler, L. Gregory Bloomquist, and Duane Frederick Watson (Harrisburg, Pa.: Trinity Press International, 2003), 111.

17. The use of the first person suggests that Matthew's version was closer to the original, which related a direct encounter between Jesus and the centurion.

18. Robert C. Tannehill, *The Narrative Unity of Luke-Acts: A Literary Interpretation* (Philadelphia: Fortress Press, 1986).

19. For additional studies on Paul's elite status in Acts, see Jerome Neyrey, "Luke's Social Location of Paul: Cultural Anthropology and the Status of Paul in Acts," in *History, Literature, and Society in the Book of Acts*, ed. Ben Witherington (Cambridge, England: Cambridge University Press, 1996), 251–79; and John Clayton Lentz, *Luke's Portrait of Paul* (Cambridge, England: Cambridge University Press, 1993).

20. For an interpretation of Bar-Jesus/Elymus as a representative of Satan, see Susan R. Garrett, *The Demise of the Devil: Magic and the Demonic in Luke's Writings* (Minneapolis: Fortress Press, 1989).

21. See also D'Angelo, "The ANHP Question in Luke-Acts," 57.

22. Lentz, *Luke's Portrait of Paul*, 85.

23. Ibid., 83.

24. Ibid., 144.

25. Penner, "Civilizing Discourse," 93–94.

26. See for example, Philip Francis Esler, *Community and Gospel in Luke-Acts: The Social and Political Motivations of Lucan Theology* (Cambridge, England: Cambridge University Press, 1987); Robert L. Brawley, *Luke-Acts and the Jews: Conflict, Apology, and Conciliation* (Atlanta: Scholars Press, 1987); and J. Bradley Chance, *Jerusalem, the Temple, and the New Age in Luke-Acts* (Macon, Ga.: Mercer University Press, 1988). The more recent work of Allen Brent is an exception. Brent argues that Luke's presentation of the Jerusalem cult should be viewed in relation to the imperial cult. He argues that Luke was offering a reformed Jewish cult (Christianity) as a countercultural response to the pagan cult practice. Allen Brent, *The Imperial Cult and the Development of Church Order: Concepts and Images of Authority in Paganism and Early Christianity before the Age of Cyprian*, Supplements to Vigiliae Christianae, vol. 45 (Boston: Brill, 1999).

27. S. R. F. Price, *Rituals and Power: The Roman Imperial Cult in Asia Minor* (Cambridge, England: Cambridge University Press, 1986); Inez Scott Ryberg, *Rites of*

the State Religion in Roman Art, Memoirs of the American Academy in Rome, vol. 22 (Rome: American Academy in Rome, 1955).

28. Beard, North, and Price, *Religions of Rome,* 186.

29. J. Rufus Fears, "The Cult of Virtues and Roman Imperial Theology," *Aufstieg und Niedergang der römischen Welt* II.17.2 (1981): 850.

30. For a more extensive argument for the influence of Virgil's *Aeneid* on Luke-Acts, see Marianne Palmer Bonz, *The Past as Legacy: Luke-Acts and Ancient Epic* (Minneapolis: Fortress Press, 2000).

31. Sherk, *Rome and the Greek East to the Death of Augustus,* 79b.

32. Brent, *The Imperial Cult and the Development of Church Order,* 90.

33. Notably, the one other New Testament text in which ἀρχηγός is used, the letter to the Hebrews, also features Jesus explicitly as a high priest (Hebrews 2:10, 2:17, 3:1, 12:2, 4:14–5:10). Here Jesus' high priestly role appears firmly set in a Jewish context, as Jesus offers sacrifice for the atonement of sins. Yet the notion of expiation of sins is also found in the Roman imperial setting. Consider Horace's *Odes* 3.6.1–4: "Thy fathers' sins, O Roman, thou, though guiltless, shall expiate, till you have restored the crumbling temples and shrines of the gods and their statues soiled with grimy smoke."

34. Lee I. Levine, "Second Temple Jerusalem: A Jewish City in the Greco-Roman Orbit," in *Jerusalem: Its Sanctity and Centrality to Judaism, Christianity, and Islam,* ed. Lee I. Levine (New York: Continuum, 1999), 56–60.

35. Ramsay MacMullen, *Romanization in the Time of Augustus* (New Haven, Conn.: Yale University Press, 2000), 22–23.

36. This euergetic practice also extended to diaspora. According to Josephus, the gates of the Temple were plated with gold by a certain Alexander the Alabarch, from Alexandria (*BJ* 5, 205–206). See Martin Goodman, "The Pilgrimage Economy of Jerusalem," in *Jerusalem: Its Sanctity and Centrality to Judaism, Christianity, and Islam,* ed. Lee I. Levine (New York: Continuum, 1999), 69–76.

37. Duane W. Roller, *The Building Program of Herod the Great* (Berkeley: University of California Press, 1998).

38. Adela Yarbro Collins, "Jesus' Actions in Herod's Temple," in *Antiquity and Humanity: Essays on Ancient Religion and Philosophy,* ed. Adela Yarbro Collins and Margaret M. Mitchell (Tübingen, Germany: Mohr Siebeck, 2001), 57.

39. Ya'akov Meshorer, "One Hundred Years of Tyrian Shekels," in *Festschrift Für Leo Mildenberg: Numismatik, Kunstgeschichte, Archäologie = Studies in Honor of Leo Mildenberg: Numismatics, Art History, Archeology,* ed. Leo Mildenberg and Arthur Houghton (Wetteren, Belgium: Editions NR, 1984), 170–79. For an opposing argument, see A. M. Burnett, Michel Amandry, P. P. Ripollés Alegre, and Bibliothèque Nationale (France), *Roman Provincial Coinage,* vol. 1, pt. 1 (Paris: British Museum Press with Bibliothèque Nationale [France], 1992).

40. Adela Collins uses Meshorer's work to interpret the "temple cleansing" scenes in the Gospels, with Jesus looking to purify the Temple of pagan influences such as the use of these coins. Collins, "Jesus' Actions in Herod's Temple." Her interpretation would assume that Jesus would be concerned with "pagan influence," but nothing in the Jesus traditions corroborates this theory.

41. J. G. Szemler, "Priesthood and Priestly Careers in Ancient Rome," *Aufstieg und Niedergang der römischen Welt* II.16.3 (1972): 2314–31.

42. Beard, North, and Price, *Religions of Rome*, 192.

43. Meir Bar-Ilan, "Writing in Ancient Israel and Early Judaism Part II: Scribes and Books in the Late Second Commonwealth and Rabbinic Period," in *Mikra: Text, Translation, Reading, and Interpretation of the Hebrew Bible in Ancient Judaism and Early Christianity*, ed. M. J. Mulder and Harry Sysling (Minneapolis: Fortress Press, 1990), 22.

44. Matthew follows Mark in putting the saying in the context of the last passion prediction (Mark 10:42–44, Matthew 20:25–28). Neither of them relates the conferring of a kingdom on the disciples here or elsewhere in their narratives.

CHAPTER 8

1. J. N. D. Kelly, *Early Christian Doctrines*, 4th ed. (London: Black, 1968), 339.

2. My count is only of occurrences of "the Son." I omit references to Son of Man, Son of God, or Son of David that run through the synoptic tradition, because here I am interested in the father/son relationship.

3. Adele Reinhartz, " 'And the Word Was Begotten': Divine Epigenesis in the Gospel of John," *Semeia* 85 (1999): 83–103.

4. Ibid., 92.

5. Ibid., 94.

6. Ibid., 99.

7. For discussion of the betrothal type-scene, see Robert Alter, *The Art of Biblical Narrative* (New York: Basic Books, 1981), 51–52. For the presence of this type-scene in John, see also P. Joseph Cahill, "Narrative Art in John IV," *Religious Studies Bulletin* 2 (1982): 44–47; Paul D. Duke, *Irony in the Fourth Gospel* (Atlanta: John Knox Press, 1985), 103; Lyle Eslinger, "The Wooing of the Woman at the Well: Jesus, the Reader and Reader-Response Criticism," *Literature and Theology* 1 (1987): 167–83; Adele Reinhartz, "The Gospel of John," in *Searching the Scriptures*, ed. Elisabeth Schüssler Fiorenza (New York: Crossroad, 1993), 572.

8. Lyle Eslinger, "The Wooing of the Woman at the Well."

9. M. Cambre, "L'influence Due Cantique Des Cantique Sur Le Nouveau Testament," *Revue Thomiste* 62 (1962): 5–26; Ann Roberts Winsor, *A King Is Bound in the Tresses: Allusions to the Song of Songs in the Fourth Gospel* (New York: Peter Lang, 1999).

10. Craig S. Keener, *The Gospel of John: A Commentary*, vol. 2 (Peabody, Mass: Hendrickson Publishers, 2003), 846.

11. At issue is whether ἐκάθισεν should be read transitively (he set him) or intransitively (he sat).

12. Though influenced by Christological readings of Isaiah, early church tradition suggests otherwise. Stephen D. Moore, "Ugly Thoughts: On the Face and Physique of the Historical Jesus," in *Biblical Studies/Cultural Studies* (Sheffield, England: Sheffield University Press, 1998), 376–99.

13. Dominic Montserrat, "Experiencing the Male Body in Roman Egypt," in *When Men Were Men: Masculinity, Power and Identity in Classical Antiquity*, ed. Lin Foxhall and J. B. Salmon (London: Routledge, 1998).

14. Ibid., 158–59.

15. Ibid., 160.

16. Raymond Edward Brown, *The Gospel According to John*, vol. 29A, The Anchor Bible (Garden City, N.Y.: Doubleday, 1970), 950.

17. For examples of the standard confession, "God raised him," see Mt. 20:19; Acts 3.15, 4:10, 5.30; 1 Cor. 6:14; Rom 4.24–25, 8.11, 10.9; 1 Pet 1.21.

18. Dale B. Martin, *Slavery as Salvation: The Metaphor of Slavery in Pauline Christianity* (New Haven, Conn.: Yale University Press, 1990).

19. Raymond Edward Brown, *The Gospel According to John*, vol. 29A, The Anchor Bible (Garden City, N.Y.: Doubleday, 1966), cxxii–cxxv; James D. G. Dunn, "Let John Be John—A Gospel for Its Time," in *Evangelium Und Die Evangelien* (Tübingen, Germany: J. C. B. Mohr [Paul Siebeck], 1983); Michael E. Willett, *Wisdom Christology in the Fourth Gospel* (San Francisco: Mellen Research University Press, 1992); and Martin Scott, *Sophia and the Johannine Jesus*, Journal for the Study of the New Testament Supplement 71 (Sheffield, England: Sheffield Academic Press, 1992).

20. Brown, *The Gospel According to John*, cxxiv.

21. Ibid., cxxii.

22. Joan Chamberlain Engelsman, *The Feminine Dimension of the Divine* (Philadelphia: Westminster Press, 1979), 199.

23. Elizabeth A. Johnson, *She Who Is: The Mystery of God in Feminist Theological Discourse* (New York: Crossroad, 1992), 172.

24. Scott, *Sophia and the Johannine Jesus*, 174. Scott's own imagination appears reluctant to drift too far in this direction. In the end, it seems that he envisions not a gender blend but a gender split—Jesus' inherent maleness is preserved and his feminine side is reflected in (or projected on to?) the Gospel's female characters (250).

25. Schüssler Fiorenza draws here on Norman Petersen, who, although not concerned with gender categories, nevertheless focuses on the way the Gospel's use of Wisdom traditions displaces Sophia (which has already displaced Moses in Second Temple Jewish literature) in favor of Jesus. Norman R. Petersen, *The Gospel of John and the Sociology of Light: Language and Characterization in the Fourth Gospel* (Valley Forge, Pa.: Trinity Press, 1993), 114–19.

26. Elisabeth Schüssler Fiorenza, *Jesus: Miriam's Child, Sophia's Prophet: Critical Issues in Feminist Christology* (New York: Continuum, 1994), 153.

27. Wayne A. Meeks, "Man from Heaven in Johannine Sectarianism," *Journal of Biblical Literature* 91 (1972): 72.

28. Judith E. McKinlay, *Gendering Wisdom the Host: Biblical Invitations to Eat and Drink*, Journal for the Study of the Old Testament Supplement 216 (Sheffield, England: Sheffield Academic Press, 1996), 206; Luise Schottroff, *Lydia's Impatient Sisters: A Feminist Social History of Early Christianity* (Louisville, Ky.: Westminter John Knox Press, 1995), 85.

29. Willett, *Wisdom Christology in the Fourth Gospel*, 147–48.

30. Jane S. Webster, "Sophia: Engendering Wisdom in Proverbs, Ben Sira and the Wisdom of Solomon," *Journal for the Study of the Old Testament* 78 (1998): 63–79.

31. Judith M. Lieu, "Scripture and the Feminine in John," in *Feminist Companion to the Hebrew Bible in the New Testament* (Sheffield, England: Sheffield Academic Press, 1996), 228–29.

32. Webster, "Sophia," 67.

33. Petersen, *The Gospel of John and the Sociology of Light*, 110–32.

34. Bill Salier suggests that the adjective ἀλήθιεα (true) suggests a polemic against claims made about the emperor. For this and other potential associations between the Johannine Jesus and imperial ideology, see "Jesus, the Emperor, and the Gospel According to John," in *Challenging Perspectives on the Gospel of John*, ed. John Lierman (Tübingen, Germany: Mohr Siebeck, 2006), 284–301.

35. Webster, "Sophia," 76.

36. Raymond E. Brown, "Roles of Women in the Fourth Gospel," *Theological Studies* 36 (1975): 688–99; Sandra M. Schneiders, "Women in the Fourth Gospel and the Role of Women in the Contemporary Church," *Biblical Theology Bulletin* 12 (1982): 35–45; Scott, *Sophia and the Johannine Jesus*.

37. See Colleen M. Conway, *Men and Women in the Fourth Gospel: Gender and Johannine Characterization* (Atlanta: Society of Biblical Literature, 1999), 163–77.

38. I develop this idea in my article "Gender Matters in John," in *The Feminist Companion to the Gospel of John*, ed. Amy-Jill Levine (Sheffield, England: Sheffield Academic Press, 2003), 79–103.

CHAPTER 9

1. While Adela Yarbro Collins's work on the ancient Near Eastern combat myth as background for Revelation is likely on target, it does not reduce the resonance that battle imagery would have with the contemporary Roman context. Adela Yarbro Collins, *The Combat Myth in the Book of Revelation*, Harvard Dissertations in Religion, no. 9 (Missoula, Mont.: Scholars Press, 1976).

2. For the angelic characteristics of the Son of Man in Revelation 1, see Matthias Reinhard Hoffmann, *The Destroyer and the Lamb: The Relationship between Angelomorphic and Lamb Christology in the Book of Revelation* (Tübingen, Germany: Mohr Siebeck, 2005), 219–46.

3. David E. Aune, *Revelation 1–5*, Word Biblical Commentary, vol. 52a (Dallas: Word Books, 1997), 128. Aune's argument builds on the work of Margareta Benner, *The Emperor Says: Studies in the Rhetorical Style in Edicts of the Early Empire* (Göteborg, Sweden: Acta Universitatis Gothoburgensis, 1975).

4. Gunnar Rudberg, "Zu Den Sendschreiben Der Johannes-Apokalypse," *Eranos* 11 (1911): 170–79. Rudberg was the first to make the association between the letters of Revelation and imperial edicts.

5. Aune, *Revelation 1–5*, 129. See also David E. Aune, "The Form and Function of the Proclamations to the Seven Churches (Rev 2–3)," *New Testament Studies* 36 (1990): 182–204.

6. Aune, *Revelation 1–5*, 129.

7. So Leif Vaage notes of Aune's conclusions, "One might just as easily conclude on the basis of the same comparison, that God and Jesus in Revelation are mirror-imitations of the Roman emperor." Leif E. Vaage, "Why Christianity Succeeded (in) the Roman Empire," in *Religious Rivalries in the Early Roman Empire and the Rise of Christianity*, ed. Leif E. Vaage (Waterloo, Ont.: Wilfrid Laurier University Press, 2006), 268.

8. There are now multiple studies on the relationship of Revelation to its imperial context. See, for instance, Leonard L. Thompson, *The Book of Revelation: Apocalypse and Empire* (New York: Oxford University Press, 1990); Steven J. Friesen, *Imperial Cults and the Apocalypse of John: Reading Revelation in the Ruins* (New York: Oxford University Press, 2001); and Stephen D. Moore, *Empire and Apocalypse: Postcolonialism and the New Testament* (Sheffield, England: Sheffield Phoenix Press, 2006).

9. Recent interpreters who discuss the sexual overtones of the action include Greg Carey, *Elusive Apocalypse: Reading Authority in the Revelation to John* (Macon, Ga.: Mercer University Press, 1999), 158, and Christopher A. Frilingos, *Spectacles of Empire: Monsters, Martyrs, and the Book of Revelation* (Philadelphia: University of Pennsylvania Press, 2004), 109.

10. Many interpreters argue against an interpretation that emphasizes the violent imagery in Revelation.

11. This phrase, "another angel," is another clear indication that the author had angelic imagery in mind in his depiction of the Son of Man.

12. Or 189 miles, to be more precise, as a Roman stadium is equivalent to 625 feet.

13. Robert H. Mounce, *The Book of Revelation*, rev. ed. (Grand Rapids, Mich.: Eerdmans, 1998), 356.

14. See the discussion of anger in chapter 2, "Acting Like a Man: Masculinity, Sexuality, and the Virtues."

15. Gregory M. Stevenson, "Conceptual Background to Golden Crown Imagery in the Apocalypse of John (4:4,10 14:14)," *Journal of Biblical Literature* 114 (1995): 257–72.

16. Mitchell G. Reddish, *Revelation* (Macon, Ga.: Smyth & Helwys, 2001), 368.

17. Ronald H. Preston and Anthony T. Hanson, *The Revelation of Saint John the Divine: An Introduction and Commentary* (London: SCM Press, 1949), 120. More recently, see also Gerhard Krodel, *Revelation* (Minneapolis: Augsburg, 1989), 323.

18. "Among the variant readings βεβαμμένον appears to be the best supported (A 046 051 most minuscules cop^sa arm *al*) and most likely to provoke change." Bruce M. Metzger, *A Textual Commentary on the Greek New Testament*, 3rd ed. (London: United Bible Societies, 1971), 761.

19. Jürgen Roloff, *The Revelation of John* (Minneapolis: Fortress Press, 1993), 218; David E. Aune, *Revelation 17–22*, Word Biblical Commentary, vol. 52c (Nashville: T. Nelson, 1998), 1048, 57; and Mounce, *The Book of Revelation*, 353–54.

20. Elizabeth Cornelia Evans, *Physiognomics in the Ancient World*, vol. 59, Transactions of the American Philosophical Society (Philadelphia: American Philosophical Society, 1969), 8–9.

21. Loren L. Johns, *The Lamb Christology of the Apocalypse of John: An Investigation into Its Origins and Rhetorical Force*, Wissenschaftliche Untersuchungen Zum Neuen Testament. 2. Reihe, 167 (Tübingen, Germany: Mohr Siebeck, 2003), 168. For a similar response to the text, see David L. Barr, "Apocalypse as the Symbolic Transformation of the World: A Literary Analysis," *Interpretation* 38 (1984): 41.

22. Johns, *The Lamb Christology of the Apocalypse of John*, 161.

23. Brian K. Blount, *Can I Get a Witness? Reading Revelation through African American Culture* (Louisville, Ky.: Westminster John Knox Press, 2005).

24. Frilingos, *Spectacles of Empire*, 78.

25. For readings that represent such communites, see Allan Aubrey Boesak, *Comfort and Protest: Reflections on the Apocalypse of John of Patmos* (Philadelphia: Westminster Press, 1987) and Miroslav Volf, *Exclusion and Embrace: A Theological Exploration of Identity, Otherness, and Reconciliation* (Nashville: Abingdon Press, 1996), 275–306. For a range of interpretations of Revelation from a variety of social locations, see David M. Rhoads, ed., *From Every People and Nation: The Book of Revelation in Intercultural Perspective* (Minneapolis: Fortress Press, 2005).

26. David L. Barr, "The Lamb Who Looks Like a Dragon? Characterizing Jesus in John's Apocalypse," in *The Reality of Apocalypse: Rhetoric and Politics in the Book of Revelation*, ed. David L. Barr (Atlanta: Society of Biblical Literature, 2006), 209.

27. Blount, *Can I Get a Witness*, 82.

28. Ibid.

29. Barr, "The Lamb Who Looks Like a Dragon," 215.

30. Mounce, *The Book of Revelation*, 133.

31. David E. Aune, "The Influence of Roman Imperial Court Ceremonial on the Apocalypse of John," *Biblical Research* 18 (1983): 5–26.

32. For a sustained reading of Revelation alongside 4 Maccabees (and Irish nationalism), see Stephen D. Moore, *God's Beauty Parlor: And Other Queer Spaces in and around the Bible* (Stanford, Calif.: Stanford University Press, 2001), 191–99.

33. Janice Capel Anderson and Stephen D. Moore, "Taking It Like a Man: Masculinity in 4 Maccabees," *Journal of Biblical Literature* 117 (1998): 264, 272.

34. Moore, *God's Beauty Parlor*, 199.

35. Frilingos, *Spectacles of Empire*, 81.

36. Janice Capel Anderson and Stephen D. Moore, "Taking It Like a Man: Masculinity in 4 Maccabees," *Journal of Biblical Literature* 117 (1998): 267. For analysis of the images of women in Revelation, see Tina Pippin, *Death and Desire: The Rhetoric of Gender in the Apocalypse of John* (Louisville, Ky.: Westminster John Knox Press, 1992), and Tina Pippin, *Apocalyptic Bodies: The Biblical End of the World in Text and Image* (London: Routledge, 1999). Also Paul B. Duff, "Wolves in Sheep's

Clothing: Literary Opposition and Social Tension in the Revelation of John," in *Reading the Book of Revelation: A Resource for Students*, ed. David L. Barr (Leiden, the Netherlands: Brill, 2004) and Edith M. Humphrey, "A Tale of Two Cities and (at Least) Three Women: Transformation, Continuity, and Contrast in the Apocalypse," in *Reading the Book of Revelation: A Resource for Students*, ed. David L. Barr (Leiden, the Netherlands: Brill, 2004).

37. Moore, *Empire and Apocalypse*, 106.

38. Many have suggested that these redeemed are symbolically chaste insofar as they have not participated in the imperial cult.

39. Adela Yarbro Collins, *Crisis and Catharsis: The Power of the Apocalypse* (Philadelphia: Westminster Press, 1984), 130. See also John W. Marshall, *Parables of War: Reading John's Jewish Apocalypse* (Waterloo, Ont.: Wilfrid Laurier University Press, 2001), 155–63. References to purity in the camp are found in Leviticus 14:1–8 and Numbers 5:1–4. Especially Deuteronomy 23:9–14 suggests the sexual purification required for those who enter the war camp. David points to the sexual abstinence of his men on expedition (1 Samuel 21:5), and Uriah refuses to have intercourse with his wife while his comrades are in the war camp (2 Samuel 11:11).

40. Marshall, *Parables of War*, 162.

41. For an alternative argument regarding the "arrested masculinity" of the lamb, see Frilingos, *Spectacles of Empire*, 87–88.

42. Collins, *Crisis and Catharsis*.

43. Robert M. Royalty, *The Streets of Heaven: The Ideology of Wealth in the Apocalypse of John* (Macon, Ga.: Mercer University Press, 1998), 246.

44. Moore, *Empire and Apocalypse*, 120.

45. Moore, *God's Beauty Parlor*, 198–99.

CHAPTER 10

1. Michele Renee Salzman, *The Making of a Christian Aristocracy: Social and Religious Change in the Western Roman Empire* (Cambridge, Mass.: Harvard University Press, 2002).

2. Carlin A. Barton, *The Sorrows of the Ancient Romans: The Gladiator and the Monster* (Princeton, N.J.: Princeton University Press, 1993), and Maud W. Gleason, *Making Men: Sophists and Self-Presentation in Ancient Rome* (Princeton, N.J.: Princeton University Press, 1995).

3. Matthew Kuefler, *The Manly Eunuch: Masculinity, Gender Ambiguity, and Christian Ideology in Late Antiquity* (Chicago: University of Chicago Press, 2001), 209.

4. Ibid., 208.

5. See chapter 2.

6. For further discussion of Scott's work in relation to New Testament interpretation, see Richard A. Horsley, *Hidden Transcripts and the Arts of Resistance: Applying the Work of James C. Scott to Jesus and Paul* (Atlanta: Society of Biblical Literature, 2004).

7. James C. Scott, *Domination and the Arts of Resistance: Hidden Transcripts* (New Haven, Conn.: Yale University Press, 1990), 102–103.

8. Greg Woolf, *Becoming Roman: The Origins of Provincial Civilization in Gaul* (Cambridge, England: Cambridge University Press, 1998), 55.

9. Leif E. Vaage, "Why Christianity Succeeded (in) the Roman Empire," in *Religious Rivalries in the Early Roman Empire and the Rise of Christianity*, ed. Leif E. Vaage (Waterloo, Ont.: Wilfrid Laurier University Press, 2006), 255. In my 2004 SBL presentation, "Imperial Masculinity and the Jesus Traditions," I spoke of the Gospel writers' strategies of resistance through accommodation in much the same way.

10. See chapter 5, "The Markan Jesus as Noble Martyr."

11. Jonathan Dollimore, *Sexual Dissidence: Literatures, Histories, Theories* (New York: Oxford University Press, 1991), 52.

Bibliography

Alter, Robert. *The Art of Biblical Narrative*. New York: Basic Books, 1981.

Anderson, Graham. *Philostratus: Biography and Belles Lettres in the Third Century A.D.* London: Croom Helm, 1986.

Anderson, Janice Capel, and Stephen D. Moore. "Matthew and Masculinity." In *New Testament Masculinities*, edited by Stephen D. Moore and Janice Capel Anderson, 67–91. Atlanta: Society of Biblical Literature, 2003.

———. "Taking It Like a Man: Masculinity in 4 Maccabees." *Journal of Biblical Literature* 117 (1998): 249–73.

Ariès, Philippe, and André Béjin. *Western Sexuality: Practice and Precept in Past and Present Times*. Oxford: Blackwell, 1985.

Aspegren, Kerstin. *The Male Woman: A Feminine Ideal in the Early Church*, edited by René Kieffer. Uppsala, Sweden: Uppsala University, 1990.

Atherton, Catherine. "Children, Animal, Slaves and Grammar." In *Pedagogy and Power: Rhetorics of Classical Learning*, edited by Yun Lee Too and Niall Livingstone, 214–44. Cambridge, England: Cambridge University Press, 1998.

Aune, David E. "The Form and Function of the Proclamations to the Seven Churches (Rev 2–3)." *New Testament Studies* 36 (1990): 182–204.

———. "The Influence of Roman Imperial Court Ceremonial on the Apocalypse of John." *Biblical Research* 18 (1983): 5–26.

———. *Revelation 1–5*. Word Biblical Commentary. Vol. 52a. Dallas: Word Books, 1997.

———. *Revelation 17–22*. Word Biblical Commentary. Vol. 52c. Nashville: T. Nelson, 1998.

Baer, Richard Arthur. *Philo's Use of the Categories Male and Female*. Leiden, the Netherlands: Brill, 1970.

Bar-Ilan, Meir. "Writing in Ancient Israel and Early Judaism Part II: Scribes and Books in the Late Second Commonwealth and Rabbinic Period." In *Mikra: Text, Translation, Reading, and Interpretation of the Hebrew Bible in Ancient Judaism and Early Christianity*, edited by M. J. Mulder and Harry Sysling. Minneapolis: Fortress Press, 1990.

Barr, David L. "Apocalypse as the Symbolic Transformation of the World: A Literary Analysis." *Interpretation* 38 (1984): 39–50.

———. "The Lamb Who Looks Like a Dragon? Characterizing Jesus in John's Apocalypse." In *The Reality of Apocalypse: Rhetoric and Politics in the Book of Revelation*, edited by David L. Barr, 205–20. Atlanta: Society of Biblical Literature, 2006.

Barton, Bruce. *The Man Nobody Knows: A Discovery of Jesus*. Indianapolis: Bobbs-Merrill, 1925.

Barton, Carlin A. *Roman Honor: The Fire in the Bones*. Berkeley: University of California Press, 2001.

———. *The Sorrows of the Ancient Romans: The Gladiator and the Monster*. Princeton, N.J.: Princeton University Press, 1993.

Barton, Stephen C. *Discipleship and Family Ties in Mark and Matthew*. Cambridge, England: Cambridge University Press, 1994.

Barton, Tamsyn. *Power and Knowledge: Astrology, Physiognomics, and Medicine under the Roman Empire*. Ann Arbor: University of Michigan Press, 1994.

Basil. *Ascetical Works*, translated by Monica Wagner. Vol. 9, The Fathers of the Church. Washington, D.C.: Catholic University of America Press, 1950.

Beard, Mary, and John Henderson. "The Emperor's New Body: Ascension from Rome." In *Parchments of Gender: Deciphering the Bodies of Antiquity*, edited by Maria Wyke, 191–219. Oxford: Oxford University Press, 1998.

Beard, Mary, John A. North, and S. R. F. Price. *Religions of Rome: Volume 1: A History*. Cambridge, England: Cambridge University Press, 1998.

Beker, Johan Christiaan. *Paul the Apostle: The Triumph of God in Life and Thought*. Philadelphia: Fortress Press, 1980.

Bellemore, Jane, ed. *Nicolaus of Damascus Life of Augustus*. Bristol, England: Bristol Classical Press, 1984.

Benner, Margareta. *The Emperor Says: Studies in the Rhetorical Style in Edicts of the Early Empire*. Göteborg, Sweden: Acta Universitatis Gothoburgensis, 1975.

Best, Ernest. *The Temptation and the Passion: The Markan Soteriology*. 2nd ed. Cambridge, England: Cambridge University Press, 1990.

Betz, Hans Dieter. *The Sermon on the Mount: A Commentary on the Sermon on the Mount, Including the Sermon on the Plain (Matthew 5:3–7:27 and Luke 6:20–49)*. Hermeneia. Minneapolis: Fortress Press, 1995.

Bhabha, Homi K. *The Location of Culture*. London: Routledge, 1994.

Blevins, James L. *The Messianic Secret in Markan Research, 1901–1976*. Washington, D.C.: University Press of America, 1981.

Bloomer, W. Martin. "Schooling in Persona: Imagination and Subordination in Roman Education." *Classical Antiquity* 16 (1997): 58–78.

Blount, Brian K. *Can I Get a Witness? Reading Revelation through African American Culture*. Louisville, Ky.: Westminster John Knox Press, 2005.

Boer, Roland, and Gerald O. West, eds. *A Vanishing Mediator? The Presence/Absence of the Bible in Postcolonialism*. Atlanta: Society of Biblical Literature, 2001.

Boesak, Allan Aubrey. *Comfort and Protest: Reflections on the Apocalypse of John of Patmos*. Philadelphia: Westminster Press, 1987.

Bonz, Marianne Palmer. *The Past as Legacy: Luke-Acts and Ancient Epic*. Minneapolis: Fortress Press, 2000.

Boring, M. Eugene. *Mark: A Commentary*. Louisville, Ky.: Westminster John Knox Press, 2006.

———. "Narrative Christology in the Apocalypse." *Catholic Biblical Quarterly* 54 (1992): 702–23.

Bosworth, Brian. "Augustus, the *Res Gestae* and Hellenistic Theories of Apotheosis." *Journal of Roman Studies* 89 (1999): 1–18.

Bowersock, G. W. "The Mechanics of Subversion in the Roman Provinces." In *Opposition Et Résistances À L'empire D'auguste À Trajan: Neuf Exposés Suivis De Discusssions*, edited by Kurt A. Raaflaub and Adalberto Giovannini, 291–320. Vandœuvres-Genève, Switzerland: Fondation Hardt, 1987.

———. "The Pontificate of Augustus." In *Between Republic and Empire: Interpretations of Augustus and His Principate*, edited by Kurt A. Raaflaub, Mark Toher, and G. W. Bowersock, 380–94. Berkeley: University of California Press, 1990.

Bowie, E. L. "Apollonius of Tyana: Tradition and Reality." *Aufstieg und Niedergang der römischen Welt* II.16.2 (1978): 1652–99.

Brakke, David. "The Passions and the Social Construction of Masculinity." Paper presented at the annual meeting of the Society of Biblical Literature. Orlando, November 21–24, 1998.

Brannigan, John. *New Historicism and Cultural Materialism*. New York: St. Martin's Press, 1998.

Brawley, Robert L. *Luke-Acts and the Jews: Conflict, Apology, and Conciliation*. Atlanta: Scholars Press, 1987.

Brent, Allen. *The Imperial Cult and the Development of Church Order: Concepts and Images of Authority in Paganism and Early Christianity before the Age of Cyprian*. Supplements to Vigiliae Christianae. Vol. 45. Boston: Brill, 1999.

Brod, Harry, ed. *The Making of Masculinities: The New Men's Studies*. Boston: Allen & Unwin, 1987.

Brod, Harry, and Michael Kaufman. *Theorizing Masculinities*. Thousand Oaks, Calif.: Sage Publications, 1994.

Brown, Peter R. *The Body and Society: Men, Women, and Sexual Renunciation in Early Christianity*. New York: Columbia University Press, 1988.

Brown, Raymond E. "Roles of Women in the Fourth Gospel." *Theological Studies* 36 (1975): 688–99.

Brown, Raymond E. *The Gospel According to John*. Vols. 29, 29A, The Anchor Bible. Garden City, N.Y.: Doubleday, 1966, 1970.

Burnett, A. M., Michel Amandry, P. P. Ripollés Alegre, and Bibliothèque Nationale (France). *Roman Provincial Coinage*. Vol. 1, pt. 1. Paris: British Museum Press with Bibliothèque Nationale (France), 1992.

Burridge, Richard A. "From Titles to Stories: A Narrative Approach to the Dynamic Christologies of the New Testament." In *Person of Christ*, edited by Stephen R. Holmes and Rae Murray, 37–60. London: T & T Clark, 2005.

Butler, Judith. *Gender Trouble: Feminism and the Subversion of Identity*. New York: Routledge, 1990.

Bynum, Caroline Walker. *Jesus as Mother: Studies in the Spirituality of the High Middle Ages*. Berkeley: University of California Press, 1982.

Cahill, P. Joseph. "Narrative Art in John IV." *Religious Studies Bulletin* 2 (1982): 41–48.

Cambre, M. "L'influence Due Cantique Des Cantique Sur Le Nouveau Testament." *Revue Thomiste* 62 (1962): 5–26.

Carey, Greg. *Elusive Apocalypse: Reading Authority in the Revelation to John*. Macon, Ga.: Mercer University Press, 1999.

Carr, Anne E. *Transforming Grace: Christian Tradition and Women's Experience*. San Francisco: Harper & Row, 1990.

Carr, David M., and Colleen M. Conway. "The Divine-Human Marriage Matrix and Constructions of Gender and 'Bodies' in the Christian Bible." In *Sacred Marriages: The Divine-Human Sexual Metaphor from Sumer to Early Christianity*, edited by Martti Nissinen and Risto Uro. Winona Lake, Ind.: Eisenbrauns, 2008.

Carrigan, Tim, Bob Connell, and John Lee. "Toward a New Sociology of Masculinity." In *The Making of Masculinities: The New Men's Studies*, edited by Harry Brod, 63–111. Boston: Allen & Unwin, 1987.

Carter, Warren. *Matthew and Empire: Initial Explorations*. Harrisburg, Pa.: Trinity Press International, 2001.

———. *Matthew and the Margins: A Sociopolitical and Religious Reading*. Maryknoll, N.Y.: Orbis Books, 2000.

Chance, J. Bradley. *Jerusalem, the Temple, and the New Age in Luke-Acts*. Macon, Ga.: Mercer University Press, 1988.

Choi, Hee An, and Katheryn Pfisterer Darr, eds. *Engaging the Bible: Critical Readings from Contemporary Women*. Minneapolis: Fortress Press, 2006.

Chronis, Harry L. "To Reveal and to Conceal: A Literary-Critical Perspective on 'the Son of Man' in Mark." *New Testament Studies* 51 (2005): 459–81.

Clare, Anthony W. *On Men: Masculinity in Crisis*. London: Chatto & Windus, 2000.

Coleridge, Mark. *The Birth of the Lukan Narrative: Narrative as Christology in Luke 1-2*. Sheffield, England: JSOT Press, 1993.

Collins, Adela Yarbro. *The Combat Myth in the Book of Revelation*. Harvard Dissertations in Religion. No. 9. Missoula, Mont.: Scholars Press, 1976.

———. *Crisis and Catharsis: The Power of the Apocalypse*. Philadelphia: Westminster Press, 1984.

———. ed. *Feminist Perspectives on Biblical Scholarship*. Chico, Calif.: Scholars Press, 1985.

————. "Jesus' Actions in Herod's Temple." In *Antiquity and Humanity: Essays on Ancient Religion and Philosophy*, edited by Adela Yarbro Collins and Margaret M. Mitchell, 45–61. Tübingen, Germany: Mohr Siebeck, 2001.

Combes, Isobel. "Nursing Mother, Ancient Shepherd, Athletic Coach: Some Images of Christ in the Early Church." In *Images of Christ: Ancient and Modern*, edited by Stanley E. Porter, Michael A. Hayes, and David Tombs, 113–25. Sheffield, England: Sheffield Academic Press, 1997.

Conant, Robert Warren. *The Virility of Christ: A New View*. Chicago: The author, 1915.

Connolly, Joy. "Like the Labors of Heracles: *Andreia* and *Paideia* in Greek Culture under Rome." In *Andreia: Studies in Manliness and Courage in Classical Antiquity*, edited by Ralph Mark Rosen and I. Sluiter, 287–317. Leiden, the Netherlands: Brill, 2003.

————. "Mastering Corruption: Constructions of Identity in Roman Oratory." In *Women and Slaves in Greco-Roman Culture: Differential Equations*, edited by Sandra R. Joshel and Sheila Murnaghan, 130–51. London: Routledge, 2001.

Conway, Colleen M. "Gender Matters in John." In *The Feminist Companion to the Gospel of John*, edited by Amy-Jill Levine, 79–103. Sheffield, England: Sheffield Academic Press, 2003.

————. "Imperial Masculinity and the Jesus Traditions." Paper presented at the annual meeting of the Society of Biblical Literature. San Antonio, November 2004.

————. *Men and Women in the Fourth Gospel: Gender and Johannine Characterization*. Atlanta: Society of Biblical Literature, 1999.

————. "New Historicism and the Historical Jesus in John: Friends or Foes?" In *John, Jesus and History: Critical Appraisals of Critical Views*, edited by Paul Anderson, Felix Just and Tom Thatcher, 203–19. Atlanta: Scholars Press, 2007.

————. "Philo of Alexandria and Divine Relativity." *Journal for the Study of Judaism* 34 (2003): 471–91.

Cotter, Wendy J. "Greco-Roman Apotheosis Traditions and the Resurrection Appearances in Matthew." In *The Gospel of Matthew in Current Study: Studies in Memory of William G. Thompson S.J*, edited by David E. Aune, 127–53. Grand Rapids, Mich.: Eerdmans, 2001.

Cousar, Charles B. *A Theology of the Cross: The Death of Jesus in the Pauline Letters*. Minneapolis: Fortress Press, 1990.

Cribiore, Raffaella. *Gymnastics of the Mind: Greek Education in Hellenistic and Roman Egypt*. Princeton, N.J.: Princeton University Press, 2001.

Cullmann, Oscar. *The Christology of the New Testament*. Translated by Shirley C. Guthrie and Charles A.M. Hall. Rev. ed. Philadelphia: Westminster Press, 1959.

Cullyer, Helen. "Socratic Echoes in Stoic 'Manly Courage.'" In *Andreia: Studies in Manliness and Courage in Classical Antiquity*, edited by Ralph Mark Rosen and I. Sluiter, 213–33. Leiden, the Netherlands: Brill, 2003.

D'Angelo, Mary Rose. "The ANHP Question in Luke-Acts: Imperial Masculinity and the Deployment of Women in the Early Second Century." In *A Feminist*

Companion to Luke, edited by Amy-Jill Levine and Marianne Blickenstaff, 44–69. London: Sheffield Academic Press, 2002.

Danove, Paul. "The Rhetoric of Characterization of Jesus as the Son of Man and Christ in Mark." *Biblica* 84 (2003): 16–34.

Davies, W. D., and Dale C. Allison. *A Critical and Exegetical Commentary on the Gospel According to Saint Matthew*. Vol. 1. Edinburgh: T. & T. Clark, 1988.

Day, Linda, and Carolyn Pressler, eds. *Engaging the Bible in a Gendered World: An Introduction to Feminist Biblical Interpretation in Honor of Katharine Doob Sakenfeld*. Louisville, Ky.: Westminster John Knox Press, 2006.

de Jonge, Henk J. "The Original Setting of the χριστός ἀπέθανεν ὑπερ Formula." In *The Thessalonian Correspondence*, edited by Raymond Collins, 229–35. Louvain, Belgium: Leuven University Press, 1990.

de Jonge, Marinus. *Christology in Context: The Earliest Christian Response to Jesus*. Philadelphia: Westminster Press, 1988.

Derrett, J. Duncan M. "Contributions to the Study of the Gerasene Demoniac." *Journal for Study of the New Testament* 3 (1979): 2–17.

Deutsch, Celia. *Lady Wisdom, Jesus, and the Sages: Metaphor and Social Context in Matthew's Gospel*. Valley Forge, Pa.: Trinity Press International, 1996.

Dewey, Arthur J. "The Unkindest Cut of All? Matthew 19:11–12." *Forum* 8 (1992): 113–22.

Dewey, Johanna. "The Gospel of Mark." In *Searching the Scriptures*. Vol. 2. *A Feminist Commentary*, edited by Elisabeth Schüssler Fiorenza, Shelly Matthews, and Ann Graham Brock, 470–509. New York: Crossroad, 1994.

Dollimore, Jonathan. *Sexual Dissidence: Literatures, Histories, Theories*. New York: Oxford University Press, 1991.

Donahue, John R., and Daniel J. Harrington. *The Gospel of Mark*. Collegeville, Minn.: Liturgical Press, 2005.

Donaldson, Terrence L. "The Vindicated Son: A Narrative Approach to Matthean Christology." In *Contours of Christology in the New Testament*, edited by Richard N. Longenecker, 100–121. Grand Rapids, Mich.: Eerdmans, 2005.

Doss, Erika. "Making a 'Virile, Manly Christ': The Cultural Origins and Meanings of Warner Sallman's Religious Imagery." In *Icons of American Protestantism: The Art of Warner Sallman*, edited by David Morgan, 61–94. New Haven, Conn.: Yale University Press, 1996.

Downing, F. Gerald. "A Bas Les Aristos: The Relevance of Higher Literature for the Understanding of the Earliest Christian Writings." *Novum Testamentum* 30 (1988): 212–30.

———. *Cynics and Christian Origins*. Edinburgh: T & T Clark, 1992.

Dubu, Musa W. *Postcolonial Feminist Interpretation of the Bible*. St. Louis: Chalice Press, 2000.

Duff, Paul B. "Wolves in Sheep's Clothing: Literary Opposition and Social Tension in the Revelation of John." In *Reading the Book of Revelation: A Resource for Students*, edited by David L. Barr, 65–79. Leiden, the Netherlands: Brill, 2004.

Duke, Paul D. *Irony in the Fourth Gospel*. Atlanta: John Knox Press, 1985.

Dunn, J. D. G. "Paul's Understanding of the Death of Jesus." In *Sacrifice and Redemption*, edited by S. W. Sykes, 35–56. Cambridge, England: Cambridge University Press, 1990.

Dunn, James D. G. "Let John Be John—A Gospel for Its Time." In *Evangelium Und Die Evangelien*, 309–39. Tübingen, Germany: J. C. B. Mohr (Paul Siebeck), 1983.

Dupont, Florence. "The Emperor-God's Other Body." In *Fragments for a History of the Human Body: Part Three*, edited by Michael Feher, 397–419. New York: Zone, 1989.

Dzielska, Maria. *Apollonius of Tyana in Legend and History*. Rome: "L'Erma" di Bretschneider, 1986.

Edwards, Catharine. *The Politics of Immorality in Ancient Rome*. Cambridge, England: Cambridge University Press, 1993.

———. "The Suffering Body: Philosophy and Pain in Seneca's Letters." In *Constructions of the Classical Body*, edited by James I. Porter, 252–68. Ann Arbor: University of Michigan Press, 1999.

Edwards, Tim. *Cultures of Masculinity*. London: Routledge, 2006.

Ehrenberg, Victor, A. H. M. Jones, and D. L. Stockton, eds. *Documents Illustrating the Reigns of Augustus and Tiberius*. 2nd ed. Oxford: Clarendon Press, 1976.

Eilberg-Schwartz, Howard. *God's Phallus and Other Problems for Men and Monotheism*. Boston: Beacon Press, 1994.

Elliott, Neil. *Liberating Paul: The Justice of God and the Politics of the Apostle*. Maryknoll, N.Y.: Orbis Books, 1994.

Elsner, Jas. *Art and the Roman Viewer: The Transformation of Art from the Pagan World to Christianity*. Cambridge, England: Cambridge University Press, 1995.

Elsner, John. "Cult and Sculpture: Sacrifice in the Ara Pacis Augustae." *Journal of Roman Studies* 81 (1991): 50–61.

Engelsman, Joan Chamberlain. *The Feminine Dimension of the Divine*. Philadelphia: Westminster Press, 1979.

Esler, Philip Francis. *Community and Gospel in Luke-Acts: The Social and Political Motivations of Lucan Theology*. Cambridge, England: Cambridge University Press, 1987.

Eslinger, Lyle. "The Wooing of the Woman at the Well: Jesus, the Reader and Reader-Response Criticism." *Literature and Theology* 1 (1987): 167–83.

Evans, Elizabeth Cornelia. *Physiognomics in the Ancient World*. Vol. 59, Transactions of the American Philosophical Society. Philadelphia: American Philosophical Society, 1969.

Faxon, Alicia Craig. *Women and Jesus*. Philadelphia: United Church Press, 1973.

Fears, J. Rufus. "The Cult of Virtues and Roman Imperial Theology." *Aufstieg und Niedergang der römischen Welt* II.17.2 (1981): 825–948.

Foucault, Michel. *The History of Sexuality*. Vol. 3, *The Care of the Self*. New York: Vintage Books, 1988.

Friesen, Steven J. *Imperial Cults and the Apocalypse of John: Reading Revelation in the Ruins*. New York: Oxford University Press, 2001.

Frilingos, Christopher A. *Spectacles of Empire: Monsters, Martyrs, and the Book of Revelation*. Philadelphia: University of Pennsylvania Press, 2004.

Fuller, Reginald Horace. *The Foundations of New Testament Christology*. New York: Scribner, 1965.

Galen. *On the Usefulness of the Parts of the Body*. Translated by Margaret Tallmadge May. Ithaca, N.Y.: Cornell University Press, 1968.

Galinsky, Karl. *The Cambridge Companion to the Age of Augustus*. Cambridge, England: Cambridge University Press, 2005.

Gallagher, Catherine. "Marxism and the New Historicism." In *The New Historicism*, edited by H. Aram Veeser, 37–48. New York: Routledge, 1989.

Gallagher, Catherine, and Stephen Greenblatt. *Practicing New Historicism*. Chicago: University of Chicago Press, 2000.

Gardner, Jane. "Sexing a Roman: Imperfect Men in Roman Law." In *When Men Were Men: Masculinity, Power, and Identity in Classical Antiquity*, edited by Lin Foxhall and J. B. Salmon, 136–52. London: Routledge, 1998.

Garnsey, Peter, and Richard P. Saller. *The Roman Empire: Economy, Society, and Culture*. Berkeley: University of California Press, 1987.

Garrett, Susan R. *The Demise of the Devil: Magic and the Demonic in Luke's Writings*. Minneapolis: Fortress Press, 1989.

Garrison, Daniel H. *Sexual Culture in Ancient Greece*. Norman: University of Oklahoma Press, 2000.

Gibson, Jeffrey B. "Paul's 'Dying Formula': Prolegomena to an Understanding of Its Import and Significance." In *Celebrating Romans: Template for Pauline Theology*, edited by Sheila E. McGinn, 20–41. Grand Rapids, Mich.: Eerdmans, 2004.

Gilbert, Gary. "Roman Propaganda and Christian Identity in the Worldview of Luke-Acts." In *Contextualizing Acts: Lukan Narrative and Greco-Roman Discourse*, edited by Todd C. Penner and Caroline Vander Stichele, 233–56. Leiden, the Netherlands: Brill, 2004.

Gilmore, David D. *Manhood in the Making: Cultural Concepts of Masculinity*. New Haven, Conn.: Yale University Press, 1990.

Glancy, Jennifer A. "Boasting of Beatings (2 Corinthians 11:23–25)." *Journal of Biblical Literature* 123 (2004): 99–135.

———. "Protocols of Masculinity in the Pastoral Epistles." In *New Testament Masculinities*, edited by Stephen D. Moore and Janice Capel Anderson, 235–64. Atlanta: Society of Biblical Literature, 2003.

Gleason, Maud W. *Making Men: Sophists and Self-Presentation in Ancient Rome*. Princeton, N.J.: Princeton University Press, 1995.

———. "The Semiotics of Gender: Physiognomy and Self-Fashioning in the Second Century C.E." In *Before Sexuality: The Construction of Erotic Experience in the Ancient Greek World*, edited by John J. Winkler, David M. Halperin, and Froma I. Zeitlin, 399–402. Princeton, N.J.: Princeton University Press, 1990.

———. "Truth Contests and Talking Corpses." In *Constructions of the Classical Body*, edited by James I. Porter, 287–313. Ann Arbor: University of Michigan Press, 1999.

Good, Deirdre Joy. *Jesus the Meek King*. Harrisburg, Pa.: Trinity Press International, 1999.

Goodenough, E. Ramsdell. *By Light, Light: The Mystic Gospel of Hellenistic Judaism*. New Haven, Conn.: Yale University Press, 1935.

Goodman, Martin. "The Pilgrimage Economy of Jerusalem." In *Jerusalem: Its Sanctity and Centrality to Judaism, Christianity, and Islam*, edited by Lee I. Levine, 69–76. New York: Continuum, 1999.

Gowler, David B. "Texture, Culture, and Ideology in Luke 7:1–10: A Dialogic Reading." In *Fabrics of Discourse: Essays in Honor of Vernon K. Robbins*, edited by David B. Gowler, L. Gregory Bloomquist, and Duane Frederick Watson, 89–125. Harrisburg, Pa.: Trinity Press International, 2003.

Gradel, Ittai. *Emperor Worship and Roman Religion*. Oxford: Oxford University Press, 2004.

Grant, Michael. *From Imperium to Auctoritas: A Historical Study of Aes Coinage in the Roman Empire, 49 B.C.–A.D. 14*. Cambridge, England: Cambridge University Press, 1946.

Grassi, Joseph A., and Carolyn Grassi. *Mary Magdalene and the Women in Jesus' Life*. Kansas City, Mo.: Sheed & Ward, 1986.

Gundry, Robert H. *Mark: A Commentary on His Apology for the Cross*. Grand Rapids, Mich.: Eerdmans, 1993.

Hahn, Ferdinand. *The Titles of Jesus in Christology: Their History in Early Christianity*. New York: World Publishing Co., 1969.

Hallett, Judith P. "Perusinae Glandes and the Changing Image of Augustus." *American Journal of Ancient History* 2 (1977): 151–71.

Halperin, David M., John J. Winkler, and Froma I. Zeitlin. *Before Sexuality: The Construction of Erotic Experience in the Ancient Greek World*. Princeton, N.J.: Princeton University Press, 1990.

Harrington, Daniel J. *The Gospel of Matthew*. Sacra Pagina. Collegeville, Minn.: Liturgical Press, 1991.

Harris, William V. *Restraining Rage: The Ideology of Anger Control in Classical Antiquity*. Cambridge, Mass.: Harvard University Press, 2001.

Hartsock, Nancy. "Foucault on Power: A Theory for Women?" In *Feminism/Postmodernism*, edited by Linda J. Nicholson, 157–75. New York: Routledge, 1990.

Hemelrijk, Emily A. "Masculinity and Femininity in the Laudatio Turiae." *Classical Quarterly* 54 (2004): 185–97.

Hemelrijk, Emily Ann. *Matrona Docta: Educated Women in the Roman Élite from Cornelia to Julia Domna*. London: Routledge, 1999.

Hezser, Catherine. *Jewish Literacy in Roman Palestine*. Tübingen, Germany: Mohr Siebeck, 2001.

Himmelfarb, Martha. *Ascent to Heaven in Jewish and Christian Apocalypses*. New York: Oxford University Press, 1993.

Hobbs, Angela. *Plato and the Hero: Courage, Manliness, and the Impersonal Good*. Cambridge, England: Cambridge University Press, 2000.

Hoffmann, Matthias Reinhard. *The Destroyer and the Lamb: The Relationship between Angelomorphic and Lamb Christology in the Book of Revelation*. Tübingen, Germany: Mohr Siebeck, 2005.

Holladay, Carl R. *Theios Aner in Hellenistic-Judaism: A Critique of the Use of This Category in New Testament Christology*. Missoula, Mont.: Scholars Press, 1977.

Hooker, Morna Dorothy. *The Son of Man in Mark: A Study of the Background of the Term "Son of Man" and Its Use in St. Mark's Gospel.* Montreal: McGill University Press, 1967.

Hopkins, Julie M. *Towards a Feminist Christology: Jesus of Nazareth, European Women, and the Christological Crisis.* Grand Rapids, Mich.: Eerdmans, 1995.

Hopkins, Julie M., and Elisabeth Dieckmann. *Feministiche Christologie: Wie Frauen Heute Von Jesus Reden Können.* Mainz, Germany: Matthais-Grünewald Verlag, 1996.

Horrell, David G. *The Social Ethos of the Corinthian Correspondence: Interests and Ideology from 1 Corinthians to 1 Clement.* Studies of the New Testament and Its World. Edinburgh: T & T Clark, 1996.

Horsley, Richard A. *Hearing the Whole Story: The Politics of Plot in Mark's Gospel.* Louisville, Ky.: Westminster John Knox Press, 2001.

———. *Hidden Transcripts and the Arts of Resistance: Applying the Work of James C. Scott to Jesus and Paul.* Atlanta: Society of Biblical Literature, 2004.

———, ed. *Paul and Empire: Religion and Power in Roman Imperial Society.* Harrisburg, Pa.: Trinity Press International, 1997.

———, ed. *Paul and Politics: Ekklesia, Israel, Imperium, Interpretation.* Harrisburg, Pa.: Trinity Press International, 2000.

———, ed. *Paul and the Roman Imperial Order.* Harrisburg, Pa.: Trinity Press International, 2004.

Humphrey, Edith M. "A Tale of Two Cities and (at Least) Three Women: Transformation, Continuity, and Contrast in the Apocalypse." In *Reading the Book of Revelation: A Resource for Students,* edited by David L. Barr, 81–96. Leiden, the Netherlands: Brill, 2004.

Hurtado, Larry W. *One God, One Lord: Early Christian Devotion and Ancient Jewish Monotheism.* 2nd ed. Edinburgh: T&T Clarke, 1998.

Isherwood, Lisa. *Introducing Feminist Christologies.* London: Sheffield Academic Press, 2001.

Johns, Loren L. *The Lamb Christology of the Apocalypse of John: An Investigation into Its Origins and Rhetorical Force.* Wissenschaftliche Untersuchungen Zum Neuen Testament. 2. Reihe, 167. Tübingen, Germany: Mohr Siebeck, 2003.

Johnson, Elizabeth A. *She Who Is: The Mystery of God in Feminist Theological Discourse.* New York: Crossroad, 1992.

Kahl, Brigitte. "'No Longer Male': Masculinity Struggles Behind Galatians 3:28?" *Journal for the Study of the New Testament* 79 (2000): 37–49.

Kantorowicz, Ernst Hartwig. *The King's Two Bodies: A Study in Mediaeval Political Theology.* Princeton, N.J.: Princeton University Press, 1957.

Kaster, Robert A. "Controlling Reason: Declamation in Rhetorical Education at Rome." In *Education in Greek and Roman Antiquity,* edited by Yun Lee Too, 317–37. Leiden/Boston: Brill, 2001.

Kee, Howard Clark. *Jesus in History: An Approach to the Study of the Gospels.* New York: Harcourt Brace & World, 1970.

Keener, Craig S. *The Gospel of John: A Commentary.* 2 vols. Peabody, Mass.: Hendrickson Publishers, 2003.

Kellum, Barbara. "The Phallus as Signifier: The Forum of Augustus and Rituals of
    Masculinity." In *Sexuality in Ancient Art: Near East, Egypt, Greece, and Italy*,
    edited by Natalie Kampen, 170–83. Cambridge, England: Cambridge University
    Press, 1996.

Kelly, J. N. D. *Early Christian Doctrines*. 4th ed. London: Black, 1968.

Kiley, Mark Christopher. *Colossians as Pseudepigraphy*. Sheffield, England: JSOT Press,
    1986.

King, Karen L. "Sophia and Christ in the Apocryphon of John." In *Images of the
    Feminine in Gnosticism*, edited by Karen L. King, 158–76. Philadelphia: Fortress
    Press, 1988.

Knust, Jennifer Wright. *Abandoned to Lust: Sexual Slander and Ancient Christianity*.
    New York: Columbia University Press, 2006.

Koskenniemi, Erkki. *Apollonios Von Tyana in Der Neutestamentlichen Exegese*.
    Tübingen, Germany: Mohr, 1994.

———. "Apollonius of Tyana: A Typical Theios Anhr?" *Journal of Biblical Literature*
    117 (1998): 455–67.

Kraft, Konrad. "Der Sinn Des Mausoleum Des Augustus." *Historia* 16 (1967):
    186–202.

Krause, Deborah. "School's in Session: The Making and Unmaking of Docile
    Disciple Bodies in Mark." In *Postmodern Interpretations of the Bible: A Reader*,
    edited by A. K. A. Adam, 177–86. St. Louis: Chalice Press, 2000.

Krodel, Gerhard. *Revelation*. Minneapolis: Augsburg, 1989.

Kuefler, Mathew. *The Manly Eunuch: Masculinity, Gender Ambiguity, and Christian
    Ideology in Late Antiquity*. Chicago: University of Chicago Press, 2001.

Laporte, Jean. "Philo in the Tradition of Biblical Wisdom Literature." In *Aspects of
    Wisdom in Judaism and Early Christianity*, edited by Robert Louis Wilken, 103–41.
    Notre Dame, Ind.: University of Notre Dame Press, 1975.

Laqueur, Thomas W. *Making Sex: Body and Gender from the Greeks to Freud*.
    Cambridge, Mass.: Harvard University Press, 1990.

Larson, Jennifer. "Paul's Masculinity." *Journal of Biblical Literature* 123 (2004): 85–97.

Lenski, Gerhard E. *Power and Privilege: A Theory of Social Stratification*. New York:
    McGraw-Hill, 1966.

Lentz, John Clayton. *Luke's Portrait of Paul*. Cambridge, England: Cambridge
    University Press, 1993.

Levine, Amy-Jill. *The Social and Ethnic Dimensions of Matthean Salvation History*.
    Lewiston, N.Y.: E. Mellen Press, 1988.

Levine, Lee I. "Second Temple Jerusalem: A Jewish City in the Greco-Roman Orbit."
    In *Jerusalem: Its Sanctity and Centrality to Judaism, Christianity, and Islam*, edited
    by Lee I. Levine, 53–68. New York: Continuum, 1999.

Lieu, Judith M. "Scripture and the Feminine in John." In *Feminist Companion to
    the Hebrew Bible in the New Testament*, 225–40. Sheffield, England: Shef-
    field Academic Press, 1996.

Liew, Tat-siong Benny. *Politics of Parousia: Reading Mark Inter(Con)Textually*. Leiden,
    the Netherlands: Brill, 1999.

————. "Re-Mark-Able Masculinities: Jesus, the Son of Man, and the (Sad) Sum of Manhood?" In *New Testament Masculinities*, edited by Stephen D. Moore and Janice Capel Anderson, 93–135. Atlanta: Society of Biblical Literature, 2003.

Lutz, Cora E. *Musonius Rufus, "The Roman Socrates."* New Haven, Conn.: Yale University Press, 1947.

Luz, Ulrich. *Matthew 1–7: A Commentary.* Minneapolis: Augsburg, 1989.

MacMullen, Ramsay. *Romanization in the Time of Augustus.* New Haven, Conn.: Yale University Press, 2000.

Malbon, Elizabeth Struthers. "The Christology of Mark's Gospel: Narrative Christology and the Markan Jesus." In *Who Do You Say That I Am? Essays on Christology*, edited by Mark Allan Powell and David R. Bauer, 33–48. Louisville, Ky.: Westminster John Knox Press, 1999.

————. "Narrative Christology and the Son of Man: What the Markan Jesus Says Instead." *Biblical Interpretation* 11 (2003): 373–85.

Marcus Aurelius. *Meditations.* Translated by Maxwell Staniforth. Baltimore: Penguin Books, 1964.

Marshall, John W. *Parables of War: Reading John's Jewish Apocalypse.* Waterloo, Ont.: Wilfrid Laurier University Press, 2001.

Martin, Dale B. "Contradictions of Masculinity: Ascetic Inseminators and Menstruating Men in Greco-Roman Culture." In *Generation and Degeneration: Tropes of Reproduction in Literature and History from Antiquity through Early Modern Europe*, edited by Valeria Finucci and Kevin Brownlee, 81–108. Durham, N.C.: Duke University Press, 2001.

————. *Sex and the Single Savior: Gender and Sexuality in Biblical Interpretation.* Louisville, Ky.: Westminster John Knox Press, 2006.

————. *Slavery as Salvation: The Metaphor of Slavery in Pauline Christianity.* New Haven, Conn.: Yale University Press, 1990.

Martin, Ralph P. *Philippians.* Grand Rapids, Mich.: Eerdmans, 1980.

Matera, Frank J. *New Testament Christology.* Louisville, Ky.: Westminster John Knox Press, 1999.

Mattila, Sharon Lea. "Wisdom, Sense Perception, Nature and Philo's Gender Gradient." *Harvard Theological Review* 89 (1996): 103–29.

Mattingly, Harold. "Virgil's Fourth Eclogue," *Journal of the Warburg and Courtauld Institutes* 10 (1947): 14–19.

McEwen, Indra Kagis. *Vitruvius: Writing the Body of Architecture.* Cambridge, Mass.: MIT Press, 2003.

McGuire, Anne. "Women, Gender, and Gnosis in Gnostic Texts and Traditions." In *Women and Christian Origins*, edited by Ross Kraemer and Mary Rose D'Angelo, 257–99. New York: Oxford University Press, 1999.

McKinlay, Judith E. *Gendering Wisdom the Host: Biblical Invitations to Eat and Drink.* Journal for the Study of the Old Testament Supplement 216. Sheffield, England: Sheffield Academic Press, 1996.

McNay, Lois. *Foucault and Feminism: Power, Gender and Self.* Cambridge, England: Polity, 1992.

Meeks, Wayne. "The Prophet-King: Moses Traditions and the Johannine Christology." In *Religions in Antiquity: Essays in Memory of Erwin Ramsdell Goodenough*, edited by Jacob Neusner, 354–71. Leiden, the Netherlands: Brill, 1968.

Meeks, Wayne A. "The Image of the Androgyne: Some Uses of a Symbol in Early Christianity." *History of Religion* 13 (1974): 165–208.

———. "Man from Heaven in Johannine Sectarianism." *Journal of Biblical Literature* 91 (1972): 44–72.

Mellor, Ronald. *Augustus and the Creation of the Roman Empire: A Brief History with Documents.* New York: Palgrave Macmillan, 2006.

Meshorer, Ya'akov. "One Hundred Years of Tyrian Shekels." In *Festschrift Für Leo Mildenberg: Numismatik, Kunstgeschichte, Archäologie = Studies in Honor of Leo Mildenberg: Numismatics, Art History, Archeology*, edited by Leo Mildenberg and Arthur Houghton, 170–79. Wetteren, Belgium: Editions NR, 1984.

Metzger, Bruce M. *A Textual Commentary on the Greek New Testament.* 3rd ed. London: United Bible Societies, 1971.

Millar, Fergus, and Erich Segal. *Caesar Augustus: Seven Aspects.* Oxford: Clarendon Press, 1984.

Moltmann-Wendel, Elisabeth. *The Women around Jesus.* New York: Crossroad, 1992.

Mommsen, Theodor, Paul Krueger, and Alan Watson, eds. *The Digest of Justinian.* Philadelphia: University of Pennsylvania Press, 1985.

Montserrat, Dominic. "Experiencing the Male Body in Roman Egypt." In *When Men Were Men: Masculinity, Power and Identity in Classical Antiquity*, edited by Lin Foxhall and J. B. Salmon. London: Routledge, 1998.

Moore, Stephen D. *Empire and Apocalypse: Postcolonialism and the New Testament.* Sheffield, England: Sheffield Phoenix Press, 2006.

———. *God's Beauty Parlor: And Other Queer Spaces in and around the Bible.* Stanford, Calif.: Stanford University Press, 2001.

———. " 'O Man, Who Art Thou?': Masculinity Studies and New Testament Studies." In *New Testament Masculinities*, edited by Stephen D. Moore and Janice Capel Anderson, 1–22. Atlanta: Society of Biblical Literature, 2003.

———. "Ugly Thoughts: On the Face and Physique of the Historical Jesus." In *Biblical Studies/Cultural Studies*, 376–99. Sheffield, England: Sheffield University Press, 1998.

Moore, Stephen D., and Janice Capel Anderson, eds. *New Testament Masculinities.* Atlanta: Society of Biblical Literature, 2003.

Moore, Stephen D., and Fernando F. Segovia. *Postcolonial Biblical Criticism: Interdisciplinary Intersections.* London: T & T Clark International, 2005.

Morgan, David. *Visual Piety: A History and Theory of Popular Religious Images.* Berkeley: University of California Press, 1998.

Morgan, Teresa. *Literate Education in the Hellenistic and Roman Worlds.* Cambridge, England: Cambridge University Press, 1998.

Mounce, Robert H. *The Book of Revelation.* Rev. ed. Grand Rapids, Mich.: Eerdmans, 1998.

Mowery, Robert L. "Son of God in Roman Imperial Titles and Matthew." *Biblica* 83 (2002): 100–110.

Moxnes, Halvor. *Putting Jesus in His Place: A Radical Vision of Household and Kingdom.* Louisville, Ky.: Westminster John Knox Press, 2003.

Myers, Ched. *Binding the Strong Man: A Political Reading of Mark's Story of Jesus.* Maryknoll, N.Y.: Orbis Books, 1988.

Nanos, Mark D. *The Irony of Galatians: Paul's Letter in First-Century Context.* Minneapolis: Fortress Press, 2002.

———. *The Mystery of Romans: The Jewish Context of Paul's Letter.* Minneapolis: Fortress Press, 1996.

Needham, Anuradha Dingwaney. *Using the Master's Tools: Resistance and the Literature of the African and South-Asian Diasporas.* New York: St. Martin's Press, 2000.

Neyrey, Jerome. "Luke's Social Location of Paul: Cultural Anthropology and the Status of Paul in Acts." In *History, Literature, and Society in the Book of Acts*, edited by Ben Witherington, 251–79. Cambridge, England: Cambridge University Press, 1996.

Neyrey, Jerome H. "Jesus, Gender and the Gospel of Matthew." In *New Testament Masculinities*, edited by Stephen D. Moore and Janice Capel Anderson, 43–66. Atlanta: Society of Biblical Literature, 2003.

Nolland, John. *The Gospel of Matthew: A Commentary on the Greek Text.* Grand Rapids, Mich./Bletchley, England: Eerdmans/Paternoster Press, 2005.

Penella, Robert J. *The Letters of Apollonius of Tyana: A Critical Text with Prolegomena, Translation and Commentary.* Leiden, the Netherlands: Brill, 1979.

Penner, Todd C. "Civilizing Discourse: Acts, Declamation, and the Rhetoric of the *Polis*." In *Contextualizing Acts: Lukan Narrative and Greco-Roman Discourse*, edited by Todd C. Penner and Caroline Vander Stichele, 65–104. Leiden, the Netherlands: Brill, 2004.

Perkins, Judith. *The Suffering Self: Pain and Narrative Representation in the Early Christian Era.* London: Routledge, 1995.

Petersen, Norman R. *The Gospel of John and the Sociology of Light: Language and Characterization in the Fourth Gospel.* Valley Forge, Pa.: Trinity Press, 1993.

Pickett, Raymond. *The Cross in Corinth: The Social Significance of the Death of Jesus.* Sheffield, England: Sheffield Academic Press, 1997.

Pilch, John J. "Death with Honor: The Mediterranean Style Death of Jesus in Mark." *Biblical Theology Bulletin* 25 (1995): 65–70.

Pippin, Tina. *Apocalyptic Bodies: The Biblical End of the World in Text and Image.* London: Routledge, 1999.

———. *Death and Desire: The Rhetoric of Gender in the Apocalypse of John.* Louisville, Ky.: Westminster John Knox Press, 1992.

Pogoloff, Stephen M. *Logos and Sophia: The Rhetorical Situation of 1 Corinthians.* Atlanta: Scholars Press, 1992.

Pollini, J. "Man or God: Divine Assimilation and Imitation in the Late Republic and Early Principate." In *Between Republic and Empire: Interpretations of Augustus and His Principate*, edited by Kurt A. Raaflaub, Mark Toher, and G. W. Bowersock, 334–57. Berkeley: University of California Press, 1990.

Pollini, John. "The Augustus from Prima Porta and the Transformation of the
     Polykleitan Heroic Ideal: The Rhetoric of Art." In *Polykleitos, the Doryphoros, and
     Tradition*, edited by Warren G. Moon, 262–82. Madison, Wis.: University of
     Wisconsin Press, 1995.

Powell, Anton, ed. *Roman Poetry and Propaganda in the Age of Augustus*. London:
     Bristol Classical Press, 1992.

Preston, Ronald H., and Anthony T. Hanson. *The Revelation of Saint John the Divine:
     An Introduction and Commentary*. London: SCM Press, 1949.

Price, S. R. F. *Rituals and Power: The Roman Imperial Cult in Asia Minor*. Cambridge,
     England: Cambridge University Press, 1986.

Raaflaub, Kurt A., Mark Toher, and G. W. Bowersock, eds. *Between Republic and
     Empire: Interpretations of Augustus and His Principate*. Berkeley: University of
     California Press, 1990.

Räisänen, Heikki. *The "Messianic Secret" in Mark*. Edinburgh: T. & T. Clark, 1990.

Rajak, Tessa. "Dying for the Law: The Martyr's Portrait in the Jewish-Greek
     Literature." In *Portraits: Biographical Representation in the Greek and Latin
     Literature of the Roman Empire*, edited by M. J. Edwards and Simon Swain, 39–67.
     Oxford: Clarendon Press, 1997.

Ramage, Edwin S. *The Nature and Purpose of Augustus' "Res Gestae."* Weisbaden,
     Germany: Franz Steiner Verlag, 1987.

Ramazanoglu, Caroline. *Up against Foucault: Explorations of Some Tensions between
     Foucault and Feminism*. London: Routledge, 1993.

Reddish, Mitchell G. *Revelation*. Macon, Ga.: Smyth & Helwys, 2001.

Reinhartz, Adele. "The Gospel of John." In *Searching the Scriptures*, edited by Elisabeth
     Schüssler Fiorenza, 561–600. New York: Crossroad, 1993.

———. "'And the Word Was Begotten': Divine Epigenesis in the Gospel of John."
     Semeia 85 (1999): 83–103.

Reiser, Marius. "Love of Enemies in the Context of Antiquity." *New Testament Studies*
     47 (2001): 411–27.

Rhoads, David M., ed. *From Every People and Nation: The Book of Revelation in
     Intercultural Perspective*. Minneapolis: Fortress Press, 2005.

Ricci, Carla. *Mary Magdalene and Many Others: Women Who Followed Jesus*.
     Minneapolis: Fortress Press, 1994.

Richlin, Amy. "Foucault's *History of Sexuality*: A Useful Theory for Women?" In
     Rethinking Sexuality: Foucault and Classical Antiquity, edited by David H. J.
     Larmour, Paul Allen Miller, and Charles Platter, 128–70. Princeton, N.J.:
     Princeton University Press, 1998.

———. *The Garden of Priapus: Sexuality and Aggression in Roman Humor*. Rev. ed.
     New York: Oxford University Press, 1992.

———. "Gender and Rhetoric: Producing Manhood in the Schools." In *Roman
     Eloquence: Rhetoric in Society and Literature*, edited by William J. Dominik, 90–
     110. London: Routledge, 1997.

Robinson, Sally. *Marked Men: White Masculinity in Crisis*. New York: Columbia
     University Press, 2000.

———. "Pedagogy of the Opaque: Teaching Masculinity Studies." In *Masculinity Studies and Feminist Theory: New Directions*, edited by Judith Kegan Gardiner, 141–60. New York: Columbia University Press, 2002.

Roller, Duane W. *The Building Program of Herod the Great*. Berkeley: University of California Press, 1998.

Roloff, Jürgen. *The Revelation of John*. Minneapolis: Fortress Press, 1993.

Rosen, Ralph M., and I. Sluiter, eds. *Andreia: Studies in Manliness and Courage in Classical Antiquity*. Leiden, the Netherlands: Brill, 2003.

Rothschild, Clare K. *Luke-Acts and the Rhetoric of History: An Investigation of Early Christian Historiography*, Wissenschaftliche Untersuchungen Zum Neuen Testament. 2. Reihe, 175. Tübingen, Germany: Mohr Siebeck, 2004.

Roueche, Charlotte. "Acclamations in the Later Roman Empire: New Evidence from Aphrodisias." *Journal of Roman Studies* 74 (1984): 181–99.

Rowe, C. Kavin. *Early Narrative Christology: The Lord in the Gospel of Luke*. Berlin: Walter de Gruyter, 2006.

Royalty, Robert M. *The Streets of Heaven: The Ideology of Wealth in the Apocalypse of John*. Macon, Ga.: Mercer University Press, 1998.

Ruane, Nicole. *Sacrifice, Purity and Gender in Priestly Law*. Cambridge, England: Cambridge University Press, forthcoming.

Rudberg, Gunnar. "Zu Den Sendschreiben Der Johannes-Apokalypse." *Eranos* 11 (1911): 170–79.

Ruether, Rosemary Radford. *Sexism and God-Talk: Toward a Feminist Theology*. London: SCM, 1983.

Russell, Letty M. *Feminist Interpretation of the Bible*. Philadelphia: Westminster Press, 1985.

Ryberg, Inez Scott. *Rites of the State Religion in Roman Art*. Memoirs of the American Academy in Rome. Vol. 22. Rome: American Academy in Rome, 1955.

Said, Edward W. *Orientalism*. London: Routledge and Kegan Paul, 1978. Reprinted as a twenty-fifth anniversary edition with a new preface by the author. New York: Vintage Books, 2003.

Salier, Bill. "Jesus, the Emperor, and the Gospel According to John." In *Challenging Perspectives on the Gospel of John*, edited by John Lierman, 284–301. Tübingen, Germany: Mohr Siebeck, 2006.

Salzman, Michele Renee. *The Making of a Christian Aristocracy: Social and Religious Change in the Western Roman Empire*. Cambridge, Mass.: Harvard University Press, 2002.

Sanders, E. P. *Paul and Palestinian Judaism: A Comparison of Patterns of Religion*. Philadelphia: Fortress Press, 1977.

Schaberg, Jane "Feminist Interpretation of the Infancy Narrative in the Gospel of Matthew." *Journal of Feminist Studies in Religion* 13 (1997): 35–62.

Schnackenburg, Rudolf. *The Gospel of Matthew*. Grand Rapids, Mich.: Eerdmans, 2002.

Schneiders, Sandra M. "Women in the Fourth Gospel and the Role of Women in the Contemporary Church." *Biblical Theology Bulletin* 12 (1982): 35–45.

Schottroff, Luise. *Let the Oppressed Go Free: Feminist Perspectives on the New Testament.* Louisville, Ky.: Westminster John Knox Press, 1993.

———. *Lydia's Impatient Sisters: A Feminist Social History of Early Christianity.* Louisville, Ky.: Westminster John Knox Press, 1995.

Schüssler Fiorenza, Elisabeth. *Bread Not Stone: The Challenge of Feminist Biblical Interpretation.* Boston: Beacon Press, 1984.

———. *In Memory of Her: A Feminist Theological Reconstruction of Christian Origins.* New York: Crossroad, 1983.

———. *Jesus: Miriam's Child, Sophia's Prophet: Critical Issues in Feminist Christology.* New York: Continuum, 1994.

Schüssler Fiorenza, Elisabeth, and Shelly Matthews, eds. *Searching the Scriptures.* Vol. I. *A Feminist Introduction.* New York: Crossroad, 1993.

Schüssler Fiorenza, Elisabeth, Shelly Matthews, and Ann Graham Brock, eds. *Searching the Scriptures.* Vol. 2. *A Feminist Commentary.* New York: Crossroad, 1994.

Scott, Bernard Brandon. "The Birth of the Reader: Matthew 1:1–4:16." In *Faith and History: Essays in Honor of Paul W. Meyer,* edited by John T. Carroll, Charles H. Cosgrove, and E. Elizabeth Johnson, 35–54. Atlanta: Scholars Press, 1991.

Scott, James C. *Domination and the Arts of Resistance: Hidden Transcripts.* New Haven, Conn.: Yale University Press, 1990.

Scott, Martin. *Sophia and the Johannine Jesus,* Journal for the Study of the New Testament Supplement 71. Sheffield, England: Sheffield Academic Press, 1992.

Seeley, David. *The Noble Death: Graeco-Roman Martyrology and Paul's Concept of Salvation,* Journal for the Study of the New Testament Supplement 28. Sheffield, England: JSOT Press, 1990.

———. "Rulership and Service in Mark 10:41–45." *Novum Testamentum* 35 (1993): 234–50.

Shaw, Brent D. "Body/Power/Identity: Passions of the Martyrs." *Journal of Early Christianity Studies* 4 (1996): 269–312.

Sherk, Robert K. *Rome and the Greek East to the Death of Augustus.* Cambridge, England: Cambridge University Press, 1984.

Shipley, Frederick W., trans. *Velleius Paterculus. Res Gestae Divi Augusti,* Loeb Classical Library. Cambridge, Mass./London: Harvard University Press; W. Heinemann, 1979.

Silverman, Kaja. *Male Subjectivity at the Margins.* New York: Routledge, 1992.

Skinner, Marilyn B. *Sexuality in Greek and Roman Culture.* Oxford: Blackwell, 2005.

———. "Zeus and Leda: The Sexuality Wars in Contemporary Classical Scholarship." *Thamyris* 3 (1996): 103–23.

Sly, Dorothy. *Philo's Perception of Women.* Atlanta: Scholars Press, 1990.

Spivak, Gayatri Chakravorty. "Can the Subaltern Speak?" In *Marxism and the Interpretation of Culture,* edited by Cary Nelson and Lawrence Grossberg, 271–313. Urbana: University of Illinois Press, 1988.

Stendahl, Krister. "The Apostle Paul and the Introspective Conscience of the West." *Harvard Theological Review* 56 (1963): 199–215.

————. *The Bible and the Role of Women: A Case Study in Hermeneutics*. Philadelphia: Fortress Press, 1966.

————. *Paul among Jews and Gentiles and Other Essays*. Philadelphia: Fortress Press, 1976.

Stevens, Maryanne. *Reconstructing the Christ Symbol: Essays in Feminist Christology*. New York: Paulist Press, 1993.

Stevenson, Gregory M. "Conceptual Background to Golden Crown Imagery in the Apocalypse of John (4:4,10 14:14)." *Journal of Biblical Literature* 114 (1995): 257–72.

Stichele, Caroline Vander, and Todd Penner. "'All the World's a Stage': The Rhetoric of Gender in Acts." In *Luke and His Readers: Festschrift A. Denaux*, edited by R. Bieringer, Gilbert van Belle, and Jozef Verheyden, 373–96. Louvain, Belgium: Leuven University Press, 2005.

Stowers, Stanley K. *A Rereading of Romans: Justice, Jews, and Gentiles*. New Haven, Conn.: Yale University Press, 1994.

Sugirtharajah, R. S. *The Bible and Empire: Postcolonial Considerations*. Cambridge, England: Cambridge University Press, 2005.

————. *The Postcolonial Bible*. Sheffield, England: Sheffield Academic Press, 1998.

Sumney, Jerry L. "'I Fill Up What Is Lacking in the Afflictions of Christ': Paul's Vicarious Suffering in Colossians." *Catholic Biblical Quarterly* 68 (2006): 664–80.

Swancutt, Diana M. "'The Disease of Effemination': The Charge of Effeminacy and the Verdict of God (Romans 1:18–2:16)." In *New Testament Masculinities*, edited by Stephen D. Moore and Janice Capel Anderson, 193–233. Leiden, the Netherlands: Brill, 2004.

Szemler, J. G. "Priesthood and Priestly Careers in Ancient Rome." *Aufsteig und Niedergang der römischen Welt* II. 16.3 (1972): 2314–31.

Szesnat, Holger. "'Pretty Boys' in Philo's De Vita Contemplativa." *Studia Philonica Annual* 10 (1998): 87–107.

Talbert, Charles H. "Biographies of Philosophers and Rulers as Instruments of Religious Propaganda in Mediterranean Antiquity." *Aufsteig und Niedergang der römischen Welt* II.16.2 (1978): 1619–51.

Tannehill, Robert C. *The Narrative Unity of Luke-Acts: A Literary Interpretation*. Philadelphia: Fortress Press, 1986.

Taylor, Brian. *Responding to Men in Crisis: Masculinities, Distress and the Postmodern Political Landscape*. London: Routledge, 2006.

Theissen, Gerd. "The Political Dimension of Jesus' Activities." In *The Social Setting of Jesus and the Gospels*, edited by Wolfgang Stegemann, Bruce Malina, and Gerd Theissen, 225–50. Minneapolis: Fortress Press, 2002.

Thompson, Leonard L. *The Book of Revelation: Apocalypse and Empire*. New York: Oxford University Press, 1990.

Thurman, Eric. "Looking for a Few Good Men: Mark and Masculinity." In *New Testament Masculinities*, edited by Stephen D. Moore and Janice Capel Anderson, 137–61. Atlanta: Society of Biblical Literature, 2003.

Tolbert, Mary Ann. *Sowing the Gospel: Mark's World in Literary-Historical Perspective.* Minneapolis: Fortress Press, 1989.

Traister, Bryce. "Academic Viagra: The Rise of American Masculinity Studies." *American Quarterly* 52 (2000): 274–304.

Trible, Phyllis. *God and the Rhetoric of Sexuality.* Philadelphia: Fortress Press, 1978.

———. *Texts of Terror: Literary-Feminist Readings of Biblical Narratives.* Philadelphia: Fortress Press, 1984.

Turnbull, Percival. "The Phallus in the Art of Roman Britain." *Bulletin of the Institute of Archeology* 15 (1978): 199–206.

Usener, Hermannus, ed. *Epicurea.* Studia Philologica 3. "L'Erma" di Bretchschneider: Rome, 1963.

Vaage, Leif E. "Why Christianity Succeeded (in) the Roman Empire." In *Religious Rivalries in the Early Roman Empire and the Rise of Christianity,* edited by Leif E. Vaage, 253–78. Waterloo, Ont.: Wilfrid Laurier University Press, 2006.

van den Hoek, Annewies. "Endowed with Reason or Glued to the Senses: Philo's Thoughts on Adam and Eve." In *The Creation of Man and Woman,* edited by G. P. Luttikhuizen. Leiden, the Netherlands: Brill, 2000.

van Kooten, George H. *Cosmic Christology in Paul and the Pauline School: Colossians and Ephesians in the Context of Graeco-Roman Cosmology, with a New Synopsis of the Greek Texts,* Wissenschaftliche Untersuchungen Zum Neuen Testament 2. Reihe, 171. Tübingen, Germany: Mohr Siebeck, 2003.

Vander Stichele, Caroline, and Todd C. Penner. *Her Master's Tools? Feminist and Postcolonial Engagements of Historical-Critical Discourse.* Atlanta: Society of Biblical Literature, 2005.

Versnel, Henk S. "Making Sense of Jesus' Death: The Pagan Contribution." In *Deutungen Des Todes Jesu Im Neuen Testament,* edited by Jörg Frey and Jens Schröter, 213–94. Tübingen, Germany: Mohr Siebeck, 2005.

Volf, Miroslav. *Exclusion and Embrace: A Theological Exploration of Identity, Otherness, and Reconciliation.* Nashville: Abingdon Press, 1996.

Wainwright, Elaine. "The Gospel of Matthew." In *Searching the Scriptures,* edited by Elisabeth Schüssler Fiorenza, 635–77. New York: Crossroad, 1993.

Walker, Donald Dale. *Paul's Offer of Leniency (2 Cor 10:1): Populist Ideology and Rhetoric in a Pauline Letter Fragment.* Tübingen, Germany: Mohr Siebeck, 2002.

Walters, Jonathan. "Invading the Roman Body: Manliness and Impenetrability in Roman Thought." In *Roman Sexualities,* edited by Judith P. Hallett and Marilyn B. Skinner, 29–43. Princeton: Princeton University Press, 1997.

Ward, Graham. "Mimesis: The Measure of Mark's Christology." *Journal of Literature and Theology* 8 (1994): 1–29.

Washington, Harold C., Susan Lochrie Graham, Pamela Lee Thimmes, eds. *Escaping Eden: New Feminist Perspectives on the Bible.* Sheffield: Sheffield Academic Press, 1998.

Webster, Jane S. "Sophia: Engendering Wisdom in Proverbs, Ben Sira and the Wisdom of Solomon." *Journal for the Study of the Old Testament* 78 (1998): 63–79.

Weeden, Theodore J. *Mark: Traditions in Conflict*. Philadelphia: Fortress Press, 1971.

Wengst, Klaus. *Christologische Formeln Und Lieder Des Urchristentums*. Studien Zum Neuen Testament 7. Gütersloh, Germany: Gütersloher Verlagshaus Gerd Mohn, 1972.

Willett, Michael E. *Wisdom Christology in the Fourth Gospel*. San Francisco: Mellen Research University Press, 1992.

Williams, Craig A. *Roman Homosexuality: Ideologies of Masculinity in Classical Antiquity*. New York: Oxford University Press, 1999.

Williams, Demetrius K. *Enemies of the Cross of Christ: The Terminology of the Cross and Conflict in Philippians*. London: Sheffield Academic Press, 2002.

Williams, Michael A. "Uses of Gender Imagery in Ancient Gnostic Texts." In *Gender and Religion: On the Complexity of Symbols*, edited by Caroline Walker Bynum, Stevan Harrell, and Paula Richman, 196–227. Boston: Beacon Press, 1986.

———. "Variety in Gnostic Perspectives on Gender." In *Images of the Feminine in Gnosticism*, edited by Karen L. King, 2–22. Philadelphia: Fortress Press, 1988.

Williams, Sam K. *Jesus' Death as Saving Event: The Background and Origin of a Concept*. Missoula, Mont.: Scholars Press for *Harvard Theological Review*, 1975.

Wilson, R. McL. *A Critical and Exegetical Commentary on Colossians and Philemon*. London: T & T Clark International, 2005.

Winkler, John J. *The Constraints of Desire: The Anthropology of Sex and Gender in Ancient Greece*. New York: Routledge, 1990.

———. "Laying Down the Law: The Oversight of Men's Behavior in Classical Athens." In *Before Sexuality: The Construction of Erotic Experience in the Ancient Greek World*, edited by John J. Winkler, David M. Halperin, and Froma I. Zeitlin, 171–209. Princeton, N.J.: Princeton University Press, 1990.

Winsor, Ann Roberts. *A King Is Bound in the Tresses: Allusions to the Song of Songs in the Fourth Gospel*. New York: Peter Lang, 1999.

Wondra, Ellen K. *Humanity Has Been a Holy Thing: Toward a Contemporary Feminist Christology*. Lanham, Md.: University Press of America, 1994.

Woolf, Greg. "Becoming Roman, Staying Greek: Culture, Identity and the Civilizing Process in the Roman East." *Proceedings of the Cambridge Philological Society* 40 (1994): 116–43.

———. *Becoming Roman: The Origins of Provincial Civilization in Gaul*. Cambridge, England: Cambridge University Press, 1998.

Yavetz, Zvi. "The *Res Gestae* and Augustus' Public Image." In *Caesar Augustus: Seven Aspects*, edited by Fergus Millar and Erich Segal, 1–36. Oxford: Clarendon Press, 1984.

Zanker, Paul. *The Power of Images in the Age of Augustus*. Ann Arbor: University of Michigan Press, 1990.

Zeller, Dieter. "New Testament Christology in Its Hellenistic Reception." *New Testament Studies* 47 (2001): 312–33.

Subject Index

Index of Citations